Development and Underdevelopment

Garrett Nagle

Nelson

PO31913

Contents

Chapter 1
What is development?

'Development' is a term that is widely used and widely misunderstood. It is a complex, often emotional issue. How do you think it feels to be called 'less developed' or 'developing'? It is not just countries that are called 'underdeveloped' but regions and peoples: in Britain the north-south divide is often used as an example of contrasts in levels of development, and in some countries there is a striking difference in the levels of development between different racial groups. The USA and South Africa illustrate this last point clearly. Even in Britain there are differences in the well-being of different ethnic and racial groups.

So, in this chapter we discuss:
- what development is
- how we measure it
- how it occurs.

A number of case studies are used to show differences in levels of development and processes of development. These include India, South Korea and South Africa. The main models which help to explain the development process are discussed – these include some quite simple models, such as the sector model, and other more complex ones such as the dependency theory. The importance of trade and aid is analysed, and we look at some of the controversies regarding the use of aid: a case study of South Africa illustrates these points.

DEFINING DEVELOPMENT

The term 'development' is difficult to define. In geography, development refers to a number of characteristics such as demographic change, economic growth, increased use of resources, modernisation, higher levels of technology and political freedom.

Many 'development reports' provide statistical 'evidence' of levels of development. Generally they refer to such characteristics as population growth, life expectancy, health, education, urbanisation, income distribution, industrialisation and energy consumption. Using these features, geographers and developers have produced maps to show levels of world development. The gap between the wealthy and the poor is great (Figure 1.1). The geographic pattern is quite complex (Figure 1.2). The map presents a more accurate picture of development than the 1950s view, which classified every country as belonging to either the First, Second or Third Worlds.

ABBREVIATIONS
GNP - Gross National Product
IMR - Infant Mortality Rates
HDI - Human Development Index

These were defined as:
- the **First World** comprising Western Europe, North America, Australia, New Zealand and Japan
- the **Second World** consisting of the state-controlled Communist countries such as the former USSR
- the **Third World** containing all the other less developed countries.

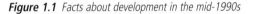

- over the last 30 years, the poorest 30% of the population have seen their share of world income fall from 2.3% to 1.4%, whereas the wealthiest 20% have seen their income rise from 70% to 85%
- the average income in India is one-twentieth of the average income in the USA
- 25% of the world's population live in extreme poverty
- the poorest 50 countries account for 20% of the world's population, and less than 2% of the world's income
- African countries account for 10% of the world's population, 1% of world trade and 0.4% of manufacturing
- each day 35 000 children die from preventable diseases

Figure 1.1 Facts about development in the mid-1990s

In the 1960s and 1970s the terms **Less Developed Countries (LDCs)** and **Developed Countries (DCs)** were used. This classification was not very useful because of its simplistic nature and emotive language: in many so-called LDCs, peoples such as the Mayas in central Mexico and the Shona in Zimbabwe, were quite advanced socially and politically. In the early 1980s, the terms **North (Developed World)** and **South (Less Developed World)** were used. Although not as emotive, the classification was still too simple: the oil rich countries of the Middle East and the Newly Industrialising Countries such as South Korea did not fit into either category very well.

In the 1990s the following classifications have been adopted:

Economically More Developed Countries (EMDCs) such as the UK and the USA. These are the most 'developed' countries and have a high standard of living.

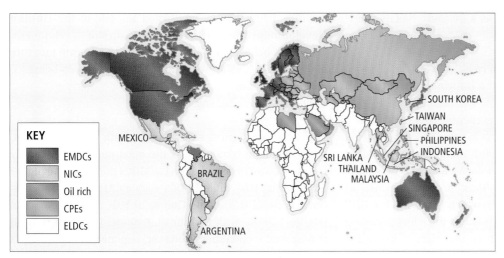

Figure 1.2
Classification of countries – 1990s

KEY
- EMDCs
- NICs
- Oil rich
- CPEs
- ELDCs

SOUTH KOREA
TAIWAN
SINGAPORE
PHILIPPINES
INDONESIA
MEXICO
BRAZIL
SRI LANKA
THAILAND
MALAYSIA
ARGENTINA

Figure 1.3
Gross National Product/head, 1993
Source: Nagle G. and Spencer, K., 1997,
Advanced Geography Revision Handbook,
OUP

KEY
High		$8626 or more
Upper middle		$2786–8625
Lower middle		$696–2785
Low		$695 or less
No data		

Economically Less Developed Countries (ELDCs), for example Namibia and India. These countries are at an earlier stage of development and have a lower quality of life.
Centrally Planned Economies (CPEs) are countries such as North Korea whose economies are strictly controlled by socialist governments. Living standards can be higher than ELDCs.
Oil rich countries such as Saudi Arabia and Libya. These countries are very rich in terms of gross national product (GNP) per head although the wealth may not be distributed evenly. Without oil, many of these countries would be ELDCs.
Newly Industrialising Countries (NICs) include South Korea and Taiwan. These are countries which have experienced rapid industrial, social and economic growth since the 1960s, largely as a result of government policy. (By contrast, **Old Industrial Countries (OICs)** are usually EMDCs.)

MEASURING DEVELOPMENT

The commonest way of measuring development is to use GNP/head. GNP is the total value of goods and services produced in a country in a single year. GNP/head gives an average value for the wealth of the total population. It is found by dividing the total GNP of the country by its population size. The world map of GNP/head (Figure 1.3) shows that the EMDCs of Western Europe, Japan, North America and Australia have much higher values, over US$8626, than the ELDCs such as India, Bangladesh, Nigeria and Zimbabwe, less than US$695. Only 15% of the world's population live in areas with a high GNP/head, whereas 56% of the world's population live in areas with a low GNP/head. Some countries, including Rwanda, Burundi, Ethiopia, Tanzania and Mozambique, have a GNP/head of less than US$200.

QUESTIONS

1 What do you understand by the term 'development'? How would you decide whether a country is developed? Explain your answer.

2 Are there any features of an EMDC, such as the UK, that you dislike? Are there any features of an ELDC that you find attractive? What do your responses suggest to you about the terms 'more developed' and 'less developed'?

3 Which of the methods of classifying countries do you think is best? Explain your answer.

However, average GNP/head as a measure has its short-comings. It:

- hides regional variations
- fails to take into account local costs of living
- does not take into account the informal (unregistered) economy
- ignores the social and environmental cost of economic growth.

Other measures of development include the **Physical Quality of Life Index (PQLI)** and the **Measure of Economic Welfare (MEW)**. The World Bank prefers the use of **Purchasing Power Parity (PPP)**, which is the level of GNP adjusted to local costs of living. This has the effect of raising the position of most ELDCs, where the costs of living are lower, and depressing the wealth of EMDCs where the costs of living are higher (Figure 1.4).

Since 1990 the UN has urged the use of the **Human Development Index (HDI)** as a measure of development. This, they believe, is a more reliable and accurate measure of development as it includes three indices of well-being:

- life expectancy
- literacy and schooling
- PPP.

The 1994 HDI figures show Canada with the highest HDI, with a value of 0.932 (1.0 is the maximum value), closely followed by Switzerland, 0.931. EMDCs dominate the higher levels of the HDI while ELDCs such as Afghanistan, 0.208, Burkina Faso, 0.203, and Guinea, 0.191, are at the bottom (Figure 1.5). As with GNP/head, national HDIs can conceal widespread inequalities. However, regional and racial HDIs can be developed, and these show very interesting patterns within a country (Figure 1.6).

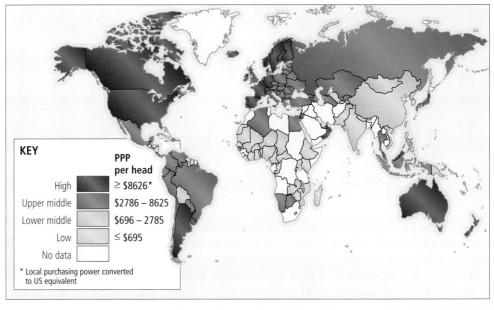

Figure 1.4 *Purchasing Power Parity per Capita, 1993*
Source: Nagle G. and Spencer K., 1997, Advanced Geography Revision Handbook, OUP

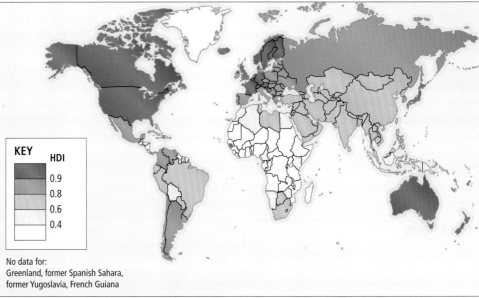

Figure 1.5
Human Development Index
Source: Nagle G. and Spencer K., 1997, Advanced Geography Revision Handbook, OUP

Regional disparities in Brazil and Mexico
Percentage of overall national HDI

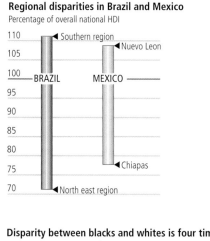

Regional disparities needing urgent attention in Nigeria

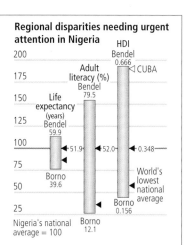

Nigeria's national average = 100

Figure 1.6 *Regional and racial variations in the HDI*
Source: Nagle G. and Spencer K., 1997, Advanced Geography Revision Handbook, OUP

Figure 1.7 *Part of the 'underclass' in South Africa*

Disparity between blacks and whites is four times larger in South Africa than in the USA

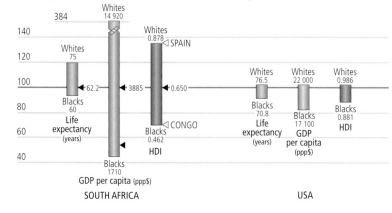

SOUTH AFRICA   USA

Figure 1.8 *White housing in the foreground, black housing in the background in South Africa*

QUESTIONS

1 Study Figures 1.4 and 1.5.

a) Describe the global variations in **(i)** PPP and **(ii)** HDI.

b) What evidence is there to suggest **(i)** a world North-South divide, and **(ii)** an EMDC-ELDC gap? Support your answers with evidence from the maps.

2 Study Figure 1.5.
There is no HDI for Greenland, the former Yugoslavia and the former Spanish Sahara. Choose any two of these countries and state why you think that a HDI has not been produced.

3 Study Figure 1.6.

a) Compare the USA and South Africa in terms of racial differences in HDI. In which country are educational standards and PPP highest?

b) What do these graphs tell us about **(i)** racial differences in the USA and South Africa, and **(ii)** levels of development between the USA and South Africa?

Inset 1.1
Spearman's Rank Correlation Coefficient (Rs)

Spearman's Rank Correlation Coefficient (Rs) is one of the most widely used statistics in geography: because of its simplicity, it is commonly used by examination boards. It allows us to decide whether or not there is a significant **statistical correlation (relationship)** between two sets of data. In some cases it is clear whether a correlation exists or not (Figure 1.11). However, in most cases it is less clear cut and to avoid subjective comments we use Rs to bring in a level of objectivity. It is relatively quick and easy to do and only requires that data are available on the **ordinal (ranked)** scale. More complex data can be transformed into ranks very simply. It is called a 'rank' correlation because only the ranks are correlated not the actual values.

Worked example: GNP and infant mortality rates (IMR)
Procedure:

1 **State null hypothesis (Ho)**, i.e. there is **no relationship** between infant mortality rate and GNP. The **alternative hypothesis (H1)** is that there is a relationship between infant mortality rate and GNP.

2 **Rank both sets of data** from high to low, i.e. highest value gets rank 1, second highest 2, and so on. In the case of **joint** or **tied ranks** find the average rank, e.g. if two values occupy positions two and three they both take on rank 2.5. If three values occupy positions four, five and six, they all take rank 5.

3 **Work out the correlation** using the formula $Rs = 1 - \dfrac{6\Sigma d^2}{n^3 - n}$ where d is the difference between ranks and n is the number of observations (Figure 1.9).

4 **Compare the computed Rs with the critical values** for a given level of significance in the statistical tables (Figure 1.10). ('Critical values' are the levels above which the result is statistically significant – usually 95% or 99%.)

If the computed value exceeds the critical values for levels of significance in the table, we can say that we are 95% or 99% sure that there is a relationship between the sets of data. In other words, there is only a 5% or 1% chance that there is no relationship between the data.

It is convention to accept 95% and 99% levels of significance. For a sample of ten, these values are 0.56 for 95% significance and 0.75 for 99% significance. In this example, it is clear that the relationship is strong, i.e. there is a more than 95% chance that there is a relationship between the data. The fact that the correlation is –0.84 shows that it is an **inverse relationship**, i.e. that as one variable increases the other decreases, thus as GNP increases infant mortality rate decreases. The next stage would be to offer explanations for the relationship.

n	Significance level	
(no. of values)	95%	99%
4	1.00	–
5	0.90	1.00
6	0.83	0.94
7	0.71	0.89
8	0.64	0.83
9	0.60	0.78
10	0.56	0.75
12	0.51	0.71
14	0.46	0.65
16	0.43	0.60
18	0.40	0.56
20	0.38	0.53
22	0.36	0.51
24	0.34	0.49
26	0.33	0.47
28	0.32	0.45
30	0.31	0.42

Figure 1.10 *Critical values for levels of significance*

	GNP ($)	IMR* (‰)	Rank GNP	Rank IMR	Difference	Difference^2
Brazil	3020	58	5	3	2	4
China	490	31	8	6	2	4
Germany	23 560	6	3	9	–6	36
India	290	79	10	2	8	64
Japan	31 450	5	1	10	–9	81
Namibia	1660	57	7	4	3	9
Nigeria	310	84	9	1	8	64
South Africa	2900	53	6	5	1	1
UK	17 970	8	4	7.5	–3.5	12.25
USA	24 750	8	2	7.5	–5.5	30.25
						$\Sigma = 303.5$

$$Rs = 1 - \frac{6\Sigma d^2}{n^3 - n} = 1 - \frac{6 \times 303.5}{10^3 - 10} = 1 - \frac{1821}{990} = 1 - 1.84 = -0.84$$

*IMR: the number of deaths in children aged under 1 year per 1000 live births

Figure 1.9 *Worked example*
Sources: United Nations Development Programme, 1994; Human Development Report and World Bank Atlas, 1996

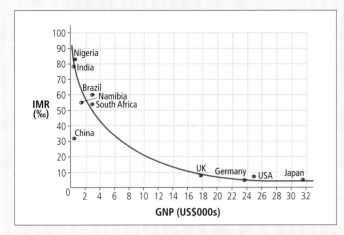

Figure 1.11 *Scatter graph to show the relationship between GNP and IMR*

Spearman's rank has a number of limitations:
- it requires a **sample size** of at least seven
- it tests for **linear** relationships and would give an answer of 0 for data such as river discharge and frequency (Figure 1.12c), which follows a curvilinear pattern, with few very low or very high flows and a large number of medium flows
- it is easy to make **false correlations**, as between summer temperatures in the UK and infant mortality rates in India, thus a **significant** relation does not necessarily indicate a **causal** one
- the question of **scale** is always important. For example, a survey of river sediment rates and discharge for the whole of a drainage system, may give a strong correlation whereas analysis of just the upper catchments gives a much lower result (Figure 1.12d).

As always, statistics are tools to be used. They are only part of the analysis, and we must be aware of their limits.

Correlation matrix

In some cases we can make multiple correlations. We do this to see if some variables are more correlated than others. For example, all of the variables in Figure 1.33 (except one pair) have been tested for statistical correlations. The answers are shown in Figure 1.13. On the left of the diagram the result is shown. On the right, the level of significance is shown. We can see quite clearly that the infant mortality rate is very closely correlated with all other variables.

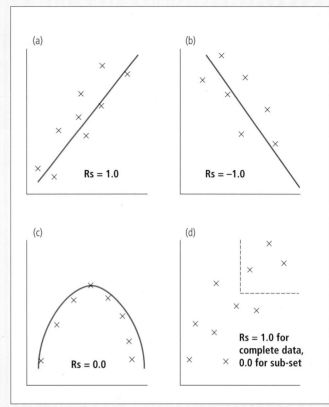

Figure 1.12 *Some Spearman's rank correlation coefficients (Rs)*
Source: Nagle, G. and Spencer, K., 1997, Geographical enquiries, Stanley Thornes

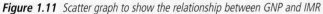

	GNP	IMR	TFR	GR	Ag	En
Gross national product (US$)	–	99%	95%	95%		99%
Infant mortality rate (‰)	–0.84	–	99%	99%	99%	99%
Total fertility rate	–0.70	0.87	–	99%	99%	95%
Growth rate (%/year)	–0.72	0.82	0.93	–	95%	95%
Agri. share of GDP (%)		0.89	0.75	0.72	–	99%
Use of energy (kg/person)	0.87	–0.81	–0.66	–0.73	–0.91	–

Figure 1.13 *A correlation matrix*

QUESTIONS

Using the data for GNP and percentage share of agriculture, complete the correlation matrix. Follow these guidelines:

1. State the null hypothesis.
2. Set out the data in a table as shown in Figure 1.9.
3. Rank both sets of data from high to low (highest = rank 1).
4. Work out the difference in ranks.
5. Find the square of the differences.
6. Add up the figures in the final column to find Σd^2
7. Using this figure, work out the correlation between GNP and percentage share of agriculture

$$Rs = 1 - \frac{6\Sigma d^2}{n^3 - n}$$

8. Compare your answer with the critical values in the table (Figure 1.10). How significant is your result?

DEVELOPMENT STRATEGIES

This section looks at development strategies in a number of countries. The first example is India, chosen because it is a former British colony which has recently (1997) celebrated fifty years of independence from Britain. Such a length of time might have allowed India to make the transition from less developed to more developed.

Development in India, an ELDC

Characteristics of ELDCs

Most ELDCs are characterised by:

- a large proportion of the workforce engaged in primary industries
- a large rural sector
- rapid population growth
- high rates of urbanisation
- low standards of living.

When India gained independence from Great Britain in 1947 it was a very poor country: infant mortality rates (IMR) were high, life expectancy was less than thirty years, and only about 30% of the population were literate. In 1995, India was still among the world's poorest countries. It had a low HDI, 0.382, an IMR of 89 per thousand and less than 50% of the population were literate. Nearly three-quarters of the population lived in rural areas and were largely unaffected by **industrialisation** and **development**. This was despite India's huge economy.

The main political leaders at the time of Independence, were Gandhi and Nehru. These two leaders stood for two contrasting approaches to development. Gandhi favoured development centred in rural villages which would create **self-sufficiency** in food, clothing and housing. By contrast, Nehru was a firm believer in national and industrial growth. Nehru became Prime Minister in 1947 and started a series of Five Year Plans which enabled India to follow a path of **large-scale industrial development**. India now has one of the world's largest economies and a skilled labour force that is second in size only to the USA.

Nehru believed that the benefits of growth would **trickle down** to rural areas: increased demand from the industrial workforce for agricultural products would stimulate rural areas. This did not happen. From the 1970s, a series of **Rural Development Programmes, Food for Work Programmes** and a **National Minimum Needs Programme** were introduced in an attempt to improve the standards of living among the poor, especially those in rural areas. Their success has been very limited since the size of the problem is so great. In some areas, development projects have been planned and organised by the rural communities themselves. These projects are far more **appropriate** since they take into account the needs, ideas and resources of the people.

The Indian government's strategy for **economic modernisation** is to attract foreign investment. Although it has been quite successful and the economy and exports are growing, there has been little development for the poor. For example, the educational system is still little developed, especially in rural areas: on average most Indians spend just two and a half years at school. Also, child labour is widespread. There may be as many as 55 million children aged between 5 and 15 years working between fourteen and sixteen hours a day, in hazardous conditions, for minimal wages.

Inset 1.2
Child labour in 1998

- There are many abusive forms of child labour such as slavery, debt bondage, child prostitution and hazardous work.
- About 250 million children aged 5 years and over are working in ELDCs. Nearly half of these work full-time.
- Up to 153 million children in Asia work.
- 40% of children in Africa work.
- Child labour is increasing in Eastern Europe.
- India employs 100 million children, the largest in any country.
- In India there are fines of US$750 for employing children.
- Many children are employed in diamond polishing, match and fireworks making, slate, glass and textiles industries.
- In the Philippines, 60% of working children were exposed to chemicals and 40% suffered serious injury.
- In 1996 a ban on the use of child labour was imposed upon Bangladesh's garment industry. The ban was the result of intense US pressure. The US imports 60% of Bangladesh's garment exports. In addition Bangladesh supplies 50% of the T-shirts sold in Europe. The use of child labour has been crucial in the spectacular growth of Bangladesh's textile industry.

QUESTIONS

1 How can the benefits of development 'trickle down' to rural areas?

2 'Economic success without human development is unlikely to provide India with a strong platform for development in the twenty-first century.' Discuss this statement.

Development in South Korea, a NIC

	1 **Traditional society**	2 **Import substitution industries (ISIs)**	3 **Export orientated industries (EOIs)**
	Labour-intensive industries, low levels of technology, local raw materials are used in industries such as food processing and textiles.	The development of home industries reduces expensive imports. Industries are protected by policies such as high trade tariffs on manufactured goods.	High technology, capital intensive industries with Research and Development (R&D) functions. Rapid growth and development of the economy.

Figure 1.14 *Stages in the emergence of a NIC*
Source: Nagle G. and Spencer K., 1997, Advanced Geography Revision Handbook, OUP

Characteristics of NICs

An NIC is characterised by:

- an increasing proportion of the workforce in manufacturing industries
- significant average annual growth in manufacturing production
- a significant increase in GDP provided by manufacturing (Figure 1.14)
- an increasing share of the world manufacturing output.

Three main groups of NICs have been identified:

1 Asian 'tigers' such as Hong Kong, Singapore, South Korea (Figures 1.15 and 1.16) and Taiwan
2 Latin American NICs such as Brazil and Mexico
3 European NICs including Portugal, Greece and the former Yugoslavia.

Figure 1.15 *The location of South Korea on the West Pacific Rim*

Population	43 million	Urban population	74%
Birth rate	16‰	Manufacturing	
Death rate	6‰	(av. annual growth)	15.6%
Infant mortality rate	21‰	Employment	
GNP per head	US$7670	Agriculture	11%
PPP	US$9810	Industry	43%
HDI	0.859	Services	46%
Literacy	90%		

Korea was the scene of a bitter war during the 1950s which resulted in the creation of two countries, communist North Korea and capitalist South Korea. During the war, South Korea was supported by the USA and there is still a large US military presence in the country. However, South Korea is increasingly extending links with other countries, especially in Europe. South Korea has shown spectacular growth since the early 1960s, helped by aid from the USA and Japan, loans and grants from development banks, government incentives to promote economic growth and investment by multinational companies.

The first industries developed by South Korea were **import substitution industries (ISIs)**. These aimed to reduce dependence upon expensive foreign imports. Iron and steel, shipbuilding, textiles and chemicals were expanded, based on:

- a skilled and cheap labour force
- an excellent geographic location
- large modern factories, owned by family-run conglomerates known as *chaebol*.

Access to raw cotton from neighbouring countries aided the textile industry, while artificial fibres were generated by the rapidly expanding chemicals industry.

As development proceeded, South Korea turned its attention to **export orientated industries (EOIs)** in an attempt to secure foreign currency and export earnings. Computers, televisions and microwave equipment were at the forefront of the country's electronics industry.

South Korea's future growth industries are likely to be in research and development, and high-value industries, including computers, biotechnology and aerospace. In order to become more flexible and competitive, the government is helping small and medium sized industries to compete in specialised markets.

Figure 1.16 *South Korea: key facts*
Source: United Nations Development Programme 1994 Human Development Report

---

QUESTIONS

1 Using a map, show why South Korea's geographic location is 'excellent'.

2 How typical is South Korea as an NIC? Give reasons for your answer.

3 Explain why South Korea's workforce is so important for its economic development.

SPREADING DEVELOPMENT

Development often occurs in specific locations. These developments grow by attracting investment, people and new economic opportunities. Governments may try to spread development, for a variety of reasons:

- **Economic** reasons – such as reducing unemployment, raising productivity and using resources more efficiently
- **Social** reasons – such as increasing standards of living, slowing migration, and reducing regional inequalities
- **Political** motives – such as attempting to win votes before an election
- **Strategic** reasons – important in times of military conflict and threats to national security
- **Environmental** concerns – dereliction, blight and contamination may cause governments to intervene.

Attempts to spread development vary with the type of development. For example, economic development is frequently associated with industrialisation, whereas human development may be more affected by the provision of clean water (Figure 1.18) or an education system.

Development is often associated with a change in a country's employment structure, from largely rural and agricultural to urban and industrial. These stages of growth do not, however, tell us how growth occurs.

How and where development occurs

There are three broad ways in which development occurs:

- **Natural** – under free market conditions countries exploit their resources and base their growth on their advantages. Most EMDCs have taken this route
- **Forced** – in socialist countries, such as North Korea and the former USSR, the government controls all the resources and dictates the type and place of growth that it desires
- **Planned** – Newly Industrialising Countries such as South Korea have progressed from using import substitution industries (ISIs), which reduce debt, into developing export orientated industries (EOIs) which gain valuable currency.

These three ways tell us how a country develops, but fail to tell us which regions prosper and which fail. Regional inequalities develop over time due to economic forces.

- Initially, development takes place in particular places. This is due to **comparative advantages** such as natural resources, location or labour supply, which stimulate industrial growth. In turn, **multiplier effects** (cumulative causation) occur. **Acquired advantages**, such as improvements in infrastructure and a skilled workforce, reinforce the area's reputation, and attract further investment. This ensures that the region grows and stays ahead.
- **Spatial interaction** increases. This means that skilled workers, investment and new developments move to the growing area, the **core**. By contrast the **peripheral** areas are flooded by manufactured goods from the core (the **backwash effect**). This prevents the development of manufacturing in the periphery. The **spread effect** occurs when the core stimulates surrounding areas to develop to meet consumer demand.

These ideas have been used extensively in planning. Places or districts which are favoured by reason of location, resources, labour or market access are economically more attractive. Consequently they are developed by planners to form natural **growth poles**, from which development can spread, and these expand faster than other districts. Generally, these are urban-industrial complexes which have good transport and accessibility.

Such an approach does not benefit rural areas. In general, resources in rural areas are spread over the whole landscape. Growth poles introduced in rural areas are usually expensive projects with concentrated resources. Classic examples include the dairy industry in the Nile Valley and the irrigation scheme at Keiskammahoek, South Africa. These benefit only a small area and a small number of people. There are very limited spread effects. Increasingly, attention is being turned to **appropriate development**, using local resources, needs and ideas, at a price which is affordable to the local community. Examples include check dams (small-scale dams), earthen terraces, and vegetable gardens.

Figure 1.17 *Development in many parts of Southern Africa is limited by access to water*

Figure 1.18 *Bringing piped water to a rural area*

The South African government's regional development policy has for many years provided industrial development points in and around a number of former homeland areas in order to stimulate employment. An array of benefits is available to attract industries and bolster economic viability. For example, in Ciskei, incentives have included relocation reimbursements, tax-free allowances and reduced tax rate, abolition of corporate tax, electricity and transport rebates, housing subsidies and cash grants for every person employed. In general, the scheme has not been a success as it has spread development too thinly on the ground and in areas that were not necessarily favoured. Hence there is very little multiplier effect to promote growth without outside help. Moreover, rationalisation of companies during recession further weakens the less favoured areas.

Figure 1.19 *Industrial policy in Ciskei (South Africa)*
Source: Nagle, G., Regional inequalities in the 'new' South Africa, Geographical, September 1994

QUESTIONS

1 What are the advantages and disadvantages of a growth pole strategy?

2 Give two examples of how the spread effect may operate in rural areas.

3 Study Figures 1.17 – 1.19 which show two types of development in a rural area in South Africa. Discuss the likely advantages and disadvantages of each scheme to **(i)** the national economy, **(ii)** local residents, and **(iii)** the environment.

EXPLAINING DEVELOPMENT AND UNDERDEVELOPMENT

There have been many attempts to explain the development process. The most basic are from the developmentalism school. These suggest that the way in which Europe and North America developed is the 'right' way, and that developing countries should copy them. More recent theories, including the dependency theory, show that EMDCs may, in fact, be the cause of underdevelopment in many ELDCs.

Clark's sector model

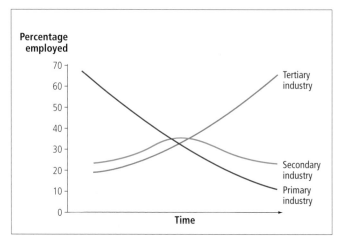

Figure 1.20 *Clark's sector model, 1950*

Clark's sector model (Figure 1.20) is the most basic of development models. It describes how EMDCs have changed from agricultural societies to industrial and post-industrial societies. Change occurs because success in one sector produces a surplus revenue. This revenue is then invested in new industries and technologies, thereby increasing the range of industries in an area.

The main weakness of this model is that it is descriptive and offers only a crude level of analysis. It does not say how or why the country developed, nor does it show regional variations within it.

Rostow's model of development

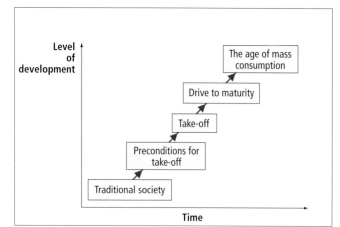

Figure 1.21 *Rostow's model of economic growth, 1955*

W. W. Rostow, a US economist, described five stages in the development of a country (Figure 1.21). His model is a simplified way of describing and understanding levels of development. These levels can be described as:

1 **Traditional subsistence economy:** agricultural basis, little manufacturing industry, few links with other countries and low levels of population growth. A few indigenous tribes, such as the Kalahari bushmen, in Africa, or the Kayapo Indians in Brazil are still at this stage.

2 **Preconditions for take-off:** links with other countries are established; resources are increasingly exploited, often by colonial countries or, nowadays, by multinational companies (MNCs); the country begins to develop an urban system (often with a primate city), and a transport infrastructure; inequalities emerge between the growing core and the underdeveloped periphery. The population continues to increase in the core. There are very few countries at this stage, but some regions within countries fit this model. Parts of Siberia or Alaska, and the Zaire and Colombian rain forests are good examples of areas where resources are being exploited and developed.

3 **Take-off to maturity** (sustained growth): the economy expands rapidly, especially manufacturing industry, population growth often accelerates. Regional inequalities

intensify because of multiplier effects. This growth can be 'natural' (as in the case of most EMDCs), 'forced' (the ex-socialist countries of Eastern Europe) or 'planned' (as in the NICs). China and India currently represent this stage.

4 **The drive to maturity:** diversification of the economy, the development of the service industry (health, education, welfare etc.); growth spreads to other sectors and to other regions in the country. Population growth begins to slow down and stabilise. Many of the less developed EMDCs, such as Ireland and Spain, are at this stage.

5 **The age of high mass consumption:** advanced urban-industrial systems, with high production and consumption of consumer goods, such as televisions, compact disc players, dishwashers. Population growth slows considerably. The UK, USA and Japan characterise this level.

The main weaknesses of Rostow's model are:

- it is **anglo-centric** – based on the experience of North America and Western Europe
- it is **aspatial** and does not look at variations within countries. For example, within the UK there are disparities in the levels of development between the north and the south – Rostow's model fails to pick this out
- it does not take into account racial differences. For example, in South Africa and the USA there are still clear differences in the relative prosperity of whites and blacks.

Myrdal's model of cumulative causation and spatial interaction

An approach which adopts a spatial pattern is the core-periphery model, based on the work of Myrdal in 1955. Myrdal believed that over time economic forces increase regional inequalities rather than reduce them (Figure 1.22). He argued that development was caused by natural advantages and regional interaction.

Initial **comparative advantages** such as location, natural resources or labour, provide the stimulus for development in a particular location. In turn, cumulative causation (the multiplier effect) occurs as acquired advantages are developed and reinforce the area's reputation, thereby attracting further investment. The **acquired advantages** include improvements in infrastructure, skilled workforce, and increased tax revenues. Further investment ensures that the core grows and stays ahead of other regions.

Regional interaction occurs as skilled workers, investment, new technologies and developments gravitate to the growing area, the core. By contrast manufactured goods from the core are sold to the peripheral areas (the backwash effect). This prevents the development of a local manufacturing base. As the core expands it may stimulate surrounding areas to develop due to increased consumer demand (the spread effect).

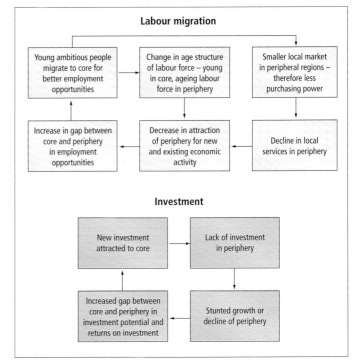

Figure 1.22 *Myrdal's model of cumulative causation*

Three main stages can be identified in Myrdal's model:

1 traditional, preindustrial stage with few regional disparities
2 increased disparities caused by multiplier and backwash effects as the country industrialises
3 a reduction in regional inequalities as spread effects occur.

Friedmann's stages of growth

Friedmann's model (1966) also adopts a spatial pattern. He shows how different parts of a country develop at different rates, and how they change over time. Four clear stages can be seen (Figure 1.23).

1 **Preindustrial economy:** independent local centres, no hierarchy.
2 **Transitional economy:** a single strong centre emerges. This dominates the colonial society as the stage of preconditions begins. A growing manufacturing sector encourages concentration of investment in only a few centres – hence a core emerges with a primate city.
3 **Industrial economy:** a single national centre, strong peripheral sub-centres, increased regional inequalities between core and periphery; upward spiral in the core, downward spiral in the periphery (Myrdal's cumulative causation). In time, as the economy expands, more balanced national development occurs – subcentres develop forming a more integrated national urban hierarchy.
4 **Post-industrial economy:** functionally interdependent urban system; the periphery is eliminated.

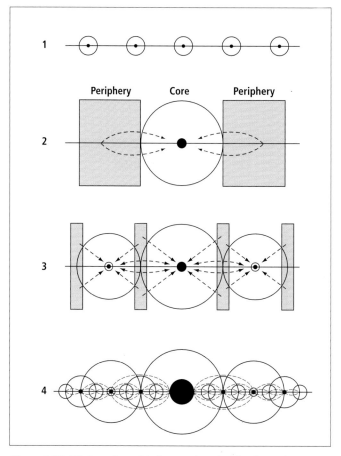

Figure 1.23 *Friedmann's model of economic and regional growth*

Friedmann believed that stage 4 had been reached in the USA, although there are still peripheral areas such as the Ozarks, Appalachians and Alaska. Friedmann's model is very simplified and does not take into account variations in the distributions of resources. It overemphasises the importance of centrality.

Top-down development
- decision making comes from the government or from large multilateral organisations outside the country
- local communities have very little say in the decisions
- projects are large, involving huge amounts of money and western technology

Bottom-up development
- decision making rests with the local community
- the local community is involved in the planning and development of the project
- projects are small-scale, appropriate to the local needs, and culturally acceptable

Sustainable development
- meets the needs of the present generation without compromising the needs of future generations
- takes into account environmental conditions

Figure 1.24 *Types of development*

AID AND DEVELOPMENT

Aid is the help given by a relatively wealthy country or organisation to another country that is less wealthy. This help can include money, goods, services, trained personnel, medicines, food, and arms. The donor country is usually an EMDC and the receiving country is usually an ELDC. However, there is a widespread mismatch between who gets the aid and who needs the aid. The poorest countries get the least amount of aid per person, and richer countries often receive more aid. For example, Malaysia receives 50% more aid from the UK than Bangladesh receives, yet Malaysia's average income is ten times greater than Bangladesh's.

There are three main forms of aid:

1 **Bilateral aid** is the assistance given by one country directly to another country.
2 **Multilateral aid** is the assistance given by large organisations such as the United Nations (UN) and the World Bank. Many countries provide funds to support the UN, which then funds projects of its choice in many countries.
3 **Non-government organisations (NGOs)** – charities such as Oxfam, Cafod and Save the Children. Most of their funds are drawn from public donations and these are used to support mostly small-scale, local, self-help projects. The main advantages of NGOs is that they:
- are more flexible
- are less dependent on political considerations
- have specialist knowledge and skills.

But, they have less money.

Aid can also be classified as project aid or programme aid. **Project aid** is given for a particular scheme, such as starting a small-scale irrigation project. **Programme aid**, such as debt repayment, is much larger in scale. In general, governments prefer programme aid, as it deals with a larger part of the total economy, whereas individuals and communities prefer project aid, because it is small-scale and can be seen to have visible local benefits.

Aid can be short-term or long-term. **Short-term aid** or **emergency relief** usually follows a natural disaster, such as a drought or a flood. It is provided to keep people alive. The aid given to the Rwandan refugees in the mid-1990s is a well-known example. **Long-term aid** or **development aid** is provided to improve the long-term standards of living in an area. Programmes to increase agricultural productivity in rural areas, and improvements to water and sanitation in a shanty town are good examples.

The amount of aid being given is falling. In 1995-96 the UK provided almost £2 billion of aid. This amounted to just 0.27% of GNP, compared with a UN target of 0.7% of GNP. (An earlier target of 1% of GNP had been lowered by the UN because few countries had any intention of reaching it.)

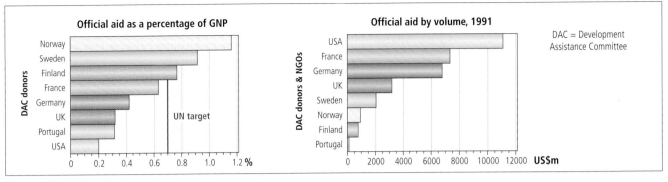

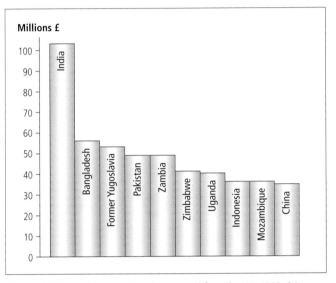

Figure 1.25 *Official aid*
Source: Uncovering the reality of aid, 1993, Action Aid

Following the election of the Labour government in 1997, the secretary of the newly-created Department for International Development gave a commitment to increase aid spending up to the UN target of 0.7% of GNP by 2000. By contrast, under the Conservative government of 1979–97, the aid budget fell from 0.51% to 0.27% of GNP. Figure 1.25 shows the amount of aid as a percentage of GNP and the amount of aid in US$ million.

The Overseas Development Agency (ODA) is the official UK aid organisation. It provides help to over 160 countries. The main receivers are shown in Figure 1.26. It provides project aid in the form of health care, education, water and sanitation, and programme aid in the form of financial and technical help. The ODA supports many voluntary organisations involved in health and education.

Figure 1.26 *Countries receiving the most aid from the UK, 1993–94*
Source: ODA

Inappropriate aid

Many aid projects have been criticised on the grounds that they are inappropriate to local needs. One example is the Akosombo Dam in Ghana, which was built to provide hydro-electric power (HEP), irrigation, and flood control, but which drowned much valuable agricultural land and led to an increase in water-borne diseases. In addition, much of the material and skills used in the building of the dam was British, not Ghanaian. The scheme is an example of **tied aid**, whereby the donor (in this case, the UK) provides the aid on the condition that the receiver (in this case, Ghana) uses the donor's raw materials.

The Pergau Dam is another example of inappropriate aid. £234 million of British aid money was spent on the dam in Kelantan in northern Malaysia. The dam was fiercely opposed by the state of Kelantan, the local people and even the Malaysian minister of energy. They wanted a smaller

gas-fired project which would have cost less than a third of the price of the Pergau Dam. So why was the dam built? Many believed that the large loan to build the dam, offered at very low rates of interest, was a 'sweetener' to the Malaysian government. In return, the British government wanted a trade deal on arms, with British manufacturers supplying the Malaysian armed forces.

Examples of inappropriate aid are numerous. They include:
- lorries sent to areas where there are no roads, as in Ethiopia
- tractors given to areas where there are no mechanics or spare parts, as in parts of Zimbabwe
- dairy cattle being introduced to desert regions
- large-scale irrigation schemes being brought to desert areas, where they cause salinisation (toxic saline crusts on the top of the soil).

QUESTIONS

1 What type of aid – project or programme – do you think people who give to charity prefer? Give reasons for your choice.

2 Look at Figure 1.24. Which type of aid is likely to be associated with **(i)** top-down development **(ii)**, bottom-up development, and **(iii)** sustainable development. Give reasons for your choice.

(It is possible for the same type of aid to appear in more than one category.)

3 Who gives aid? Explain contrasting reasons why people, charities and/or governments give aid.

When aid is effective:	When aid is ineffective:
• It provides humanitarian relief.	• Aid might allow countries to postpone improving economic management and mobilisation of domestic resources.
• It provides external resources for investment and finances projects that could not be undertaken with commercial capital.	• Aid can replace domestic saving, direct foreign investment and commercial capital as the main sources of investment and technology development.
	• The provision of aid might promote dependency rather than self-reliance.
• Project assistance helps expand much needed infrastructure.	• Some countries have allowed food aid to depress agricultural prices, resulting in greater poverty in rural areas and a dependency on food imports. It has also increased the risk of famine in the future.
• Aid contributes to personnel training and builds technical expertise.	• Aid is sometimes turned on and off in response to the political and strategic agenda of the donor country, making funds unpredictable, which can result in interruptions in development programmes.
	• The provision of aid might result in the transfer of inappropriate technologies or the funding of environmentally unsound projects.
• Aid can support better economic and social policies.	• Emergency aid does not solve the long-term economic development problems of a country.
	• Too much aid is tied to the purchase of goods and services from the donor country, which might not be the best or the most economical.
	• A lot of aid does not reach those who need it, that is, the poorest people in the poorest countries.

Figure 1.27 *The impact of aid*
Source: Baker, S. et al, Pathways in geography, 1996

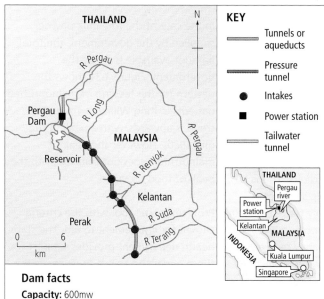

Dam facts
Capacity: 600mw
Cost: £415 million, £234 million to be paid by British taxpayer.
Area: 4 square miles.
Operation time: 20 hrs a week providing overload electricity.
Lifespan: 25–30 years
Wildlife in area: the rare Sumatran rhinoceros, elephants, tigers, leopards, tapirs, primates, sealadang.

Figure 1.28 *The Pergau Dam – ineffective and inappropriate aid*
Source: Geofile

On a much larger scale, the World Bank admits that many of its aid projects benefit multinational companies and the World Bank itself, rather than local companies. Also, it receives more money from the repayment of loans, than it lends out in the first place! British firms have also benefited: they receive orders for goods and services used in aid projects that are worth more than the total amount of British aid.

Figure 1.29 *Operation Hunger feeding scheme – effective aid*

QUESTIONS

1 Study Figure 1.25.

a) Which countries give more aid than the UN recommended limit of 0.7% of GNP? Give at least two contrasting reasons to explain why Norway gives more aid, as a percentage of GNP, than the USA.

b) Which countries give the most aid? Give at least **two** contrasting reasons to explain why the USA gives more aid than Portugal.

2 Study the list of receivers in Figure 1.26.

a) With the exception of the former Yugoslavia, what do the top five receivers have in common?

b) Why do you think the UK gives aid to China and the former Yugoslavia?

Case study:
The aid dilemma – food aid in South Africa

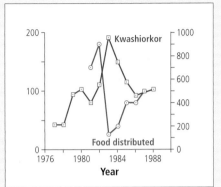

In South Africa, there have been a number of attempts by state and other non-government organisations (NGOs) to provide more food for the poorest people (Figure 1.31). However, some of these projects have had an adverse effect and have been seen as political gestures, which benefitted the urban elite at the expense of the rural poor. For example, supplementary feeding, supplied by the government or NGOs should be a positive benefit and should increase food consumption, but it can suffer from problems of targeting and access. This means that the very poor and the most infirm may not be able to receive or afford the aid. The South African government and a number of NGOs, provide skimmed milk powder and supplementary feeding, mostly to young children. However, there is no legal obligation to provide government feeding schemes at local level and these schemes do not cover all groups at risk of malnutrition.

Food aid in the Eastern Cape

Large numbers of people in the Eastern Cape (Figure 1.30) receive food aid,

some given by the state, some by voluntary organisations. Groups such as Operation Hunger, Border Council of Churches, Kinderwald and World Vision provide aid. The main forms of aid are:
- government subsidy on foods
- free milk powder provided by the government
- soup kitchens, clinic and school feeding schemes run by Operation Hunger, World Vision and Kinderwald (Figure 1.29).

The main form of state aid is the subsidy on foods, such as bread. A subsidy means that the price of food is kept artificially low. The other main form of state aid, powdered milk, is governed by attendance at a health clinic by children classified as malnourished.

By contrast, the voluntary organisation, Operation Hunger runs feeding schemes which distribute soup to all age groups via schools, crèches and clinics. This is in addition to their self-help schemes, under which groups apply for aid, and are responsible for the cooking and distribution of the food they receive. It is thus a community based project, generally organised by local women.

The wider issue of whether all such aid creates a culture of dependency, leading to long-term suffering is very real. Yet without well-fed individuals, there will be less long-term development, especially for the very poor. Without food aid, the poor and vulnerable are certain to face increased rates of morbidity and mortality, as well as a reduced quality of life. Handouts *can* be part of a programme to enable a degree of self-sufficiency, but they need to be managed carefully.

Figure 1.31 *Malnutrition and food aid in King William's Town, 1977-88*
Source: Nagle, G., 1992, Malnutrition in the Zwelitsha region of Ciskei, Unpublished D.Phil. Thesis, Univ. Oxford

In the case of the free milk powder supplied by the government, the total amount available is set by the government. Figure 1.31 shows the pattern for the feeding of malnourished patients in King William's Town. The trend is upwards, with a peak in the mid 1980s. However the peak of malnutrition does not coincide with the peak of food provided.

Problems occur, too, with the criteria chosen for entitlement to aid. The state health department provides support for those under the age of two years – this has the effect of discriminating against children with kwashiorkor (a type of malnutrition), which usually occurs only after weaning, usually in the second year of a child's life and thereafter.

Distribution of the free milk powder available varies widely with the clinics. In this scheme, the nurse in charge is given the responsibility to decide who receives aid or not. In the Welcomewood clinic in the Eastern Cape, for example, a number of complaints were made that the milk powder was not being provided to the malnourished, but kept for the nurse's family and her friends.

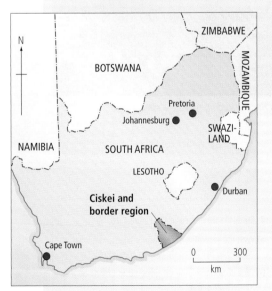

Figure 1.30 *The Ciskei and border region*

Choosing to distribute the milk powder from a clinic disadvantages those who live in the remoter areas, such as Zikhova, south of Welcomewood. Women living further away from the clinic are less likely to attend, thereby missing out on food aid.

Another set of problems relates to the food after it has been distributed. Although the milk powder is supplied for one child, there is plenty of evidence to suggest that it is used by the whole household, thereby depriving the malnourished child of its needs. Over-dilution is frequently mentioned in the clinics.

Distribution problems also exist for the health staff. The powdered milk is provided to clinics by the regional hospital, Cecilia Makiwane, once a month. This means that the clinics (and households) must budget for the month. The situation was made worse on one occasion when the transport carrying the powder broke down and many clinics in the region were without milk powder for over two weeks.

There are similar problems for those receiving soup from the voluntary organisations, since their daily attendance is necessary if they are to receive the food supplement.

Thus in theory, food aid can provide a vital role in ensuring that young children and others receive sufficient food in order to supplement their diets. Although the constraints and restrictions are many, one can only conclude that food aid is a valuable and essential commodity in the Eastern Cape.

QUESTIONS

1 **Briefly describe the ways in which food aid can be provided.**
2 **What are the advantages and disadvantages of (i) soup kitchens? and (ii) food subsidies?**

WOMEN AND DEVELOPMENT

Since the mid-1980s, many aid organisations have realised that women play a vital role in development. This is because in many ELDCs women are responsible for most of the farming, running households and providing for their children. Women's cooperatives have been set up to give women more economic and political power.

An excellent example is the Shomiti Programme in Bangladesh, set up by Action Aid. The local women have pooled their resources and set up a local development fund. The fund provides loans for individuals and organisations. A fundamental aspect is raising standards of education, seen as the key to future prosperity: a village school has been built with a teacher paid from the funds and adult education has been improved. In addition, there have been developments in health care, nutrition, sanitation, and food supply. Shomiti Programmes have become widespread in Bangladesh, and have not only improved standards of living but also empowered women.

Black women in South Africa

Many black women in South Africa are severely constrained by society. The data in this section refer to fieldwork carried out in the Eastern Cape region of South Africa from 1984-91. Most heads of household in the region are women. Many mothers are young, unmarried and experience high rates of illness. In many of these households the mother has to find work to support the family. This means that the task of child rearing is carried out by older brothers and sisters, or elderly grandparents, who may not be best suited to the role. Grandparents are often old and too infirm to cope with the demands of growing children; sisters and aunts are frequently too young, lacking the necessary maturity and responsibility.

Black women's health is not good. Most of the women in the survey claimed to be nervous, tense and worried (77%), easily tired and suffering from frequent headaches (73%), or tired all the time (69%). Other aspects of their health were also quite poor: many reported an inability to sleep well, poor appetite and in discussions with health workers, showed a general lack of emotional stability.

The status of women in South Africa, like many ELDCs, is low. Women have few rights, while at the same time bearing much of the responsibility for looking after their households. This situation is made worse, in many cases, by high fertility rates and economic dependence upon the women. Formal work opportunities for women are constrained by family ties, conditions of work and lack of crèche facilities. Yet the need for a cash income was given as a reason for entering the informal economy, which in some cases leads to problems of child minding and maternal health.

Most women are in a dilemma – go to work and risk the health and development of their children – or stay at home and exist without money. In some cases, women's cooperatives have been set up. In this area much of it was done through Operation Hunger and Oxfam. Activities include dressmaking, bead work, cultivating vegetable gardens and producing watering cans. All are low-cost, locally-based initiatives.

TRADE

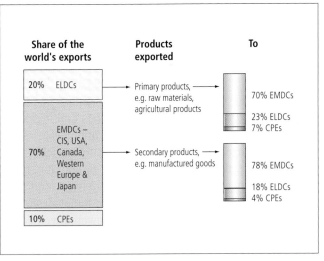

Figure 1.32 *Share of the world's exports*
Source: Adapted from Stevens, A., International trade, 1996, GeoActive 142

Trade is the import (buying) and export (selling) of goods such as food, fuel, manufactured goods, raw materials, finance, and technology. The balance of trade is the difference in money terms between imports and exports:

- a positive balance of trade means that the value of exports exceeds the value of imports
- a negative balance of trade means that the value of imports exceeds the value of exports.

Trade is vital to the development of many ELDCs. Unlike aid, which is largely one-way, trade is a two-way process which can allow countries to develop economically (Figure 1.32). However, trade can also lead to underdevelopment. According to Frank's dependency theory (Inset 1.3), ELDCs have not always been undeveloped but they become underdeveloped or less developed because of trading relations with developed countries or empires.

Patterns of trade

EMDCs and ELDCs have different export and import patterns. EMDCs export mostly machinery, transport equipment, chemicals and services, which are generally expensive. By contrast, ELDCs have a much smaller range of exports – mostly agricultural products and raw materials, which are cheaper than manufactured goods. Their range of imports is similar to EMDCs, although the goods are likely to be cheaper and less sophisticated. Hence, ELDCs are forced into a trade trap whereby they export cheap goods but import expensive products.

The pattern of **international trade** is very uneven:

- EMDCs account for the greatest amount of world trade
- ELDCs account for a decreasing amount of world trade
- Socialist countries account for a small, but increasing amount of world trade.

Inset 1.3
Dependency theory

According to the **dependency theory**, some countries become dependent upon stronger, frequently colonial, powers, as a result of exploitation, trade and 'development'. As the more powerful country exploits the resources of its weaker colony, the colony becomes dependent upon the stronger power. Goods flow from the colony to support consumers in the overseas country.

Andre Frank (1971) described the effect of capitalist development on many countries as **'the development of underdevelopment'**. The problem of poor countries is not that they lack the resources, technical know-how, modern institutions or cultural developments that lead to development, but that they are being exploited by capitalist countries.

The dependency theory is a very different approach from most models of development:

- it incorporates politics and economics in its explanation
- it takes into account the historical processes of underdevelopment, i.e. how capitalist development began in one part of the world and then expanded into other areas (Imperial expansion)
- it sees development as a revolution or a change in the political power of the people, a clash of interests between ruling classes (bourgeoisie) and the working classes (proletariat)
- it stresses that to be developed is to be self-reliant and to control national resources
- it believes that modernisation does not necessarily mean westernisation, and that underdeveloped countries must set goals of their own, appropriate to their own resources, needs and values.

Source: Nagle G. and Spencer K., 1997, Advanced Geography Revision Handbook, OUP

Trade in the 1990s is very dynamic. There are a number of new trading blocs, whose membership fluctuates, changes in tariff levels, restrictions on imports and exports, opening up of former 'closed markets' such as the Eastern Bloc and China, recession in many EMDCs, and continuing debt problems. It is in this context that ELDC countries have to find new trading partners.

Trading blocs

A trading bloc is a group of countries which protect their industries and markets. It allows free trade within the

trading bloc, but usually imposes tariffs, and places restrictions on the amount of imports, from other countries. For members of the trading bloc there are two main advantages:
- they have access to a large market
- it protects their industries against foreign competitors.

However, for many ELDCs the trading bloc they belong to does not contain a wealthy market.

Intercontinental aid: the Marshall Plan

In the history of aid, the Marshall Plan was probably the most successful example of enlightened self-interest. Established in 1947, it helped Europe recover economically after the war, and ensured that Europe was:

- politically stable
- a functioning market.

The plan pumped US$13 billion (US$88 billion at today's value) into Europe to 'jump-start' its economies. The element which contributed most to its success was the opening up of markets, and the creation of a climate favourable for private investment.

There are parallels with developments in Eastern Europe in the 1990s. The European Union and USA opened their markets to goods from Eastern Europe. This allowed those countries to earn hard foreign currency.

The Marshall Plan shows that aid can be linked to trade, and that for long-term economic success, trade is essential.

SUMMARY

In this chapter we have seen that the definition of development is complex. This makes measuring development very difficult. Nevertheless, there are certain groups of countries with shared characteristics and these countries can be identified as more developed, less developed and so on. How countries develop also varies and we have seen how some countries have developed with or without outside help. Even that help is not always in the best interests of the receiver. At the centre of the development 'debate' is the question of standards of living and quality of life – as experienced by the people.

QUESTIONS

1 Study Figure 1.33 which shows basic indicators of development.
a) Which country do you think is the most developed?
b) Give reasons for your answer.
c) Which do you think is the least developed?
d) Give reasons for your answer.
e) How useful is (i) GNP/head and (ii) the IMR as a method of measuring development? Give your reasons.
2 With the use of examples, show how governments can promote economic growth.
3 What is the difference between communism and capitalism? Why do you think capitalist countries have become NICs but communist ones have not?
4 Define these terms: import substitution industries, export orientated industries, appropriate development.
5 Explain why a successful education system is vital for long term development.
6 Development should be 'basic, appropriate, affordable, and acceptable'. What do you think these four terms mean with regard to development. Give **two** examples of development that are 'basic, appropriate, affordable, and acceptable' and **two** examples of those that are not.
7 Discuss the role of women in development.

BIBLIOGRAPHY AND RECOMMENDED READING

Brandt, W., 1980, *North-South: a programme for survival*, Pan

Chambers, R., 1983, *Rural development – putting the last first*, Longman

Corbridge, S., 1995, *Development studies: a reader*, Hodder and Stoughton

Dickenson, J. et al., 1996, *A geography of the Third World*, Routledge

International Labour Organisation, 1996, *Child labour: targeting the intolerable*, ILO

Reid, D., 1995, *Sustainable development: an introductory guide*, Earthscan

Sarre, P. and Blunden, J., 1996, *Environment, population and development*, Hodder and Stoughton

United Nations Development Programme, 1994, *Human development report*, 1994, OUP

World Bank, 1996, *The World Bank Atlas*, 1996, World Bank

WEB SITES

Africa online -
   http://www.africaonline.com/
Asia Ville - the Global Village in Asia -
   http://www.asiaville.com/
World Health Organisation -
   http://www.who.ch/

	GNP (US$)	IMR (‰)	Total fertility rate (births/woman)	Pop. growth (%)	Agri. GDP (%)	Energy use (oil equivalent) (kg/head)
Brazil	3 020	58	2.9	1.9	11	681
China	490	31	2	1.4	21	601
Germany	23 560	6	1.3	0.6	1	4358
India	290	79	3.7	2.1	31	235
Japan	31 450	5	1.5	0.4	2	3586
Namibia	1 660	57	5.4	3	11	no data
Nigeria	310	84	5.9	2.9	36	128
South Africa	2 900	53	4.1	2.4	4	2487
UK	17 970	8	1.8	0.3	2	3743
USA	24 750	8	2.1	0.9	2	7662

Figure 1.33 *Basic indicators of development*

Chapter 2
Population

Population issues are at the heart of development, and are central to the study of geography. There are constant reminders in the press and on television about human suffering, injustices, and environmental crises. To a large extent, these problems are caused by inequalities in the distribution of population and resources. Any attempt to plan for a fairer society must be based on information about how many people there are, where they live, and how fast the numbers are growing.

This chapter looks at population distribution and density on a global and local scale, population composition, population change, migration and the relationship between population and resources. Examples from Japan, South Africa, Mexico, China, India and Rwanda illustrate many of the issues in population.

POPULATION DISTRIBUTION AND DENSITY

'Population distribution' refers to where people live. On a global scale:

- 75% of the population live within 1000 kilometres of the sea
- 85% live in areas less than 500 metres high
- 85% live between latitudes 68°N and 20°N
- less than 10% live in the southern hemisphere.

The most favoured locations include fertile valleys, areas where there is a regular supply of water and the climate is not too extreme, and places with good communications. By contrast, disadvantaged areas include deserts (too dry), mountains (too steep), high latitudes (too cold) and rainforests (soil too fragile). Inequalities in population distribution can be shown by Lorenz curves (Figure 2.1).

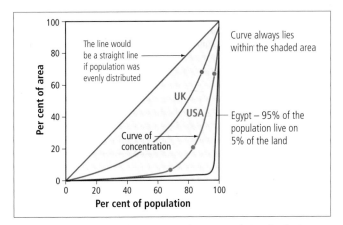

Figure 2.1 *Lorenz curve showing inequalities in population distribution*

TERMS & ABBREVIATIONS

Distribution – where the population is located

Density – the number of people per square kilometre

Natural increase – the growth in population when birth rates exceed death rates

Population growth – natural increase and migration

Dependency ratio – ratio of people who are not economically active against those who are

Migration – moving from one place to another, permanently or for a long period

AIDS (acquired immuno deficiency syndrome) – a disease which destroys the human immune system

'Population density' refers to the number of people per square kilometre. In part, it is a measure of how advantaged a place is, and in part it shows how disadvantaged alternative sites are. In the UK, population densities of over 1000 per square kilometre are found in parts of the South East, the Midlands and the North West (Figure 2.2).

In parts of London the density reaches over 4300 per square kilometre. The South East has 33% of the UK's population on 10% of the UK land area. The North West is the most densely populated region with 868 people per square kilometre. By contrast, parts of Scotland have densities of less

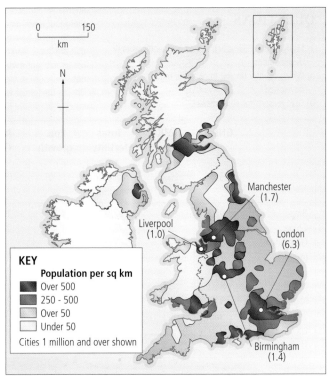

Figure 2.2 *Population density in the UK, 1991*
Source: Carr, M., 1997, New patterns: progress and change in human geography, Nelson

than 1 per square kilometre. Scotland has 10% of the UK population on 35% of the UK land area: the northern parts are remote with a relatively severe climate, communications are more difficult and there are few employment opportunities.

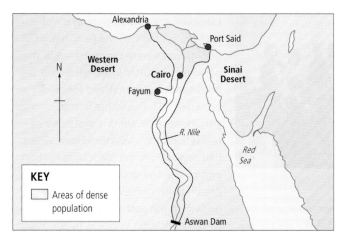

Figure 2.3 *Population distribution in Egypt, 1991*

One of the most uneven population distributions in the world is in Egypt (Figure 2.3). Up to 95% of the population is found on less than 5% of the land – the Nile Valley and its delta. The rest of Egypt is largely desert.

POPULATION COMPOSITION

'Population composition' refers to the characteristics of the population. These include age, gender, ethnic background, language, occupations and religion. Most aspects of population composition are important because they give information about population growth. They help planners provide services and facilities for the future.

In 1991 the UK figures show that 19% of the population are under the age of 15 years and 16% are over the age of 60 years. These figures hide differences between the ethnic groups. Among Caucasians (white British), 19% are in the under 15 group and 21% in the over 60 group. By contrast, among British people of Pakistani and Bangladeshi heritage, the proportions are 45% and 3%.

Inset 2.1
Dependency ratios and triangular graphs

The **dependency ratio** measures the working population and the dependent population. It is worked out by the formula:

$$\frac{\text{Population aged} < 15 + \text{population aged} > 60}{\text{Population aged } 16\text{–}59} \quad \frac{\text{the dependents}}{\text{the workers}}$$

It is a crude measure. For example, many people stay on at school after the age of 15 and many people work after the age of 60. But it is a useful measure to compare countries.

- In the developed world there is a high proportion of elderly people.
- In the developing world there is a high proportion of young people.

These ratios can be shown on a triangular graph (Figure 2.4).

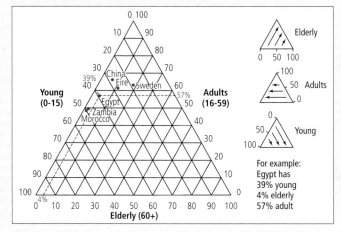

Figure 2.4 *Triangular graph to show population age structure, 1991*

Triangular graphs

Triangular graphs are used to show data that can be divided into three parts, such as population (young, adult and elderly), employment (primary, secondary and tertiary), and soil (sand, silt and clay). The data must be in the form of a percentage, totalling 100%.

Triangular graphs have many advantages.

- A large amount of data can be shown on one graph (think how many pie charts or bar charts would be used to show all the data in Figure 2.4).
- Groupings are easily recognisable. In the case of population, composition can be readily identified.
- Dominant characteristics can be shown easily.
- Classifications can be drawn up.

However, these graphs can be difficult to create and it is easy to get confused, so care must be taken.

QUESTIONS

Plot the following on a triangular graph:
1 Japan (i) elderly 13%, (ii) adult 69%, (iii) young 18%
2 South Africa (i) elderly 4%, (ii) adult 56%, (iii) young 40%
3 India (i) elderly 4%, (ii) adult 60%, (iii) young 36%
4 China (i) elderly 6%, (ii) adult 66%, (iii) young 28%
5 UK (i) elderly 16%, (ii) adult 65%, (iii) young 19%.

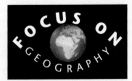

Case study:
Population composition in South Africa

South Africa's population is an interesting one to study because it shows population trends associated with an EMDC as well as an ELDC. This has arisen out of South Africa's particular type of development, apartheid, which was a racial form of development. Whites, and to a lesser extent Asians, show characteristics of EMDC populations, whereas blacks and coloureds have characteristics of ELDC populations.

South Africa's population, including the homelands, is about 40 million (1995 figures). Of the South African population, blacks (Africans) make up the majority, 76%, with whites (Europeans), coloureds (mixed race) and Asians (Indians) comprising the rest, 13%, 9% and 3% respectively.

There is a vast difference in population composition (Figure 2.6): over 18 million

Figure 2.5 *South Africa's youthful population*

South Africans are under the age of eighteen years, 80% of these are black. The age structures reveal that whites and Asians have a much smaller proportion of young people compared with coloureds and blacks (Figure 2.6). Thus the percentage annual growth rates are very different: whites, 0.77, Indians, 1.28, coloureds, 1.41, and blacks, 2.85. By the year 2000 the total population of South Africa is set to rise to 45 million and by 2010 to 60 million, 81% black.

However, population growth is not uniform spatially: in the past, higher growth rates were concentrated in the periurban squatter settlements and the homelands, areas reserved for black occupancy. The rapid rise in the periurban settlements is explained by relaxation of the apartheid laws which had severely limited black urbanisation, and by the age structure of such populations. In the homelands, rapid growth in the past can be attributed to forced relocation of blacks by the South African authorities and the youthful age structure.

The rapid growth of the population presents particular problems for the South African government. Not only are they trying to redress years of inequality under apartheid (Figure 2.8), but they are attempting to regenerate the economy in the face of unprecedented population growth.

Inset 2.2
Definitions relating to South Africa

Periurban: a large sprawling settlement lacking in most urban amenities, usually on the edge of an urban area but not necessarily so.
Urbanisation: an increase in the proportion of the population living in urban or periurban areas.
Homeland: an area formerly reserved for the exclusive occupancy of blacks. Most were peripheral, isolated and fragmented pieces of land with very high levels of population density.
Township: separate urban areas with generally low standard, crowded housing reserved for blacks, coloureds or Asians.

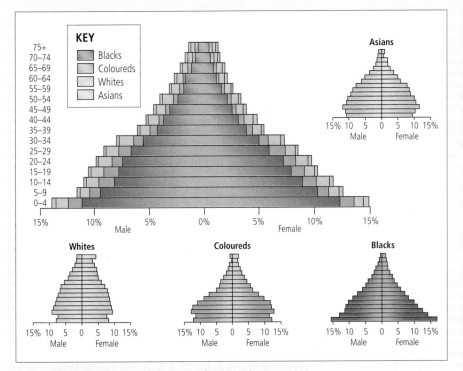

Figure 2.6 *Population pyramids for South Africa's racial groups, 1992*
Source: Nagle, G., 1994, South Africa's demographic time bomb, Geographical, 66, October 52-4

Inset 2.3
Apartheid's legacy

Apartheid was a formal system of strict racial segregation that existed in South Africa between 1948 and 1992. It was associated with the Afrikaaner National Party, which had political control of South Africa until 1994. However, segregation existed long before the apartheid era and is evident even today. As well as geographic segregation, there was also social and economic segregation: blacks and coloureds in particular were exploited as cheap labour and effectively barred from sharing South Africa's riches (Figure 2.8).

At a national level, blacks were forced to live in 'homelands', areas drawn up as a result of land acts in 1913 and 1936 (Figure 2.7). The homelands were isolated, fragmented, rural areas set aside for the sole occupancy of blacks. They accounted for just 13% of the country but were expected to accommodate up to 75% of South Africa's population. However, by 1994 only about half of the black population lived in them, with the rest in townships in 'white' South Africa.

When the National Party came to power in 1948 they introduced the policies of apartheid, or separate development, and ruthlessly pursued them. They classified all people to one of four racial groups, whites, blacks, coloureds and Asians. They believed that different races could not live in harmony, and to avoid conflict, contact between the races should be minimised. Hence, separate areas and facilities were developed for each of the groups. The Group Areas Act of 1950 dictated which urban areas each race could live in: whites had the largest and the best areas and other groups were forced to live in overcrowded townships. Many facilities were segregated under the Reservation of Separate Amenities Act of 1953: these included parks, beaches, post office counters and train carriages.

However, apartheid operated at a much more fundamental level: schools and health care facilities were also segregated. Whereas parks and beaches were among the first type of facility to be opened to all races, in 1995, schools and hospitals in the homelands were still funded by homeland authorities, rather than nationally, despite the formal abolition of the homelands in 1994.

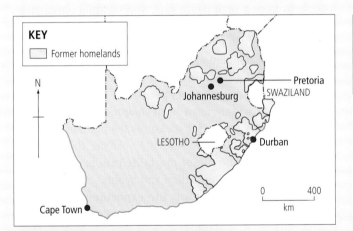

Figure 2.7 South Africa's former homelands

	Black	White	Coloured	Asian
Infant mortality rate ‰	52.8	7.3	28.0	13.5
Life expectancy (yrs)	63	73	63	67
TB cases per 100 000 people	216	15	580	53

Figure 2.8 *Selected social and economic indicators in South Africa by race, 1993*
Source: based on David Smith, 1995, Redistribution and social justice after apartheid in A. Lemon (ed.) The geography of change in South Africa, Wiley

Figure 2.9 *Many of South Africa's black population continue to live in very poor conditions*

QUESTIONS

1 Study Figure 2.6 which shows the population pyramids of the four main racial groups of South Africa. Copy and fill in the following table. (Add the percentages for male and female of each age group and divide the answer by two.)

	White	Coloured	Asian	Black
Percentage under the age of 5				
Percentage under the age of 20				
Percentage over the age of 59				

2 Define the term 'population composition'. How do you think the population composition of the four racial groups in South Africa varies and why?

3 What is meant by the term 'dependency ratio'? How does this vary between the four pyramids for the racial groups in Figure 2.6?

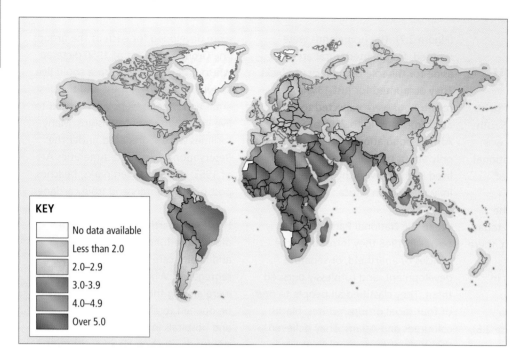

Figure 2.10 *Total fertility rates, 1990–95*
Source: Population and the environment: the challenges ahead, 1993, UNFPA

KEY

	No data available
	Less than 2.0
	2.0–2.9
	3.0–3.9
	4.0–4.9
	Over 5.0

POPULATION CHANGE

At the heart of the development question is the issue of population change. Rapid population growth puts a great strain on resources and the ability of governments to provide for their people. Population increase is brought about in a number of ways.

- high fertility rates
- declining death rates
- migration.

Birth rates and death rates

Fertility is the ability to reproduce. It is normally expressed by:

- the **crude birth rate (CBR)** – the number of live births per thousand people per year
- **total fertility rate (TFR)** – the number of children born per year per thousand women of reproductive age.

The crude birth rate is relatively easy to calculate, if the data is available. However, it does not take into account the age structure of the population. Hence the total fertility rate gives a more accurate picture. Factors affecting the birth rate include population structure, economic prosperity, material ambition, maternal health, political influences, education and literacy, availability of family planning, role of women in society, and religion.

The **crude death rate** is the number of deaths per thou-

sand people per year. It is called 'crude' because it does not take into account the age structure of the population. We would expect populations with a large number of elderly people to have a high death rate, and youthful populations to have a low death rate. Unless we know the age structure of a population, we might not be comparing like with like.

To compare populations correctly, we use the **age specific death rate**. This is the number of deaths per thousand people of a certain age group, per year.

A measure widely used in development studies is the **infant mortality rate**. This measures the number of deaths in children aged under the age of 1 year per thousand live births per year. The infant mortality rate is discussed at length in Chapter 3, Population and health.

Another useful measure is **life expectancy**. This is the average number of years a person can expect to live.

The demographic transition model

The **demographic transition model (DTM)** describes how birth rates and death rates change over time. It is divided into four or, sometimes, five stages (Figure 2.11).

Population change in the UK

In the last two decades there has been a very low rate of population growth in the UK, due mainly to the collapse of the birth rate (Figure 2.12).

QUESTIONS

1 What is the fertility rate in **(i)** India, **(ii)** Japan, and **(iii)** South Africa? (See Figure 2.10.)

2 Describe the world pattern of fertility as shown in Figure 2.10.

3 Choose any **three** factors which affect the birth rate. Explain how they influence birth rates.

There have been two periods this century when the birth rate increased, the turn of the century and in the 1960s.

The larger boom took place at the turn of the century, and this has manifested itself in the growth of people of a pensionable age in the 1960s and 1970s and the dramatic increase in the number of the very elderly in the 1980s.

The long-term trend towards smaller average household size has accelerated over the last two decades for a number of reasons, including:

- a fall in the birth rate
- the growth in the number of the elderly
- the increase in the number of young adults
- the rising divorce rate.

In addition, there have been changes in the distribution of the population and its composition in certain areas which caused a massive redistribution of population away from the largest cities to smaller settlements and more rural areas, and by an acceleration of the North-South drift.

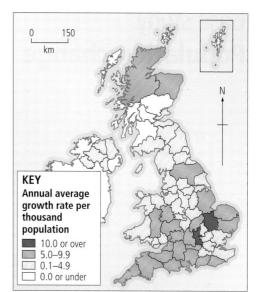

KEY
Annual average growth rate per thousand population

- 10.0 or over
- 5.0–9.9
- 0.1–4.9
- 0.0 or under

Figure 2.12 Population change in the UK, 1981-1992

Figure 2.11 The demographic transition model

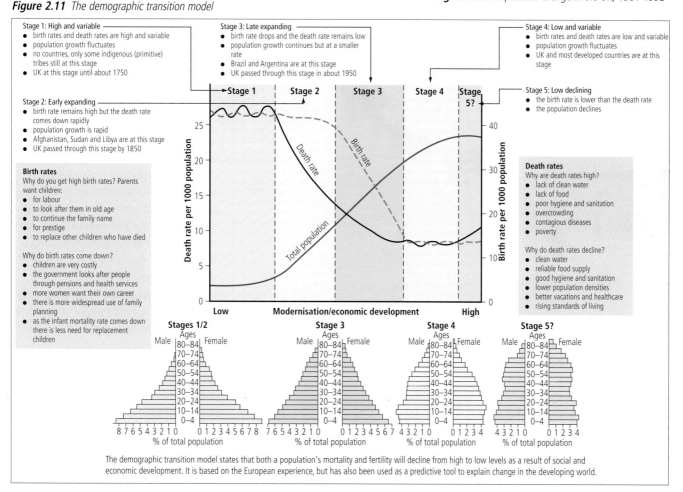

Stage 1: High and variable
- birth rates and death rates are high and variable
- population growth fluctuates
- no countries, only some indigenous (primitive) tribes still at this stage
- UK at this stage until about 1750

Stage 2: Early expanding
- birth rate remains high but the death rate comes down rapidly
- population growth is rapid
- Afghanistan, Sudan and Libya are at this stage
- UK passed through this stage by 1850

Birth rates
Why do you get high birth rates? Parents want children:
- for labour
- to look after them in old age
- to continue the family name
- for prestige
- to replace other children who have died

Why do birth rates come down?
- children are very costly
- the government looks after people through pensions and health services
- more women want their own career
- there is more widespread use of family planning
- as the infant mortality rate comes down there is less need for replacement children

Stage 3: Late expanding
- birth rate drops and the death rate remains low
- population growth continues but at a smaller rate
- Brazil and Argentina are at this stage
- UK passed through this stage in about 1950

Stage 4: Low and variable
- birth rates and death rates are low and variable
- population growth fluctuates
- UK and most developed countries are at this stage

Stage 5: Low declining
- the birth rate is lower than the death rate
- the population declines

Death rates
Why are death rates high?
- lack of clean water
- lack of food
- poor hygiene and sanitation
- overcrowding
- contagious diseases
- poverty

Why do death rates decline?
- clean water
- reliable food supply
- good hygiene and sanitation
- lower population densities
- better vacations and healthcare
- rising standards of living

Stage 1 Stage 2 Stage 3 Stage 4 Stage 5?

Death rate per 1000 population / Birth rate per 1000 population

Death rate / Birth rate / Total population

Low — Modernisation/economic development — High

Stages 1/2 **Stage 3** **Stage 4** **Stage 5?**
Ages
Male Female
80–84
70–74
60–64
50–54
40–44
30–34
20–24
10–14
0–4
% of total population

The demographic transition model states that both a population's mortality and fertility will decline from high to low levels as a result of social and economic development. It is based on the European experience, but has also been used as a predictive tool to explain change in the developing world.

QUESTIONS

1 Study figure 2.2. Describe the population density in the UK. Using an atlas, account for these variations in terms of **(i)** physical factors and **(ii)** human factors. Illustrate your answer with examples.

2 Study Figure 2.2 and 2.12. How do the maps of population density and population change compare?

Case study:
Population change in an EMDC – Japan

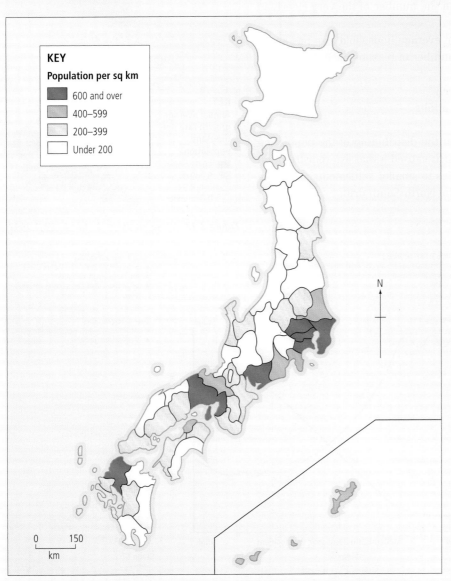

Figure 2.13 *Population density in Japan, 1990*
Source: NIPPON - a charted survey of Japan, 1992/93,
the Kokusei-Sha Corporation

KEY

Population per sq km

▓	600 and over
▒	400–599
░	200–399
☐	Under 200

0   150
km

N

1   more money is needed to support elderly people, e.g. pensions, health care, free transport

2   fewer workers are available to fill all the jobs – hence taxes on these workers may have to be increased to support the services for the elderly.

Sociologists, economists and planners forecast a number of problems, including:

● inadequate nursing facilities
● depletion of labour force
● deterioration of the economy
● trade deficit
● migration of Japanese industry overseas.

Moreover, Japan does not have many natural resources and its land and waters are already overused (Figure 2.13). In an economy where the cost of living is high, the prospect of supporting large numbers of people for decades is disturbing. So much so, that a few years ago the Japanese government investigated the possibilities of sending some of their elderly people overseas to places as far away as West Africa.

Changes in Japan's population illustrate many of the processes operating in EMDCs. The age structure of the population has changed dramatically over the last fifty years. This is largely due to a decrease in the birth rate and death rate (Figure 2.14). In 1995 the elderly population (above 65 years) accounted for 14.6% (18.3 million) of the total population. In 1970 it was only 7.1%, but by the year 2007 it will be 20%. The percentage of young people (under 15 years) has gradually declined since 1975. By 1995 they accounted for only about 16% of the population.

By the year 2025, Japan's elderly population will be larger than any other developed country. The ageing of the population structure in Japan is much more rapid than in other countries. For the government, the dual problems of a workforce declining in numbers and a dependent population increasing in numbers, are a major concern for two main reasons:

Death rates and birth rates

The death rate in Japan was relatively stable between 1975 and 1987 at 6.0-6.3 per thousand, but the ageing population is increasing the death rate. It increased to 7.1 per thousand by 1993-1994 even though life expectancy is very high – 83 years for women and 77 years for men. Japan's life expectancy is now the highest in the world. This contrasts strongly with life expectancy in 1935, when it was under 47 years for men and just over 49 years for women.

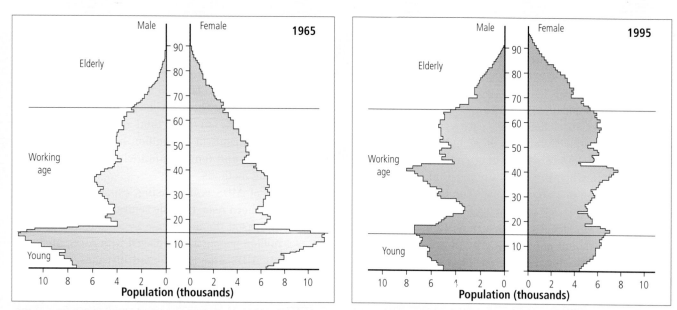

Figure 2.14 *Population pyramids for Saga, Japan, in 1965 and 1995, showing ageing population structure*
Source: Saga Prefecture, 1996, Saga

Japan's population is shrinking as well as ageing. Results from 1996 show that the birth rate in 1995 of 9.6 births per thousand is the lowest since World War II. This figure compares with a high in 1950 of 28.1. In the baby boom of 1970–1973, the birth rate reached 19 per thousand. This declined to 9.3 per thousand by 1993. In the next few years the birth rate is expected to drop very significantly. In 1995, the total fertility rate (the average number of births per woman) reached its lowest figure of 1.42. This means that on average most women have less than one and a half children.

Changes in marriage and family structure

Since World War II there have been major changes in the family structure in Japan. These have been associated with increased rural to urban migration, fewer 'arranged' marriages, more 'love' marriages and the increased number of nuclear families (husband, wife and children) rather than the vertical extended family.

In the early 1970s, the average annual number of marriages in Japan was over one million. Marriage rates were greater than 10 per thousand per year (for every one thousand people there were ten marriages). By 1993, the marriage rate was 6.3 per thousand and the average annual number of marriages was only 783 000. Although there was a slight increase in the marriage rate in 1995, to 794 000, the divorce rate was rising to its highest ever. The increasing average age of people at marriage, an increasing divorce rate and greater numbers of people choosing to remain single and childless have led to a decline in the birth rate.

Household size

Between 1920 and 1955, the average Japanese household consisted of five people, in 1994 it was just 2.95. This change is due to a decline in the birth rate and an increase in the number of nuclear families and single people. The average size of a Japanese household is expected to reach a low of 2.55 by 2010. Over 42 million households existed in Japan in 1994, an increase of 28% on the 1975 level. By contrast, the population had only increased by 11%. Moreover, the number of nuclear households is now over 25 million. This represents almost 60% of all households in Japan.

QUESTIONS

1 Compare the population problems of Japan with those of another developed country that you have studied.
2 Explain why an ageing population is a major concern to governments.
3 Using the data provided below, draw a graph to show how Japan's population has increased since the mid-1700s. When was population growth most rapid? When did it slow down? What will happen to Japan's population after 2010?

Population of Japan

1750	30 million
1868	30 million
1873	35 million
1926	60 million
1937	70 million
1967	100 million
2000	127 million
2010	130 million
2025	126 million
2050	112 million

WORLD POPULATION TRENDS

The world's population is not growing as fast as was once feared. This is mainly due to the use of contraceptives, although war and AIDS are also major factors, especially in ELDCs.

The world's population is approximately 5.85 billion and growing by over 80 million people each year. This is larger than the UK's total population of 57 million in the mid-1990s. Nevertheless this is an improvement on the mid-1980s to 1990, when the world's population increased by about 87 million people each year. The UN now believes that population will peak at about 9.4 billion people in 2050; although other predictions are as high as 12.5 billion.

Fertility rates and population growth are declining. In India, for example, the average fertility rate has declined from 4.5 children to 3.4 children per woman, as a result of better family planning. As a result population growth in India fell from 1.57% in 1994 to 1.48% in 1996. Although only a small percentage decrease, given the size of India's population, this represents a huge number of people.

In spite of this decline, the 1997 UN Population Fund report called for better reproductive health care and access to contraceptives. It estimates that 585 000 women – one every minute – die from causes related to pregnancy. 200 000 of these are related to the lack of, or failure of, contraceptive services. The UN believes that 75 million pregnancies each year, out of a total of 175 million, are unwanted, and result in 45 million abortions. In many ELDCs, abortion and female infanticide are still used as family planning methods.

The effect of AIDS is increasing, especially in central Africa and southern Asia. In some central African countries, AIDS has increased the death rate by as much as 25%. In 1996, 3.1 million people were infected with AIDS, and over 50% died of AIDS and HIV-related diseases. This total included 350 000 children under the age of 5 years.

South Asia, and India in particular, has the highest number of AIDS cases. However, the most rapid spreading of the disease is found in the former USSR; infections were almost non-existent a few years ago, but AIDS and HIV are now

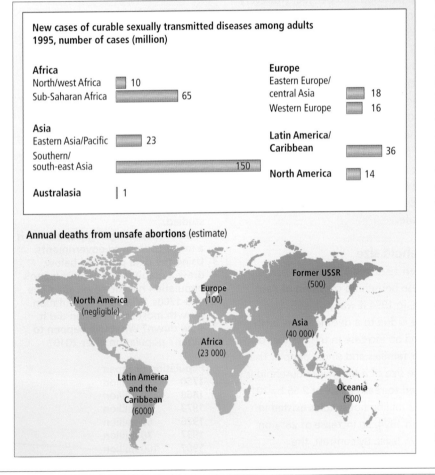

Inset 2.4
AIDS in the CIS
(Confederation of Independent States – the former USSR)

The countries of the former Soviet Union are on the brink of an AIDS epidemic. Ukraine has one of the sharpest increases in HIV infections, mostly as a result of young people injecting drugs. The cities bordering the Black Sea, where drugs are relatively easy to obtain, and where the 'holiday sex industry' is booming, have the largest number of cases. In the small town of Nikolaev, HIV infection among drug users increased dramatically from 1.7% to 56.5% in less than one year. Throughout the CIS, the number of cases increased sevenfold between 1995 and 1996.

Figure 2.15 *The world – a troubled population*
Sources: WHO, Maternal health & safe motherhood programme (Geneva), unpublished estimates

---

QUESTIONS

1 State two reasons why death rates are increasing.

2 Explain two reasons for the decline of birth rates.

3 Why do you think EMDCs did **not** give as much money, as they had agreed, to improve reproductive health care in ELDCs?

causing grave concern. Up to 70% of cases are among heterosexuals, and the majority of newly-infected people are aged between 15 and 24 years.

The UN report also shows that in ELDCs, the proportion of women under the age of 20 years who have sexual relations before the age of 20 is decreasing. By contrast, in EMDCs the number of girls under the age of 16 who are sexually active is increasing. The report blames ignorance and the lack of sexual education for unwanted pregnancies and increasing numbers of HIV infections. It also states 'sex education encourages … higher levels of abstinence, later start of sexual activity, higher use of contraceptives, and fewer sexual partners'.

The 'sex trade', which also involves trafficking in children, also fuels the HIV pandemic (global epidemic). Up to 80% of prostitutes are HIV-positive, and up to 2 million girls between the ages of 5 and 15 are brought into the commercial sex market each year. The trend is especially strong in Asia.

The international convention on population and development held in Cairo in 1994 agreed that US$17 billion would be needed annually to provide better reproductive health care. It was agreed that ELDCs would provide US$11.3 billion and EMDCs the remaining US$5.7 billion towards the UN programme. Whereas ELDCs kept close to their promise and provided US$10.7 billion, EMDCs provided less than US$2.5 billion – less than half of what they promised.

POPULATION GROWTH IN ELDCs

By the year 2050, the UN's lowest projection shows a world population of 7.8 billion and the highest projection estimates a population of 12.5 billion people. A startling reduction in fertility rates in Asia and Latin America over the past three decades has raised hopes that the world's population can be held to the UN's low projection, before stabilising some time in the next century.

To reach the UN's low projection of population growth, the average number of children per woman in the developing world would have to drop to 2.71 by 2050 from around 3.74 in 1990. Tackling population growth, says the UN, will mean reaching the estimated 350 million couples world-wide who do not have access to a full range of family-planning information or contraception.

In Ethiopia, Uganda and many parts of Africa, the average number of children a woman gives birth to remains at around seven. Mothers have more children partly because they do not know how many will survive, partly as an insurance policy for their old age, and partly because they do not have the means to exercise choice.

The prospect this raises of ungovernable, congested megacities, water and food shortages, depletion of forests and wild places and the spectre of climate change, explains why politicians – as opposed to religious leaders – almost everywhere, pay lip-service to programmes to reduce population growth.

Figure 2.16 *The battle to curb the baby boom*
Source: based on Daily Telegraph, 5 September 1994

Population control in Egypt

The last decade has been one of progress in population control, which Egypt's policy makers and aid workers consider little short of remarkable.

The population growth rate has plunged from 3% to about 2.1%. A fertility rate of 5.3 births per woman in 1980 has come down to an average of 3.9 and an average of 2.9 in urban areas. Knowledge of family planning among married couples is almost universal. In 1992 47% of women in Egypt used contraception (predominantly IUD devices and the Pill) against 24% in 1980 (Figure 2.17b).

Behind such results lie 20 years of concerted government policy, backed by foreign aid. Of this USAID has provided 75% of the costs of family planning assistance, a total of about US$170m (£113m). The money has been used to fill the media with birth control information and stock and staff hundreds of clinics, enough for 96% of all Egyptian women to be within five kilometres of a family planning centre.

At present rates, Egypt's 60 million population is growing by 1 million every 10 months. The constraints on the country's most basic resources are severe enough: all but 4% of its 1 million square kilometres is desert. A recent report by the UN's Economic and Social Commission for Western Asia stated that Egypt was consuming 95% of its available water sources and faced a water deficit by the year 2000.

Figure 2.17(b) *Family planning methods in Egypt*
Source: based on Financial Times, 2 September 1994

Method	Percentage
IUD	28
Pill	13
Traditional methods	2
Female sterilisation	1
No method	53

Figure 2.17(a) *Family planning in Egypt*

Population growth in India

India's population is growing by about 2% each year. This is creating an enormous strain on India's already stretched resources. For example, there is an urgent need to increase food production, but population growth is reducing the amount of land available. High yielding varieties of crops and intensive farming techniques can be used but these cause other problems. (This is discussed in detail in Chapter 4, Geographical issues in agriculture.)

India's population growth is fuelled by a high birth rate of about 30 per thousand. Birth rates are high for a number of reasons:

- poverty – children are needed to work on the farm and to look after their elderly parents
- relatively high infant mortality rates – hence there is a need for high birth rates to compensate for children who die
- religion – both the Hindu and Islamic religions encourage large families, and certain ceremonial functions can only be performed by males – thus there is a higher birth rate to ensure that male offspring are produced
- prestige – in many poor societies large families are a sign of importance
- lack of family planning – less than 30% of India's population use birth control methods.

India was one of the first ELDCs to encourage family planning, mainly because of the large size of its population. Despite nearly forty years of birth control, the population is still growing, and only now are there signs that growth is beginning to slow down. A number of population policies have been used in India:

1 From the 1950s, forced **sterilisations** were performed on women to reduce population growth. These operations were performed on women after their second child, and in some cases on people who had no children. Money and radios were offered to those who voluntarily underwent the treatment.

2 **Primary health care** is a form of low-cost preventative health care which is made widely available. It promotes:
- family planning
- breast feeding
- rehydration for malnourished people
- health education.

These provisions have had a profound impact in many areas. For example, the birth rates have been reduced as a result of family planning. Moreover, the infant mortality rate has been reduced as a result of better feeding practices, antenatal care and health care for infants. The need for a high birth rate has been removed.

3 Providing family planning education for women. This gives women more freedom and more choice over their future. Educated women are more likely to enter the workforce, delay the age of marriage, and aspire to a higher standard of living. This means fewer children.

Population policy in China

China has a huge population, nearly 1.3 billion people, which it is attempting to stabilise at 1.2 billion by the year 2000 (Figure 2.18). In addition, it wants to reduce its population even further by 2010. It has adopted drastic policies in an effort to achieve what it believes to be the optimum size, given its resources.

In the 1970s, China introduced a one-child policy. Families which only have one child are given better houses, better education, and better employment prospects than those which have two or more children. Compulsory sterilisations, forced abortions and female infanticide have also been used to limit population growth.

The policy has succeeded, to an extent (Figure 2.19). The fertility rate has dropped from 5.8 to 2.1. However, away from the larger, more industrialised cities, the policy has been less successful. Many rural households continue to have two or three children. The one-child policy has also introduced a new problem to China – the spoilt, overweight 'little emperors'. There has been widespread criticism of the policy, not only from foreign critics but from internal dissidents.

QUESTIONS

1 If India's population is growing by 2% each year, how long will it take for it to reach 1000 million? (Multiply India's current population of 844 million by 1.02 – this represents an increase of 2%. Multiply your answer by 1.02, and continue multiplying until you have reached 1 000 000 000.)

2 Briefly explain why population growth is so high in India whereas population growth in the UK is so low?

3 Choose an appropriate method to show the data in Figure 2.18. Comment on your results.

4 Explain how family planning can be (i) a planners' issue, (ii) an environmental issue, (iii) a women's issue, and (iv) a religious issue.

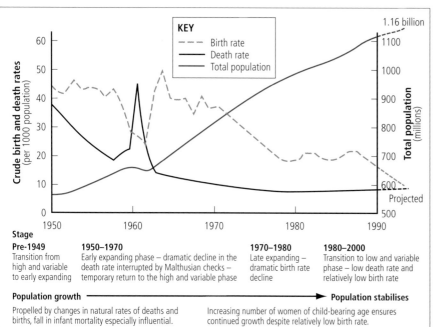

Figure 2.18 *China's birth and death rate*
Source: Jowett, J., 1989, Geography

Women of child-bearing age as a % of all women		Fertility rates	
1965	45	1970	5.8
1991	56	1991	2.1

Figure 2.19 *China's child-bearing population*
Source: Carr, New patterns: process and change in human geography, Nelson, 1997

MIGRATION

Migration is a movement which involves a permanent or relatively long-term change in residence. Hence it is different from commuting and nomadic movements which are daily and seasonal movements respectively. Migration can be classified by:

- distance – whether the migration is international or internal
- source and destination – rural to urban, urban to rural
- forced or voluntary – whether people have any choice in the decision to move and the destination.

The case study which follows, Mexico (rural to urban, and international) illustrates some of these types of migration.

Migration is often explained in terms of 'push' and 'pull' factors (Figure 2.20). Push factors are the reasons why a person wishes to leave an area – pull factors are the perceived advantages of the destination. The term 'perceived' is important – it is what the migrant believes exists, rather than what actually exists, which determines the decision to move.

Rural to urban migration

Rural to urban migration is a result of differences in standards of living between urban and rural locations, and between regions. Most migrants are young, better educated than their peers, and have higher aspirations. Young adults have less responsibilities (children, house, mortgage, employment) and so have more freedom to move. The better educated have better employment prospects which are more likely to be met in urban areas, rather than in smaller towns and rural areas.

Migration has an impact both on the source area and on the destination. For the source area, rural to urban migration removes the younger, more able people. The population left behind are the elderly, the less able and the infirm. By contrast, in the receiving area there are gains of a healthy, young, educated workforce. The influx of a young, healthy, educated workforce is very attractive for industrial development. However, if there are too many migrants, facilities and services may be overrun. The study of Mexico City is an excellent example of inward migration that has become excessive.

Urban to rural migration is increasingly common in EMDCs. This trend is analysed in detail in *Changing settlements* in this series.

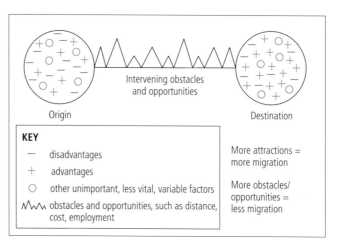

Figure 2.20 *Lee's model of migration*
Source: Everett S. Lee, 1966, A theory of migration, Demography 3

Case study:
Migration in Mexico

Mexico City is one of the largest cities in the world. It is an example of a **primate** city (the largest city, where the gap between it and the second rank cities is exceptionally wide). Its population is estimated at over 20 million people and it accounts for over 20% of Mexico's total population (Figure 2.21). The population density of Mexico City is staggering – over 17 000 per square kilometre.

The city grew at a rate of about 5% per year after 1945. Since the mid-1970s this has slowed to 3.5%. Each year about 33% of the increase is due to migration. Every day 3000 new migrants arrive, giving an annual total of just under one million migrants. As most migrants are young, this causes the birth rate to rise. Mexico City's birth rate is about 30 per thousand and the death rate is under 10 per thousand.

The migrants to Mexico City:
- are mostly young – 50% of the migrants are aged under 20 years
- show an imbalance, females to males (120:100) – many males migrate to the industrialised north and to the USA instead
- have mostly come from the nearby states of Mexico, Puebla, Morelos, Hidalgo and Tlaxcala (Figure 2.21).

Many immigrants live in very poor conditions (Figure 2.22).

The wealth gap between the industrialised north of Mexico and the rural south is very great. Average labour costs in the northern state of Nuevo Leon are three times greater than Chiapas in the south. Per capita consumption in Baja California – again in the north – is eight times greater than in Oaxaca, in the south. The rural 'misery

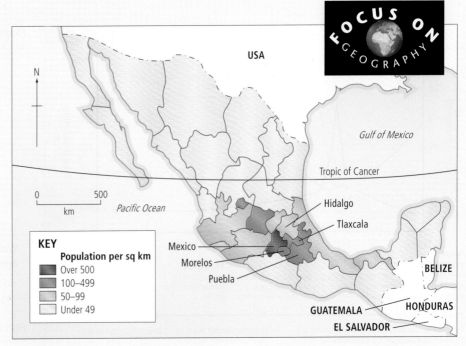

Figure 2.21 *Population density in Mexico, 1989*
Source: Regional Survey (South America/Central America/Caribbean), Europa Publications

belt' refers to the three southern states of Chiapas, Oaxaca and Guerrero: here, 25% of the population is illiterate, compared with 6% in the northern states. This is causing migration to the north as well as to Mexico City.

Another form of migration is international migration. Each year over a million Mexicans cross the US border – the main destinations being California and Texas. Although the US authorities try to keep the Mexicans out, it is impossible to guard the 3100 kilometre border. In addition, under the NAFTA agreement (see Chapter 5, pages 85-86) there has been an increase in trade between the USA and Mexico. This means that there are more vehicles crossing the border each day. Nearly 2000 trucks legally cross the bridge between Juarez (Mexico) and El Paso (USA) each day. It is impossible for customs to check them all.

About 300 000 Mexicans illegally enter the USA each year (Figure 2.23). This is largely a response to the push factors in Mexico and the perceived pull factors in the USA. The push factors include the higher unemployment, lower pay and

the poorer standards of living. The pull factors are the perceived improved conditions in the USA. However, the kinds of jobs that most migrants to the USA are given are usually low paid, unskilled and seasonal. Much of the work is as agricultural labourers. There is also a considerable amount of resentment on the part of the US population. In California there was even an attempt to deprive Mexicans of health care and education, under article 187 of Californian state law. (This bill was never passed as it was considered illegal.)

QUESTIONS

1 With the use of examples, explain why rural to urban migration is a significant influence on population distribution in Mexico.
2 What problems does rural to urban migration cause in (i) the rural areas and (ii) Mexico City? Use examples to support your answer.
3 Each year many Mexicans illegally migrate into the USA. Make a list of push factors which make them want to migrate, and a list of pull factors which attract them to the USA. What are the intervening obstacles which reduce the volume of migration from Mexico to the USA?

Figure 2.22 Slums in Mexico City

Forced migration - refugees

Refugees are people who are 'outside their own country, owing to a well-founded fear of persecution, for reasons of race, religion, nationality, membership of a particular social group or political opinion'. In 1994 there were over 23 million refugees (Figure 2.24). In many EMDCs, refugees are distinguished from 'economic migrants' – people who move to escape poverty and improve their standards of living, i.e. there is no persecution involved.

The number of refugees is increasing due to war, economic collapse and the loss of basic human rights (Figure 2.25). This increase exceeds the national and international agencies' abilities to cope and many host countries are becoming increasingly hostile to refugees.

Figure 2.23 A road sign warning drivers about Mexican migrants attempting to cross US border

Figure 2.24 Forced population removals in the 1990s
Source: Geofile, January 1992

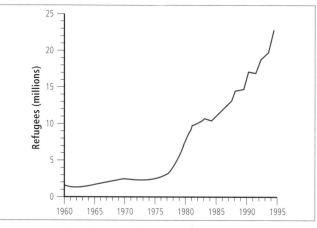

Figure 2.25 The global rise in refugees
Source: Bunce, V. and Studd, A. 1997 (eds.,) The developing world, Hodder and Stoughton

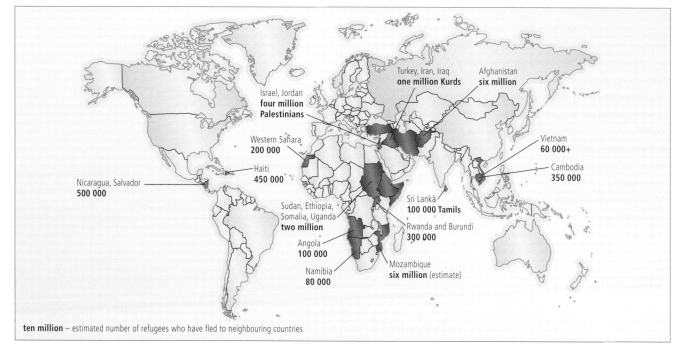
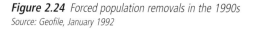

ten million – estimated number of refugees who have fled to neighbouring countries

Inset 2.5
Refugees and malnutrition

Increasing numbers of refugees, a growing gap between food needs and food supplies, and tighter relief budgets are likely to increase levels of malnutrition amongst refugees.

Three main trends dominate the humanitarian scene in the 1990s:
- An exponential increase in the number of displaced people – at present trends there could be up to 40 million internally displaced people by 2000, compared with 22 million in 1990. In addition, over 17 million refugees have crossed national boundaries.

- A widening gap between food demands and supplies. Food aid donations are set to rise to 10 million tons but the needs are over 14 million tons. The worst case scenario predicts a shortfall of 37 million tons.
- The surge in funding for relief has peaked and is beginning to decline.

POPULATION AND RESOURCES

The term **carrying capacity** refers to the number of people that an environment can support. It is a difficult concept to measure but it is useful in the discussion of overpopulation, optimum population and underpopulation.

Underpopulation occurs when there are not enough people to fully utilise resources. Examples include Rwanda and Mozambique, where war has led to declining populations, and Colombia, where the harsh environment deters settlers and thus limits exploitation.

Optimum population exists when the population utilises fully the resources of an area. It provides the highest standard of living given the resource availability. Optimum population is a balance between population density, resource availability and level of technology. Switzerland, Sweden and New Zealand are examples.

Overpopulation occurs when there are too many people for the resources available, and standards of living decline, for example in Bangladesh and Japan.

A number of simple graphs showing the relationship between population growth, overpopulation and carrying capacity are shown in Figures 2.26 and 2.27. Figure 2.27 shows that there are a number of ways in which a population can reach equilibrium with the carrying capacity of the environment. Model 1 shows an abrupt ceiling to the growth of population, model 2 a progressive slowing down of population growth to the carrying capacity, and model 3 shows that if population growth exceeds carrying capacity there will be a decline in population. In time population growth adjusts to the capacity of the environment to support it.

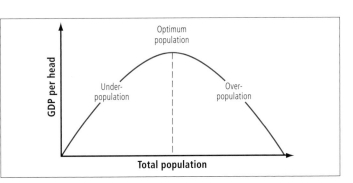

Figure 2.26 *Under-, over- and optimum population*
Source: Nagle, G. and Spencer, K., 1997, Advanced Geography Revision Handbook, OUP

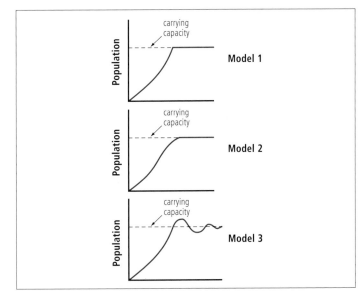

Figure 2.27 *Population growth and carrying capacity*
Source: adapted from Haggett, P., 1979, Geography: A modern synthesis, Figure 7-7, p. 151, reprinted by permission of Harper & Row Publishers Inc.

QUESTIONS

1 What do you understand by the term 'human rights'?

2 How would you distinguish between a refugee and an economic migrant?

3 Compare the benefits and disadvantages that refugees bring with them.

4 Describe the conditions associated with refugee camps.

In 1798, Thomas Malthus predicted that population growth would be greater than the growth in food and resources. He said that food supply grew at a steady pace, such as 1, 2, 3, 4, 5 and so on. By contrast, population grew at an increasing pace such as 1, 2, 4, 8, 16 and so on (Figure 2.28). If there was no attempt to reduce population growth, he declared the result would be famine, war and disease.

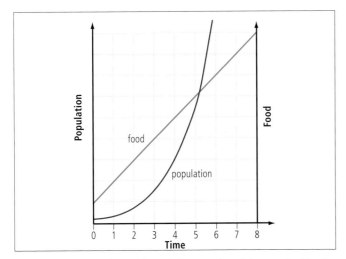

Figure 2.28 Malthus' view of population growth and the growth of food supplies

According to Malthus, population growth could be reduced by:
- delayed age of marriage
- abstinence from sex.

  (He was a vicar and was writing long before the wide-spread availability of contraceptives.)

A different view is that held by Esther Boserup, writing in 1965. She believed that people have the resources to increase food production. The greatest resource is knowledge and technology. When a need arises a solution will be found.

Since Malthus was writing, people have found many ways to increase food production. These include:
- draining marshlands
- reclaiming land from the sea
- cross breeding of cattle
- developing high yielding varieties of plants
- terracing on steep slopes
- growing crops in greenhouses
- using more sophisticated irrigation techniques
- making new foods such as soya
- making artificial fertilisers
- farming native species of crops and animals
- introducing fish farming.

SUMMARY

In this chapter we have seen many of the issues that relate to population and resources. In many ELDCs governments are faced with the problem of rapid population growth, and also with death rates increasing due to war and AIDS. Even EMDCs are not without their problems. The UK and Japan are often regarded as successful countries, yet each is facing a difficult time ahead as their population ages, bringing increased stresses on the workforce and the government. The unequal distribution of resources is one of the main reasons why migration occurs. The Mexico example illustrates some of the problems related to migration.

QUESTIONS

1 What are the world's population problems? How do they differ between ELDCs and EMDCs? What can be done to limit these problems? Use examples to support your answer.
2 What is meant by the term 'population structure'? Why is population structure important? Illustrate your answer with examples.
3 How far does migration create a balance between areas of overpopulation and areas of underpopulation? Use examples to support your answer.

4 Study Figure 2.29 which shows the impact of rural to urban migration in Zambia. What is the significance of the age-groups labelled **a)** and **b)** on the diagram. How have these shapes been caused? What will be the likely shape of the population pyramid in twenty years' time, assuming no further migration?
5 With the use of examples, explain the impact of migration on **(i)** source areas and **(ii)** destinations.

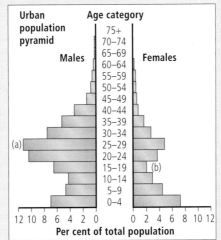

Figure 2.29 The impact of rural-urban migration in Zambia
Source: Nagle, G. and Spencer, K., 1997, Advanced Geography Revision Handbook, OUP

BIBLIOGRAPHY AND RECOMMENDED READING

Champion, T., et al., 1996, *The population of Britain in the 1990s*, OUP
Dickenson, J., et al., 1996, *Geography of the Third World*, Routledge
Japan Institute of Labour, 1996, *Japanese working life profile*
Parnwell, M., 1993, *Population movements and the Third World*, Routledge
UNDP, 1994, *Human development report 1994*, OUP

WEB SITES

Millennium Institute: State of the World Indicators -
http://www.igc.apc.org/millennium/inds/
U.S. Census Bureau - International database -
http://www.census.gov/ipc/www/idbnew.html
- http://coombs.anu.edu.au/resfacilities/demographypage.html
- http://sosig.ac.uk/subjects/demog.html

Chapter 3
Population and health

Chapter 2, Population, showed how population growth is affected by birth and death rates. These factors in turn are affected by levels of health and well-being. This chapter examines in more detail the geography of health and health care, and shows its importance in the study of population. The geography of health and health care, known as medical geography, is a good subject for project work as it can use small scale investigations, involving the use of the local press, hospital statistics, and records of the area's medical office.

This chapter looks at the health profile of the UK, as an example of an EMDC. It then looks at the problems caused by malnutrition and hunger with particular emphasis on South Africa, as an example of an ELDC. As seen in Chapter 1, What is development?, there is no such thing as a 'typical' ELDC. However, South Africa has many of the characteristics that we generally associate with ELDCs. Moreover, its pattern of development has left it with something of a dual economy, namely a rich, mainly white sector, and a largely undeveloped black sector. Patterns of health and health care reflect this.

TERMS & ABBREVIATIONS

Degenerative disease – a disease, such as strokes, cancers or heart disease, leading to a long term decline in health

Endemic – a disease native to an area

Epidemic – a severe outbreak of a disease not usually found, or prevalent, in a region

Epidemiology – the study of diseases

Infectious disease – one that can be passed through contact, for example, measles, cholera

Pandemic – a global epidemic

GDP – gross domestic product is the total value of all finished goods and products produced by a country

GNP – gross national product is GDP plus income from overseas investments, less profits from production within the country due to foreigners abroad

UNICEF – United Nations Children's Fund (originally UN International Children's Emergency Fund)

UNHCR – United Nations High Commission for Refugees

WHO – World Health Organisation

APPROACHES TO THE STUDY OF HEALTH AND HEALTH CARE

Geographical investigations into health and disease have traditionally focused upon two main aspects, **disease ecology** or **epidemiology** and the provision of **health care**.

Disease ecology is the study of how certain diseases are found in different geographic environments, for example, the clusters of higher than normal levels of leukaemia recorded around the former nuclear bomber base at Greenham Common near Newbury in Berkshire, and around the nuclear reprocessing plant at Sellafield in Cumbria.

Studies dealing with the provision of health care have traditionally considered geographic, social and racial inequalities in access to health care. Most recently, **humanistic** and **structuralist** approaches have influenced the study of medical geography. A humanistic approach stresses the importance of people's experience of, or attitude towards, illness. 'Attitude' is an increasingly important feature in project work. By contrast, a structuralist approach stresses the political and social conditions which give rise to inequalities in illness, and in access to treatment.

Essentially, the geography of health suggests that where you live affects your health and also the amount of care you receive. In the UK, for example, there are important regional contrasts in levels of health and well-being (Figure 3.1).

- Fewer babies die in East Anglia than anywhere else, 5.2 deaths per thousand in the first year of life compared with a high of 7.7 deaths per thousand in Yorkshire and Humberside.

- Allowing for the age structure of the population, cancer registrations are highest in Scotland.

- HIV is present among the major risk groups throughout Britain but the largest number are in the Thames Valley.

- The highest death rates due to heart disease are in Scotland and Northern Ireland.

Figure 3.1 *Health in the UK, 1994*
Source: Regional Trends, 1996

Inset 3.1
Data

Before looking in detail at health and healthcare, it is important to understand the nature and limitations of the available data.

- Most are **aggregate** data, that is, for groups of people rather than individuals.
- It is difficult to define 'health'. It is not just absence of illness, but complete physical, social and mental well-being (WHO, 1978).
- Data generally refer to illness and death rather than health.
- The data are often incomplete or even misleading. Diagnoses may be incorrect, secondary illnesses may be overlooked and the length or severity of the illness is rarely mentioned.
- The data may be biased. For example, some groups, such as the homeless or refugees, may be omitted from data collection.

Recently, however, the collection of statistics, in the UK at least, has improved. The 1991 census asked all UK residents about long-term illness, health problems and handicaps. Also, mortality statistics in the UK now use post-codes which enables geographic patterns to be shown more accurately.

Patterns of health vary from place to place and over time. The study of diseases, known as epidemiology, and the way in which health patterns in a country change, the epidemiological transition, can be linked with the demographic transition model discussed in Chapter 2.

The epidemiological transition model

As countries develop, health profiles change: there is a shift from infectious or contagious diseases (**epidemics**) to diseases that cause a gradual worsening in the health of an individual (**degenerative diseases**). This is known as the **epidemiological transition**. For example, a country in an early stage of development, would be expected to have a large number of deaths and illnesses from infectious diseases such as respiratory diseases, measles and gastro-enteritis (diarrhoea and vomiting) (Figure 3.2). An EMDC would be expected to have more deaths and illnesses due to heart attack, stroke, and cancers, diseases which are not infectious or communicable. The exception to this downward trend in infectious diseases is the rise in AIDS, and with it tuberculosis (TB), in EMDCs in the last decade.

HEALTH IN THE UK

There has been renewed interest in the health divide in the UK. In general, northern areas and large cities have higher rates of mortality than southern areas and rural districts. The pattern is complex, however, and varies with the type of disease. Moreover, the patterns change over time.

Figures 3.3 and 3.4 (see page 40) show the changes in the causes of death in the UK. Influenza and tuberculosis, which were the major killers in the middle part of the nineteenth century, are quite rare today. The rise in cancers, strokes and heart disease is equally striking.

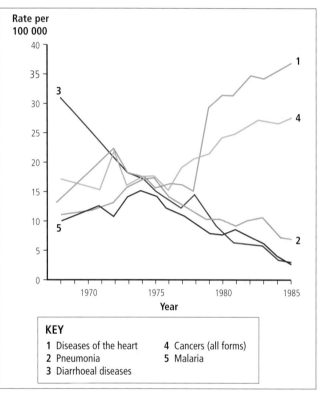

KEY

1 Diseases of the heart	4 Cancers (all forms)
2 Pneumonia	5 Malaria
3 Diarrhoeal diseases	

Figure 3.2 *Epidemiological transition for Thailand, 1968-85*

Average 1848-72		1991	
Infectious diseases	321	Diseases of the	
Tuberculosis	146	circulatory system	472
Scarlet fever	57	Heart diseases	264
Typhoid	38	Strokes	177
Respiratory diseases	148	Cancer	270
Bronchitis	66	Respiratory diseases	155
Pneumonia	57	Bronchitis	48
		Other causes	137
Diseases of the nervous system	129		
Diseases of the digestive system	83		
Diseases of the circulatory system	53		
Other causes	266		

Figure 3.3 *Principal causes of death in the UK, 1848-72 and 1991*
Sources: based on J. Beaujeu-Garnier, Geography of population, Longman 1978 and Regional Trends, 1996

(All rates per 1000 deaths)

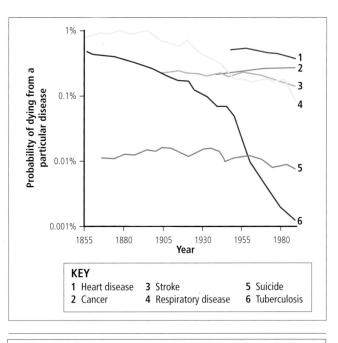

Figure 3.4 *Epidemiological transition for the UK, 1855-1990*
Source: Review of the Registrar General on deaths in England and Wales, 1941-1990

Mortality rates

The **crude mortality rate** (CMR) refers to the number of people who die per 1000 people. In a retirement coastal town, with a large proportion of elderly people, we would expect the CMR to be quite high, certainly higher than in a New Town with a youthful population. Consequently, we use the **standardised mortality rate** (SMR) or **age specific mortality rate** (ASMR) to compare the mortality rates for different places as if they had the same age population composition. Variations in the SMR are shown in Figure 3.5. Very striking geographic patterns can be seen.

SMRs attributable to heart disease, strokes, respiratory diseases and cancers show a very clear north-south divide:

- only a very small number of wards (small-scale mapping units) in the north have SMRs for heart disease below the national average; very few wards in the south have above average SMRs for heart disease

- for cancers, high death rates are found in northern towns, central Manchester, Leeds and along the Tees and Tyne valleys. Rural areas in the south of England have the lowest rates.

QUESTIONS

1 Study Figures 3.3 and 3.4. Describe the changes in the disease pattern in the UK between 1848-72 and 1991.

2 Why do disease patterns vary with levels of economic development?

	1	2	3	4	5	6
United Kingdom	472	155	270	33	137	1067
Health Authority regions						
Northern & Yorkshire	502	167	284	32	140	1125
Trent	475	158	271	32	140	1072
Anglia & Oxford	421	144	256	32	136	989
North Thames	424	165	262	29	139	1019
South Thames	430	155	259	26	139	1019
South West	429	140	254	28	111	962
West Midlands	485	151	272	33	139	1060
North West	520	178	286	33	136	1153
England	460	155	267	30	135	1048
Wales	488	155	267	30	135	1048
Scotland	567	149	307	47	161	1232
N. Ireland	549	194	267	46	110	1165

KEY
All rates per 100 000 people
1 All circulatory diseases   2 All respiratory diseases   3 Cancer
4 All injuries and poisonings   5 Other causes   6 All causes

Figure 3.5 *Standardised mortality rates for UK per 100 000 by cause of death, 1994*
Source: based upon Regional Trends, 1996

QUESTIONS

1 Study Figure 3.5. Identify the region with the highest and lowest mortality rates for each of the categories.

2 For any **two** causes of mortality, **(i)** show their distribution on a map, **(ii)** describe the geographic pattern you have shown (remember to name places and give figures in your answer), and **(iii)** attempt to explain the pattern that you have shown.

The spatial pattern of mortality in England and Wales has remained largely unchanged since World War II. The north, especially northern cities, and Wales, have above average rates of mortality whereas the south, excluding some urban areas, has below average rates of mortality.

Other geographic influences on SMR are:

- an increase from lung cancer and respiratory problems in large urban areas
- deaths from respiratory diseases are mostly found in Inner London
- an increase in deaths from strokes and heart diseases in Inner London
- increased mortality from digestive diseases in a band along the Thames in London.

Traffic accidents also have a regional variation; they are most common in rural districts, especially in the Home Counties. They are particularly important as they largely affect young people, especially males.

Inner London, Inner Manchester, central areas in Leicester and Birmingham have above average rates of suicide while the lowest rates are in south Yorkshire and the north-east of England. Of all age and gender groups, 24-year-old men are most likely to commit suicide. However, suicide accounts for less than 3% of deaths, whereas heart attacks account for almost 25% of all deaths under the age of 65. Heart disease kills men earlier than women, although its incidence is decreasing for both sexes. Cancers, on the other hand, affect more women than men, and are on the increase for both.

Area	1939	1986-9
Salford	1	1
Oldham	2	2
Blackburn	17	3
Gateshead	6	4
Manchester	15	5
St. Helens	39	6
Liverpool	5	7
Warrington	63	8
Methyr Tydfil	12	9
Halifax	19	10

Long-term illness

Long-term illness varies with:

- age (common in older people)
- gender (more common in men)
- occupation (those without jobs are far more likely to suffer long-term illness).

People living in the coalfield areas of South Wales, Yorkshire and the north-east of England experience high rates of long-term illness. Urban areas in the north and in Scotland also have high rates of long-term illness, while in the south, high rates of illness are confined to parts of London and the coast, reflecting the geographic distribution of elderly people.

Social effects on health

Death rates and disease patterns are strongly correlated with the social geography of an area, especially in terms of wealth. The distribution of mortality rates and illness shows a striking similarity to the pattern of unemployment. The link is quite straightforward: where adults are unemployed there is likely to be less income, and people are more likely to go without basic requirements, such as a healthy diet, and consequently suffer more illnesses, with greater frequency and severity.

MALNUTRITION AND HUNGER

In many ELDCs the pattern of health is very different. We have seen that people there suffer many infectious/contagious diseases. Inset 3.2 in this chapter looks at one of the most important diseases in ELDCs – malnutrition. Malnutrition is any shortfall in the quality and/or quantity of food intake (Figures 3.11 and 3.12). It is most common in ELDCs but occurs among many elderly people in EMDCs. Malnutrition is a disease in its own right as well as an important secondary disease (it is related to and accompanies other diseases). The Inset takes the opportunity to examine some of the weaknesses in relying upon published data.

Figure 3.6 *Highest ranked standardised mortality rates in England and Wales, 1986-89, with a comparison of ranks before WWII (1939)*
Source: adapted from Dorling, 1995

QUESTIONS

1 Using a local library, or a CD-ROM, investigate long-term illness in your area. Consider the following points:

- does it vary across the area?
- is it related to areas of high unemployment?
- are there any geographic factors such as poor environment, an elderly population or poverty, which may be related to it?
- what are the problems of census data?
- what are the problems of trying to find associations (correlations) between areas?

2 Figure 3.6 shows the highest standardised mortality rates in England and Wales in 1939 and 1989.

a) Using an atlas, draw a map to show the geographic distribution of the places in the table.

b) Describe the geographic pattern that you have drawn. Remember to use actual names of places, and their relative importance, in your description.

c) Explain the pattern that you have shown and described. What geographic factors are likely to explain this pattern?

Inset 3.2
Assessing the quality and bias of data

These figures are taken from nutrition surveys carried out on children under 5 in the Ciskei area of South Africa.

	Household	Clinic	Nutrition clinic	Creche
Wasting *(low weight/age)* Moderate Severe	25 5	10 1	25 6	13 <1
Stunting *(low height/age)* Moderate Severe	22 8	9 1	16 2	13 1
Wasting and stunting *(low weight/height)* Moderate Severe	17 2	9 1	15 2	11 0

Figure 3.7 *Children's nutritional status in selected surveys (percentage)*

QUESTIONS

1 Compare the data from the different sources in Figure 3.7.

a) Why do the results from the household survey differ from those of (i) the clinic survey, (ii) the nutrition clinic survey, and (iii) the creche survey in Figure 3.9?

b) How might the nutritional status of under-fives differ between those attending creches and those attending the nutrition clinic?

c) Which of the surveys is likely to give the most accurate results? Which type of survey is likely to be most biased? Give reasons for your answer.

d) What do the results above tell us about surveys, bias and accuracy?

2 What sources of data are available in the UK for studying health and disease? How accurate do you think these are? In what ways do the data for the UK or any EMDC differ from those of an ELDC such as South Africa?

Figure 3.9 *Nutritional survey in a creche*

Figure 3.8 *Measuring malnutrition*

On a global scale, about 850 million people are considered to be malnourished (Figure 3.10). The worst affected areas are Africa (Figures 3.11 and 3.13) and South Asia; by contrast, East Asia has had the most success in reducing hunger over the last thirty years or so (Figure 3.13).

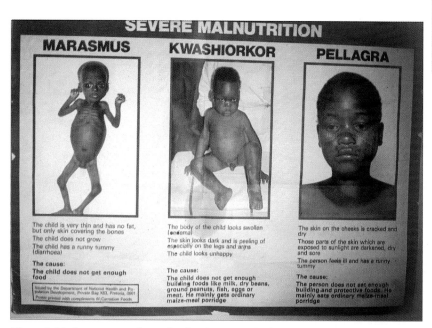

Figure 3.11 *Some common forms of malnutrition in South Africa*

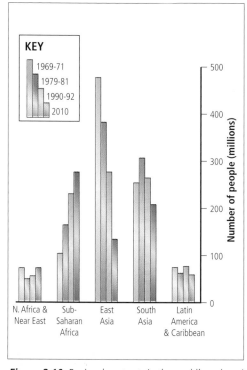

Figure 3.10 *Regional contrasts in the world's malnourished population*
Source: Financial Times, 14th November, 1996, based on data from Action Aid

Starvation	–	limited/non existent intake of food
Deficiency diseases	–	lack of specific vitamins or minerals
Kwashiorkor	–	likely to be a lack of protein
Marasmus	–	lack of calories/energy
Obesity	–	too much energy/protein foods

Figure 3.12
Types of malnutrition

Increased food production has been one of the greatest successes since World War II. Grain harvests and meat production have trebled since 1950, exceeding the rate of population growth, and the food-intake gap between rich and poor countries has narrowed. So why do some countries have such a high rate of malnutrition? Zaire and Rwanda are prime examples, where crops have rotted in fields due to a shortage of labour to harvest them.

Explaining malnutrition and hunger

Much of the early literature (pre-1970s) on malnutrition, famine and hunger consisted of reports on climate and its effect on food supplies, and on the problems of transport and storage and problems experienced by relief organisations. Such studies were often grouped under the umbrella term of Food Availability Deficit (FAD), which implied that food deficiencies were caused by local shortages due to physical factors. As such, these studies called for material remedies and, as a result, the topic of malnutrition was isolated from the internal politics of the country.

Area	Percentage malnourished	Source
Developing countries	31% (1995)	World Health Report 1996
Least developed countries	40%	
Other developing countries	30%	
South Asia	50% (86 million under 5s malnourished)	
Sub-Saharan Africa	30% (32 million children underweight)	
Bangladesh	67% (1996)	UNICEF, 1996
South Africa	25-33% (1991)	Nagle, 1992
Swaziland	50%	
Zimbabwe	33%	
Botswana, Malawi, Lesotho and Zambia	16-32%	

Figure 3.13 *Some estimates of childhood malnutrition in South Africa*

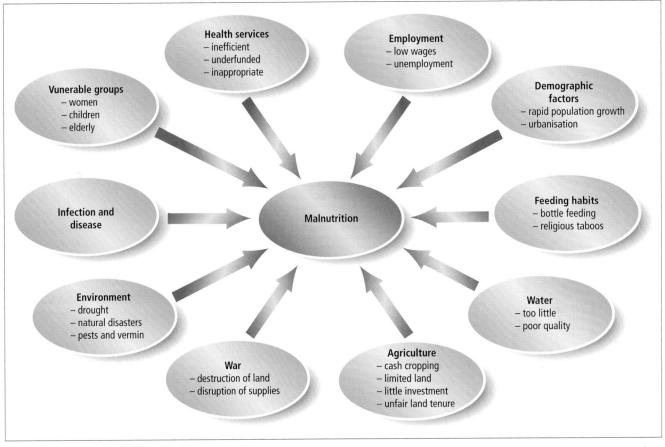

Figure 3.14 *The factors affecting malnutrition*

During the 1970s a number of nutritional studies were carried out, and from these it was possible to build models for studying malnutrition. What is immediately apparent is the multitude of factors which are involved (Figure 3.14).

More recently, the discussion of malnutrition has been heavily influenced by political and economic factors. Sen (1981) observed that not all food shortages caused hunger, and increased hunger could be observed in areas where food production was, in fact, increasing. This has been seen in India, Ethiopia and Sudan. The decline in food availability could not therefore be seen as a complete explanation of the causes of malnutrition, nor did it link hunger with the distribution of resources and poverty. In this analysis of the population 'at risk' of malnutrition, Sen felt that it was important to encompass the political and economic systems in which food was produced, distributed and consumed. This included not just the physical factors which affected yield, but also people's access to food, and the conditions which caused that access to alter. Sen's work has generally been accepted, although it is necessary to remember the physical factors, such as lack of precipitation and environmental degradation, which are also potential triggers of famines.

During the mid-1980s there was a more noticeable attempt to draw together all the factors that were related to malnutrition. This was, in part, achieved by looking at a number of discrete levels; individual, household, community, national and global. The relationship between global and local issues is clear.

More recent studies have taken into account Third World problems, north-south relations and environmental crises as having an important bearing on the incidence of malnutrition. The growing refugee problem has been identified as causing the 'new wave' of malnutrition (Inset 3.3). In certain cases, such as in Mozambique, Angola and Rwanda, war and ethnic strife are greater causes of hunger and malnutrition than shortfalls in food production and food availability. In South Asia the high prevalence of childhood malnutrition is closely linked to the low status of women.

All these approaches have something to offer, both in the identification of the causes of malnutrition and in offering solutions. A geographic approach, operating at a variety of temporal and spatial scales, from the individual health survey to global food policy, and synthesising materials from other disciplines, can offer a unique appraisal of the conditions which operate in a given location at a given time.

Inset 3.3
Refugees and ill-health

In refugee camps disease is very common. In Ethiopia in 1989 the proportion of malnourished people was 25% and among Somalian refugees in Kenya it was 29%. If the proportion of malnourished people rises, the death rate increases:

- as malnutrition rises to between 5% and 9.9% of the population the death rate doubles
- as malnutrition rises to between 10% and 19.9% of the population the death rate quadruples.

The UNHCR state that the average annual death rate (crude death rate) in ELDCs is below 18 per thousand and that if it is less than 36.5 per thousand it is 'under control'. A death rate of 2 people per day per 10 000 refugees gives a crude death rate of 73 per thousand and is classified as 'out of control'. If the level rises to 5 per day per 10 000, the death rate becomes 185 per thousand, a 'catastrophe'. In the 1980s Somalia's refugee population had a death rate of 4 per day per 10 000, 146 per thousand.

It is not always easy to provide assistance to areas where malnutrition is a problem. Food aid and distribution may be well-meaning but can be culturally unacceptable (the type of food may be unfamiliar or inappropriate, or it may be wrong to accept food). It may also create a dependency culture. Specific deficiencies may develop in certain areas, such as in Malawi in the late 1980s where there were 18 000 cases of pellagra, caused by Vitamin B deficiency, and scurvy, caused by a lack of Vitamin C.

Refugees suffer from health problems other than malnutrition. In Sudan in 1985, the death rate from measles was as high as 33%, caused largely by the lack of immunisations. There was a great need to vaccinate a high proportion of people but there was a lack of electricity and running water.

Increasingly, psychological problems are becoming apparent among refugees. These include boredom, frustration, and post traumatic stress disorder from experience of dramatic events, such as murder and rape. For example, in Malawi, where there are 8 million people and 1 million refugees, there is a chronic shortage of land and jobs. This has led to widespread boredom, alcoholism and crime.

Transmission of AIDS is a potentially serious problem in refugee populations, given the high rates of prostitution. Agencies may well play down the rate of AIDS as host countries may not want to receive the refugees.

The outlook is certainly bleak. The number of refugees doubled during the 1980s and reached 25 million in the mid-1990s. However, the income of the UNHCR remained static. There is a lack of trust between governments and non-governmental organisations (NGOs); no one is really in charge and no one is accepting responsibility.

Figure 3.15 A refugee camp in Rwanda

QUESTIONS

1 Explain why the lack of electricity and running water in refugee camps is a health concern.

2 Explain why there are health problems in refugee camps. Use Figure 3.14 to help you.

Case study:
Health and health care in South Africa

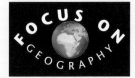

Figure 3.16 Glenmore: a site for the forced relocation of blacks in South Africa

South Africa is an ELDC characterised by:
- rapid population growth
- urbanisation
- high rates of unemployment and underemployment
- a privileged (mostly white) minority.

Hence it resembles other developing countries, such as Brazil or Mexico, although not the newly industrialising countries, such as Taiwan or Singapore.

The pattern of illness and mortality in South Africa is that of an ELDC undergoing rapid urbanisation and social transformation. For a minority of the population, which is predominantly white, the illnesses experienced and the causes of death are similar to that of a typical EMDC. However, for the majority, the diseases and the deaths are related to poor socio-economic conditions, poor housing, low incomes and overcrowding. Communicable, infectious diseases are rife. In addition there are the problems, not unique to South Africa, of social conflict. If the high level of violence and the increasing levels of drug abuse, including alcoholism, sexually transmitted diseases and HIV continue, the health care system will have increasing difficulties in serving the needs of the population.

Morbidity and mortality in South Africa

It is difficult to be certain of the health conditions of the population of South Africa before the early twentieth century, given the lack of information. However, the reports that do exist suggest that although death rates were quite high, especially in times of famine and **epidemics**, in general, physique, diet and health were good. As in nineteenth-century Britain, industrialisation in South Africa in the late nineteenth and early twentieth century was associated with 'social' diseases, notably TB and venereal disease.

By the mid-twentieth century, the disease profile of South Africa tended to follow very clearly defined racial lines and, in general, this has persisted to the present day. Nevertheless, there have been important recent changes.

For whites, the main diseases that cause morbidity and mortality are mostly **degenerative** such as:
- cerebro-vascular diseases (strokes)
- cardiovascular disease (heart)
- carcinoma (cancers).

These account for over two-thirds of all deaths among whites, while infectious and parasitic diseases account for only 2% of deaths. This is the typical pattern for a developed country.

On the other hand, a very high proportion of the coloured and black population suffer high rates of **infectious, contagious** diseases including:
- TB
- gastro-enteritis
- measles
- respiratory infections.

These have become **endemic** in black rural areas.

Definitions

Morbidity	illness
Mortality	death

In terms of the epidemiological transition model, the illnesses affecting South Africa's population are spread across the spectrum. They range from degenerative diseases (mostly among whites) to contagious ones (mostly among blacks and coloureds). However, urban blacks are increasingly taking on a pattern which mirrors that of whites: there are increasingly large proportions of stress-related diseases, strokes, heart diseases and cancers. For many households, both black and white, the pressures borne by those involved in family break-ups, single families, teenage parents, and unemployment have led to lifestyles involving drug addiction, prostitution and alcoholism, which are 'self-destructive'.

Some areas have a greater incidence of ill-health then others. In **resettlement camps**, such as Glenmore and Dimbaza in Ciskei (Figure 3.16), and periurban areas, the infectious diseases are much more dominant. This is especially so during times of rapid population in-migration, and can be largely blamed on the combination of :
- low incomes
- inadequate diets
- overcrowded housing
- poor water and sanitation facilities.

QUESTIONS

1 **Explain the meaning of the following pairs of terms: endemic and epidemic; degenerative and infectious; cardiovascular and cerebro-vascular; morbidity and mortality.**
2 **What other countries are likely to experience racial differences in morbidity and mortality? Give reasons for your answer.**

Together these create a highly unstable social and economic environment. Although the apartheid policies have ended, there are still many social and economic factors which prevent many black South Africans from achieving good health.

Mortality rates

Infant and child mortality

The **infant mortality rate** (IMR) is often taken as an indicator of a nation's development as it is affected by factors such as water supply, sanitation, housing, food supply and income levels. The lower the IMR, the more developed the country. In South Africa, however, reliable statistics relating to the IMR are scarce, although it is possible to see the main trends.

- IMR varies with race (Figure 3.17), whites having lower rates (10-15 per thousand), than blacks (50-100 per thousand), although the rates for both are decreasing. The latest data suggest rates per thousand of 52 plus for blacks, 28 for coloureds, 13.5 for Indians and 7.3 for whites.

- The IMR also varies spatially, being higher in the periurban and rural areas compared with urban areas. Nevertheless, there is considerable variation between cities, as well as within cities, ranging from 12 per thousand in Durban to 41.3 per thousand in Port Elizabeth.

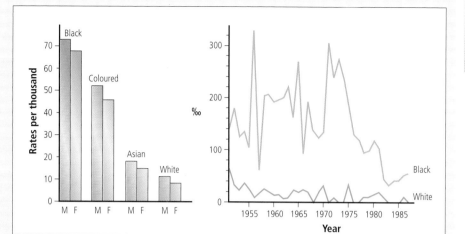

Figure 3.17 (a) *Racial contrasts in the infant mortality rate in South Africa*

Figure 3.17 (b) *Black and white infant mortality rates, King William's Town, 1950-89*

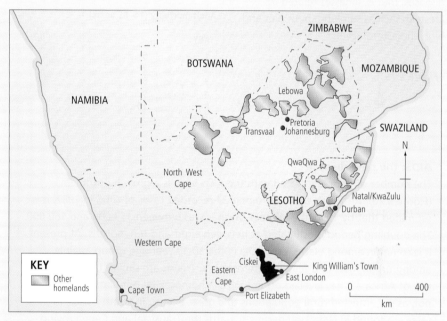

Figure 3.18 *The location of Ciskei, South Africa*

Cause and age at death among infants also varies:

- for whites, **neonatal** (0-7 days) and **peri-natal** deaths (7-28 days) were more likely, due to congenital (birth) deformities

- for blacks, they are more likely to be due to low birth-weight, gastro-enteritis, pneumonia and infections and occur at between 7-365 days, the **post-neonatal period**.

In a study of Ciskei, 1986-91, the principal causes of childhood death included gastro-enteritis (20%), kwashiorkor and marasmus (12%) and

pneumonia (12%). Similar findings were found in rural areas, where gastro-enteritis was the main cause of death, followed by malnutrition, respiratory diseases and measles. These also accounted for about 70% of black infant deaths, whereas genetic deformities and asphyxia accounted for all white infant deaths.

Similarly, the **child mortality rates** in Ciskei indicated high death rates from the enteritic, nutritional, respiratory and infectious diseases.

Mortality patterns among children in

South Africa also vary in terms of race, location and socio-economic status (Figure 3.19). Since the mid-1980s there has been an increase in the child mortality rate, linked with the deepening recession:

- for white children, mortality rates are low, consisting mainly of congenital deformities

- for black children, death rates are higher, especially in resettlement areas and periurban locations, comprising mostly gastro-enteritis, respiratory infections, and malnutrition; up to 85% of black deaths were in these categories.

Adult mortality

For adults, too, blacks tend to have much higher mortality rates compared with whites and Asians, especially from TB and respiratory infections. These diseases together with degenerative diseases, such as cancers, stress, heart attack and stroke have increased since the mid-1980s. The death rate for black adults is almost twice that of whites. Indeed, in one year, 1988, over one-quarter of the deaths of black adults aged between 35 and 64 years of age (the potentially economically productive population) were due to chronic diseases, that is, illnesses related to lifestyle, such as smoking, poor diet and high cholesterol levels.

Figure 3.19 *Crude death rates by race and age,*
South Africa
Source: based on data in Bradshaw et al., 1992

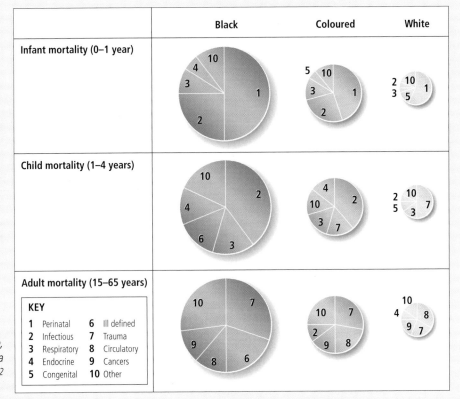

AIDS: the new disease

The number of people infected with the AIDS virus is a growing problem (Figure 3.20). Although there were only 37 recorded cases of AIDS in 1987, it is estimated that by 1990, the number of cases was between 119 000 and 160 000. The doubling period is estimated at between eight and ten months. At present it is common among blacks, especially in the 30-39 year age group, mainly among urban male and female heterosexuals. Trends are similar to those in the rest of Africa – it has levelled off among the homosexual population and has not, as yet, infected rural populations to a great extent. In South Africa, highest rates are found in Natal and decline towards the Transvaal and Cape Province.

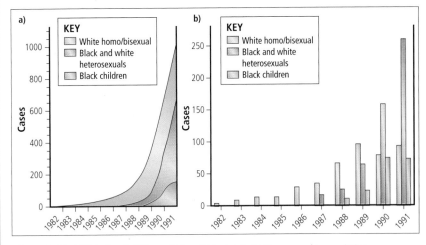

Figure 3.20 *AIDS in South Africa*   **a)** *Cumulative total*   **b)** *By year and transmission*
Source:Southall, H 1993 'South African trends and predictions of HIV infection' in Cross, S and Whiteside, A (Eds) Facing up to AIDS, Macmillan

QUESTIONS

1   **Study 3.17 a), 3.17 b) and 3.19. Compare and contrast (i) infant mortality rates, and (ii) child mortality rates among black and white children. How do you explain the differences that you have noted?**
2   **How far does South Africa fit the epidemiological transition model (ETM)? To what extent can the different racial groups be placed in different parts of the ETM? Give reasons for your answer.**
3   **What is meant by the following terms: heterosexual AIDS and homosexual AIDS?**
4   **Study Figures 3.17 a) and b). What are the implications for (i) the South African health services, and (ii) the South African economy, suggested by the data? Explain your answer.**

HEALTH CARE SERVICES IN SOUTH AFRICA AND THE HOMELANDS

Patterns of disease and health care relate directly to the nature of a country's development and to the unequal distribution of, and access to, its resources. Just as the 'development' of disease can, in part, be related to apartheid or separatist policies in South Africa, so too can the health care system.

Health care in South Africa clearly reflects the nature of society, in terms of **political developments** and **market forces**. In general, health care for whites follows a Western-world type provision, based on **curative medicine** and the use of high technology techniques. Much of this system has been privately run. By contrast, health care for most blacks is based on low technology, **preventative** measures.

In theory, health care provision should increase with the number of women, elderly and young in a population, namely the vulnerable. It should also vary with the types of disease found and be available to those who need it most, but often this is not so. Given the population structure of many black communities, especially those in the former homelands and the periurban areas, there is already an unsatisfied demand for health care. This demand will escalate greatly in the foreseeable future, owing to population growth, social upheaval, poverty and the high representation of vulnerable populations.

Health care for the majority of the population is underfunded, over-stretched and often inappropriate or inaccessible. Moreover, rural areas and periurban areas are seriously disadvantaged. For many people unable to reach official health care services, traditional practitioners offer an alternative form of health care (Figures 3.23 and 3.25).

Health care under apartheid

Under apartheid, health care in South Africa was fragmented. Each of the homelands had its own health budget and was able to allocate funds independently of the other departments. However, the Department of National Health and Population Development maintained overall responsibility for the health policy of 'white' South Africa and the homelands. Whites, coloureds and Indians were treated in segregated services, blacks in the homelands were treated by the homeland authorities, and blacks in urban areas were treated by separate services.

Health care in the new South Africa

Despite the reforms of the early 1990s, the health care system in South Africa still retains much of the apartheid plan. A number of characteristics remain:

- large-scale state intervention, i.e. government run (along racial lines)
- urban bias (more facilities in urban areas)
- excessive fragmentation (too many different health authorities)

- white dominance (blacks receive inferior health care)
- a misallocation of funds in favour of 'white' curative hospitals and the private market (most of the funding goes to hospitals in 'white' areas).

Although hospitals became 'open' to all races in May 1990, by the end of the year only a small proportion of patients admitted to previously 'white' hospitals were black (4%).

Since the 1970s, there has been an increase in state expenditure on health, which can be related both to greater state participation in the economy and an increase in GNP. Although South Africa spends 5.6% of its GDP on health services (compared with 7.5% in the UK and 13% in the USA):

- in the late 1980s, 20% of the patients, mostly whites, consumed 80% of the funds. In Johannesburg US$60 is spent per day on each white patient whereas $US12 per day is spent on each black patient
- in 1990-1991, the ten homeland areas accounted for about 45% of the total population but less than 20% of the health budget.

There is a huge bias towards **curative medicine**, which benefits the white population. Such a bias has arisen, in part, out of the **market orientation** of much of South Africa's health care. Consequently, health care is inversely related to those in most need. Hart's **inverse care law** (1971) states that those who can afford it are those who least need it, whereas those who most need it cannot afford health care, and therefore do not get it. Moreover, the cost of health care is becoming increasingly further out of the range of the poor as insurance schemes abound, medical salaries increase, and the cost of technological equipment continues to rise.

A market orientation lends itself to a neglect of rural areas and homelands, since this is where there is high representation of the poor. In the early 1990s there was one doctor for every 340 people in South Africa overall, but only one doctor for every 15 625 people in some rural areas.

Further inequalities between whites and blacks are numerous. For example:

- at least 75% of whites are covered by private medical aid compared with about 5% of blacks
- more hospital beds and doctors are available per capita for whites than for blacks. Blacks are disproportionately more dependent upon the public health services. Those in the homelands are generally worse off than other groups in South Africa (Figure 3.21).

	RSA*	Ciskei	Lebowa	QwaQwa
Hospital bed/1000 population	4	4.2	2.1	2.8
Doctor/1000 population	0.6	0.4	0.0	0.1
Nurses/1000 population	4.5	3.3	1.9	1.9

(*includes all ten homelands in the Republic of South Africa)

Figure 3.21 Health provision in South Africa
Source: South African Institute of Race Relations, 1993, 279-280

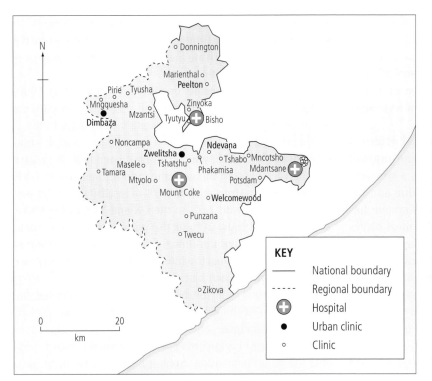

Figure 3.22 *The location of hospitals and clinics in Ciskei*

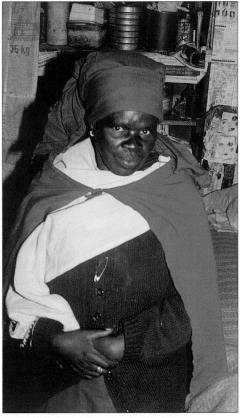

Figure 3.23 *A traditional practitioner/herbalist*

The inequalities in health care are not merely a question of the number of doctors or beds per person, but also concern the facilities available in hospitals and clinics, a feature which increases the inequalities. The age, gender, qualifications, ability to speak the local language and specialist training of medical staff, are all factors which need to be taken into account. Thus, in a country where only 17% of the population are white:

- over 90% of the doctors are white
- only 12% of the doctors are women, and likely to work part time only
- 12% of doctors are over the age of 65 years, and hence trained under the apartheid regime
- less than 2.5% of doctors are black
- the number of black doctors graduating each year is still low.

Health care in Ciskei

The provision of health care that has evolved in South Africa shows many inequalities and many constraints upon access for those most in need. An analysis of the Ciskei health services (Figure 3.24) illustrates many of the comments made above and shows how the services have developed under the constraints of the past.

Quaternary Level
– Referral and teaching hospitals, e.g. Groote Schuur (Cape Town)

Tertiary Level (main hospital)
– Regional hospitals with comprehensive specialist and training facilities, e.g. Cecilia Makiwane (Mdantsane)

Secondary Level (minor hospital)
– Health ward hospitals with limited services and/or training, e.g. Mount Coke

Primary Level (clinic)
a) Central clinics (high grade), e.g. Dimbaza, Zwelitsha
b) Satellite clinics (low grade), e.g. Ndevana, Welcomewood, Peelton
c) Sub-clinics, e.g. Zikhova

Figure 3.24 *The structure of the Ciskei health services*

The health services have a very hierarchical structure (Figure 3.24). The largest regional hospital, Cecilia Makiwane, built in 1975, is located in Mdantsane. The second tier of hospitals, including Mount Coke, developed out of small mission hospitals. Each hospital serves a number of clinics and sub-clinics in its region.

QUESTIONS

1 Explain Hart's inverse care law.

2 With the use of examples, show how governments can become involved in the provision of health care.

3 Explain why access to health care varies geographically, socially and economically. Give examples to illustrate your answer.

Figure 3.25 *The herbalist's potions – notice the inhaler!*

For example, Cecilia Makiwane hospital serves fourteen urban clinics and seven rural clinics, and Mount Coke has eighteen rural and four urban clinics. The regional hospital provides doctors, ambulance services and various health personnel to the clinics. The clinics are designed to offer a comprehensive health service providing:

- general medical care
- family planning
- nutrition education
- TB treatment
- antenatal care and obstetrics.

Generally, they comprise a waiting room, a maternity room, consulting room and toilet facilities. They also offer overnight facilities; urban clinics normally have four to five beds, whereas rural clinics usually have two. Patients who cannot be treated at the clinic are referred to the appropriate hospital. At this primary level there is a greater focus upon primary health care (PHC). This is low-cost health care which is preventative rather than curative (Figures 3.26 and 3.27).

Figure 3.26 *Health workers at the Ndevana clinic – the primary level of the hierarchy*

The aims of PHC are to promote:

- growth monitoring
- oral rehydration
- breast feeding
- provision of immunisations
- food supplementation
- female education.

However, the running of the health services is limited by a number of factors. First, the very location of clinics in Ciskei has produced a certain amount of controversy. Official documents stated that 'the siting of clinics takes into account population density, available infrastructure and accessibility'. On the other hand, it is noted that the 'location of clinics is determined in a scientific and practical way in relation to the funds available and in terms of promises made by politicians and other office bearers'.

Figure 3.27 *Queueing at the Ndevana clinic*

In practice, these services operate under a number of constraints. Staff shortages can be a serious problem as they lead to reduced efficiency and promote a poor image of the health services. When staff levels decrease, attendance at the clinics decreases, owing to increased waiting time, lack of care and attention, and reduced hours of opening. In Ciskei in 1991 the following shortfalls (%) were found:

Village health workers	25
Nursing assistants	28
Medical superintendents	40
Student nurses	34
Doctors	20
Nurses	25
Ambulance officers	85
Health inspectors	30

Figure 3.28 The Gida hospital, Keikammahoek – the second tier. Compare the level of use of the hospital with that of the clinic

Figure 3.29 Hawkers selling food outside the hospital. Even they do not suggest that the hospital is widely used. Yet the demand for health services is high - there is much inappropriate technology within the hospitals

In fact, only the posts of Director General, Deputy Director General and the nursing administrators were covered sufficiently. The same picture was seen as far back as 1984. Quality of staff also raised some concerns. Poor staff training resulted in a failure to spot potentially ill people. Staff morale was low, owing to lack of resources, poor motivation and inadequate wages. Many of the clinics were severely limited in facilities, some without electricity or piped water. Other provisions missing included transport facilities, telephone, weighing scales, stethoscopes, vaccines and proper sewage systems. The size of many clinics was inadequate for the number of people served (Figure 3.27), and the lack of accommodation for nursing staff prevented the provision of a twenty-four hour emergency service. Transport difficulties were frequent, due to the lack of equipment and the nature of the roads. Due to a high turnover of incumbents in cabinet and senior civil service positions, there has been no consistency in the development of health policies.

Planning for the future in South Africa

The new South African government is in a difficult position; funds are limited and many projects are in urgent need of funding, including housing and education.

One further problem is the rapid increase in the incidence of AIDS and its effect on other diseases, notably TB and measles. Government expenditure on AIDS has risen to over US$5 million, representing just under 2% of the health budget. This is in addition to the cost of treating other endemic diseases, not instead of them. Moreover, the medical, economic and social costs of AIDS will continue to rise well into the first decade or two of the next century as HIV cases develop into fully-blown AIDS cases.

The disease pattern in South Africa means that greater attention needs to be directed towards the infectious diseases rather than the degenerative ones. Some form of non-racial, accessible and affordable health service is desperately needed. It will prove difficult to escape from the legacy of previous decades, as the future health services will be heavily influenced by the location and nature of the existing facilities, such as hospitals and clinics. With tight constraints on government spending there is little room for large-scale improvements.

QUESTIONS

1 Study Figure 3.22 which shows the location of hospitals and clinics.

a) Explain what is meant by the term 'hierarchy of facilities'. How far does the distribution of clinics and hospitals relate to the principles of central place theory - namely, serving the maximum number of people with the least number of outlets? (See *Changing settlements* in this series.)

b) Explain the location of health care facilities in the area.

2 Distinguish between curative and preventative medicine. Which is the most appropriate for **(i)** large urban areas, and **(ii)** rural areas? Justify your answer.

3 What are the economic and social implications of the decreasing case-fatality (fewer deaths, longer survival) among AIDS victims?

4 In what ways did health services in the homelands under apartheid differ from those in the rest of South Africa? What implications does this have for differences in health services between EMDCs and ELDCs, in terms of health needs and health care types?

SUMMARY

The geography of health and health care affects us all. Where we are born, where we live and work, or go to school, has an impact on our health. We have seen this clearly in the UK, and we have seen that it takes a long time for geographic patterns to change. Some geographers claim that South Africa is a microcosm of the world's north-south divide, but on a white-black basis. Certainly the health profile and health care facilities that existed for whites before the end of the apartheid system were very similar to those in rich, capitalist EMDCs. By contrast, disease patterns among blacks, and the facilities available for their use, were more recognisable as those of an impoverished ELDC.

South Africa has many resources, great inequalities in wealth and is moving away from an authoritarian government to a more democratic one. The transition is likely to be painful and is unlikely to be accompanied by rapid economic growth. The probable consequences of low economic growth for the health of the nation will be continued social and economic disintegration leading to increases in diseases of poverty and despair – alcoholism, prostitution, drug addiction and violence.

QUESTIONS

1 Define the term 'infant mortality rate'. Why do geographers use the infant mortality rate as an indicator of development?
2 Describe the provision of health care in the UK. How does it differ from that in South Africa?
3 What can South Africa learn from the UK concerning the provision of health care?

BIBLIOGRAPHY AND RECOMMENDED READING

Black, D. and Whitehead, M., 1992, *Inequalities in health: the Black Report (new edition)*, Penguin

Dorling, D., 1995, *A new social atlas of Britain*, Wiley

HMSO, 1996, *Regional trends, 1996*, HMSO

Howe, G. M., 1976, *Man, environment and disease in Britain*, Penguin

Jones, K. and Moon, G., 1987, *Health, disease and society*, RKP

Learmouth, A., 1988, *Disease ecology*, Blackwell

Nagle, G., 1992, *Malnutrition in the Zwelitsha area of Ciskei*, unpublished D. Phil. Thesis, University of Oxford.

Nagle, G., 1997, *The geography of disease: UK focus*, GeoActive, 163

UNICEF, 1996, *Progress of Nations, 1996 World Bank Atlas*, 1996

WEB SITES

Summary of the World Health Organisation's World Health Report 1996 –
http://www.who.ch/whr/1996/exsume.htm

Chapter 4
Geographical issues in agriculture

This chapter looks at one of the world's most important industries, farming. Not only does it feed the world's population, it also employs more people than any other industry worldwide, earning valuable income for families and for nations. The four main aspects of agriculture examined here are:

- the contrasts between farming in EMDCs and ELDCs
- the world food crisis, the Green Revolution and appropriate development
- agriculture in South Africa
- environmental issues and agricultural change in an EMDC.

They show farming patterns to be a result of many forces – environmental, economic, social and political. Moreover, farming in ELDCs is closely linked with farming in EMDCs. The Green Revolution (the application of science and technology to agriculture), is affected by these same forces.

We examine agriculture in South Africa in a case study. Here, farming has evolved along political and racial lines. Another case study of the UK shows a number of the unwanted side-effects of intensive farming.

THE IMPORTANCE OF AGRICULTURE

Globally, the agricultural **workforce** is about 45% of the total workforce. Countries with a very high percentage engaged in farming include Nepal, Rwanda and Burundi (all 91%), Bhutan (90%), Niger (86%) and Mozambique (81%). At the other end of the scale, most EMDCs have less than 5% of their workforce employed in agriculture.

	1930-44	1945-64	1970	1980	1993
World	–	–	55	51	45
China	–	–	78	74	65
Egypt	71	57	52	46	39
Japan	48	27	20	10	6
South Africa	64	30	33	17	13
Thailand	89	82	80	71	62
UK	6	5	3	3	2
USA	–	7	4	4	2
Zimbabwe	–	–	77	73	67

Figure 4.1 *Agricultural workforce (%), world average and selected countries, 1930-93*

ABBREVIATIONS

FAO – Food and Agriculture Organisation
HYV – high yielding varieties of genetically altered crops
MNC – multinational company

Agriculture in ELDCs

Agriculture remains the main source of **employment** for most people in ELDCs. However, its relative economic importance has declined in recent decades, partly due to the expansion of manufacturing industry and partly due to decreased food prices. Nevertheless, it remains a vital part of many economies due to employment, **export earnings** and **food supply**.

Over three-quarters of the world's population live in ELDCs and in the poorest of these, over 70% of the population are employed in agriculture. However, much of the production in ELDCs is **subsistence**, and is not taken into account when looking at the agricultural contribution to gross dometic product (GDP).

Although most ELDCs have increased agricultural production since the 1960s, there has been a decrease in **production/head** in many African countries. The reasons are complex and include:

- deteriorating environmental conditions
- poor farming practices
- increasing population
- underpopulation, as in Rwanda in the early 1990s, where there were not enough people to harvest crops from the fields
- the neglect of the agricultural sector by governments.

The **global pattern** of agriculture in ELDCs can be divided into three main groups (Figure 4.2).

1 Tropical Africa, Iran, Iraq and Cambodia – extensive farming, shifting cultivation, low yields, limited inputs, limited mechanisation and a small proportion of irrigation.

2 Latin America – a small proportion of cultivated land, high proportion of grain, low but increasing crop yields, and limited use of high yielding varieties (HYVs) and fertilisers.

3 South and East Asia – intensive cultivation, especially of rice, high yields and much use of HYVs.

QUESTIONS

1 Choose an appropriate method to illustrate the data in Figure 4.1. Classify the countries into those which have **(i)** a small proportion of the workforce engaged in agriculture, and **(ii)** a large proportion of the workforce engaged in agriculture.

2 Which countries in Figure 4.1 have shown the greatest change **(i)** since 1930-44, and **(ii)** since 1980? How do you explain these changes and differences?

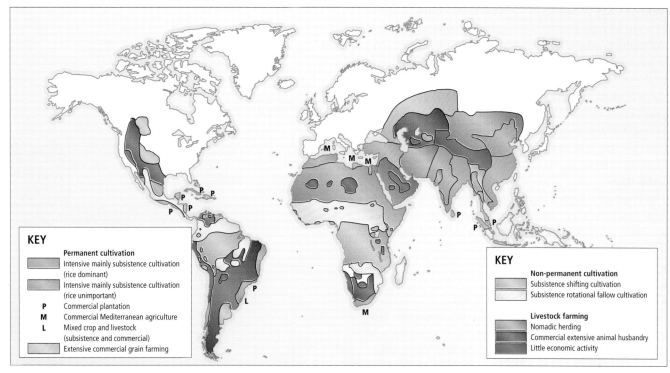

KEY

Permanent cultivation

Intensive mainly subsistence cultivation (rice dominant)

Intensive mainly subsistence cultivation (rice unimportant)

P Commercial plantation

M Commercial Mediterranean agriculture

L Mixed crop and livestock (subsistence and commercial)

Extensive commercial grain farming

KEY

Non-permanent cultivation

Subsistence shifting cultivation

Subsistence rotational fallow cultivation

Livestock farming

Nomadic herding

Commercial extensive animal husbandry

Little economic activity

Figure 4.2 *Agriculture in ELDCs*
Source: Barke and O'Hare, 1994

AN ANALYSIS OF FARMING IN EMDCs AND ELDCs

Farming systems in both EMDCs and ELDCs are very complex. They are also very different from each other (Figures 4.3 and 4.4). Agriculture in EMDCs has more in common with the manufacturing industry than it has with farming in ELDCs. For example, much of it is run by companies, and is **capital intensive**, **highly mechanised**, **large-scale**, **market orientated**, and **government involvement** is crucial. By contrast, agriculture in ELDCs is typically **small-scale**, **labour intensive** and **subsistence** by nature. In addition, EMDCs have considerable control over the price of many products, such as tea, coffee and cocoa imported from ELDCs, whereas ELDCs have little influence over price. Countries that are heavily dependent upon one or two crops are particularly vulnerable to price fluctuations and poor harvests.

Export production has been long established in ELDCs in the plantation system and it has frequently been separate from local production. Increasingly, however, agricultural systems in ELDCs are being influenced by multinational companies (MNCs), through their:

● ownership of the land

● control of marketing

● supply of inputs

● production of crops.

Figure 4.3 *Capital-intensive rice cultivation in Japan*

Figure 4.4 *Labour-intensive rice farming in India*

Although many farmers use **new techniques**, harvest new **cash crops** and are increasingly **commercial**, there are limits to which farming systems in ELDCs can adapt to external pressures for change. There are real dangers in these developments. For example, in cash cropping there is great uncertainty and there is little subsistence production to fall back on. Credit is harder to obtain because of the uncertainty and the result is increased rural poverty and environmental deterioration.

Land use

The Food and Agriculture Organisation (FAO) produces land usage data for every country, under four categories:

- arable (plus permanent crops such as coffee and fruit trees)
- permanent pasture
- forest and woodland
- other (such as urban and waste land).

Of the total land area of the world, 10% is arable, 26% natural pasture, and 3% forest. The rest is urban and waste land. Figure 4.5 shows variations in the proportions of each land use for selected countries. Arable land is the most important, as it yields more food and raw materials than permanent grassland or forest.

The **data** available for agriculture in ELDCs is at best a 'guesstimate'.

There is a very uneven distribution of **arable land per person**. Even allowing for variations in soil fertility and the practise of double cropping, the consequences for food production are great. For example, at one end of the scale there is over 3000 hectares/arable land/1000 people in Australia but only 40-50 hectares/arable land/1000 people in Japan.

The amount of arable land has increased little in recent decades. In fact, much has been lost to urbanisation and soil erosion (Figure 4.6), and there is very little opportunity to expand agricultural areas. Some exceptions exist, such as in the CIS and in areas of tropical rain forest, although these are not always suitable for agriculture. In parts of Africa, cropland deterioration is widespread. At the heart of the problem is the fact that population growth in Africa is exceeding increases in agricultural production. Potential solutions are mostly related to intensification, such as double cropping, irrigation, and increased use of

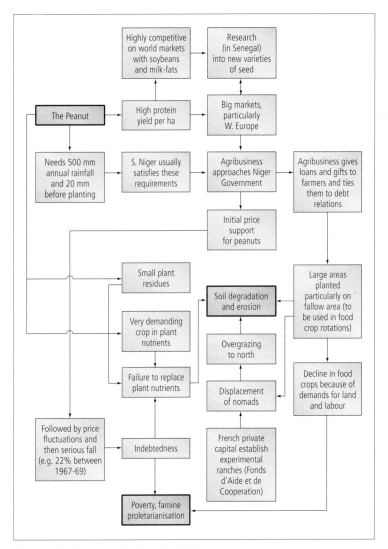

Figure 4.6 *The causes of soil erosion in Niger*
Source: Blaikie, P., 1985, The political economy of soil erosion in developing countries, Longman

	Land area (000s km²)	Arable land (%)	Permanent crops (%)	Permanent grassland (%)	Forest	Other land	Irrigated area (000s km²)	Population (million)
World	131 163	10.3	0.7	26.1	29.6	33.3	2496	5718
China	9326	10.0	0.3	42.9	14.0	32.8	490.3	1226
Egypt	995	2.2	0.4	0.0	0.0	97.4	26.5	64
Japan	377	10.8	1.2	1.7	67.0	19.3	28.0	125
South Africa	1221	10.1	0.7	66.6	3.7	18.9	11.4	44
Thailand	511	33.3	6.1	1.6	26.4	32.6	44.0	58
UK	242	27.1	0.2	46.0	10.0	16.7	1.1	58
USA	9573	19.4	0.2	25.0	29.9	25.5	203.0	263
Zimbabwe	387	7.1	0.2	12.6	49.1	1.0	2.3	11

Figure 4.5 *Global variations in agricultural land use (1992)*

fertilisers and greenhouses. But such developments are not widespread. For example, there is a very uneven global pattern of fertiliser use, with a large increase in Asia, especially China, India and Bangladesh, but not in Africa (Figure 4.11 on page 60).

QUESTIONS

1 Choose an appropriate method to show variations in land use among the countries shown in Figure 4.5. Describe the variations you have shown. What are the implications of this for food production?

2 Work out the amount of arable land per 1000 people for each of the countries in Figure 4.5. First you will need to work out the total amount of arable land in each country (i.e. Column I x Column II). Then divide the arable land by the population (Column VIII). Describe the variations in arable land per person as shown in Figure 4.5. How do you explain such variations in arable land per thousand people?

3 What effect is population growth in ELDCs having on the amount of arable land per person? What are the implications of this for food supply and productivity?

4 Give contrasting examples of, and contrasting reasons for, the loss of arable land due to urbanisation and soil erosion.

5 Study Figure 4.6 which shows some of the physical, economic, social and political factors which can lead to soil erosion. Answer the following essay question:

With the use of examples, explain the causes of soil erosion in ELDCs. How might the solutions vary with
(i) the nature of the cause, and
(ii) levels of development?

FOOD PRODUCTION IN THE 1990S: THE WORLD FOOD SUMMIT

The World Food Summit in Rome in 1996 criticised the 'physical, political and structural forces that cause hunger' and called for plans to halve the total of 850 million malnourished people in the world by 2015. It stated that each person had 'a universal right to healthy and nutritional food'.

Since most good land is already under cultivation, and population and cities are growing, yields will have to rise through **intensification** of production. Over the next 30 years, farmers will need to increase production by 75% to feed the world's population as it rises to 9 billion.

Ways of **improving food production** are well known:

- **Genetically engineered high yielding varieties**. India feeds twice as many people as Africa on just 13% of the land.
- **Fertilisers, pesticides and herbicides**. Fertiliser use in Africa is less than 10% of Chinese levels.
- **Irrigation**. The North Sinai Development Canal running from the River Nile delta to the Sinai peninsula will irrigate 62 000 square kilometres of desert.
- **Biotechnology**. This has the capacity to create another 'green revolution'. However, much of the agricultural research and development is carried out by companies in EMDCs and is concerned with food for EMDC markets not ELDCs.

The value of these developments is partly offset by negative factors, so for example:

- sub-Saharan Africa produces less food per head now than it did the 1960s
- irrigation has led to **salinisation** and/or **waterlogging**
- yields of HYVs are rising at slower rates than in the 1960s and 1970s and in some areas are **declining** due to soil exhaustion
- **agricultural policy** to reduce over-production, such as set-aside and quotas, has reduced stockpiles of grain
- in some countries, **grain stocks** have dwindled to excessively low levels, representing just 13% of annual food consumption
- food prices rose steeply in the mid-1990s
- **subsidies** in the former USSR countries have been withdrawn from inefficient state-run farms. This has reduced the amount of food being produced
- **adverse weather conditions** in the early 1990s, such as drought in southern Europe and floods in the USA, have reduced harvests and hence reserves of food
- changes to the world's **weather system** threaten once-productive grasslands in the USA, CIS and Australia. Drought and the spread of pests may become more common
- changes in **dietary patterns** in China are also having an adverse effect on global food supplies. As the Chinese population changes from a rice-based diet to a grain-based one, supplies of grain will decline. China's import of grain is likely to rise from 16 million tonnes in 1995 to 43 million tonnes in 2010, thereby reducing global stocks
- **political pressures** in EMDCs are causing farmers to reduce production. The dual combination of environmental lobbying and budgetary constraints is causing many farmers to farm in a less intensive way.

Two mechanisms which have a powerful influence on farming are **markets** and **human productivity**. Farmers will increase output in response to guaranteed prices and guaranteed markets. (In part, this was the cause of the food mountains and wine lakes in Europe in the 1980s.) In order to increase production it is necessary to pay farmers properly. Nowhere is this more needed than in ELDCs where agriculture has stagnated relative to industrialisation. To keep the better-educated, more skilled labour in rural areas, better pay and working conditions are needed, otherwise the migration of better qualified workers will continue to have the same effect as soil erosion – it reduces the ability of the land to feed the population.

QUESTIONS

1 'There is a universal right to healthy and nutritional food.' Do you agree? Give reasons for your view.

2 The market has traditionally responded to increases in demand. 'The more mouths there are to feed, the more the food companies want to fill them.' Discuss this statement.

THE GREEN REVOLUTION

Figure 4.7 *Cultivating high yielding species of rice in Indonesia*

The Green Revolution refers to the appliance of science and technology to agriculture. For example:

- genetically engineered high yielding varieties of staple crops such as rice (Figure 4.7), wheat and maize
- a package of technology of fertilisers, pesticides and herbicides, and water control combining to produce **optimum conditions**.

The Green Revolution is an **evolutionary** process. It is a dynamic system in which technology and techniques are continually developed and improved. Between 1966 and 1985, about thirty new HYVs were released. These new HYVs have overcome the problems of some of the earlier varieties and take into account variations in physical resources. Early HYVs were too **generalised** to perform well and were not suited to all areas, especially marginal 'rain fed' (non-irrigated) areas of the world, such as north-east Thailand and Orissa in India. One of the remaining challenges is to breed HYVs which can produce high yields in environmentally marginal, non-irrigated areas.

A good example of the value and limitations of an HYV is the dwarf rice which was introduced into India as early as 1965. It yielded up to 4450 kilogramme/hectare (kg/ha) under optimum conditions, compared with 3200 kg/ha of indigenous species under the same conditions, and average rice yields of just 1200 kg/ha. India's crop yield increased dramatically (Figure 4.14, on page 61). Similar developments in rice yields were recorded in the Philippines. Whereas traditional varieties had yielded 1300 kg/ha, the first HYV (IR8), yielded up to 6400 kg/ha. Both these projects were seen as successful and as models for other ELDCs. This development came at a time when many people thought the world was on the verge of a **'Malthusian' crisis** – that population growth was increasing but food production was static.

Emerging problems

However, after the initial enthusiasm for the Green Revolution, problems have become apparent:

- Only areas which are 'wealthy' in terms of soil and water are able to benefit, with the best yields on irrigated lands.
- Early species of high yielding rice and wheat were criticised because of their **poor milling** and **nutritional** qualities. In parts of Bangladesh, increased levels of **malnutrition** have been linked to the poor protein content of high yielding rice.
- The **replacement of traditional crops** by wheat for export reduces food availability for the poor who traditionally depended on root crops, such as cassava and sweet potatoes, and tree crops, such as sago and plantain. Now they have to buy much of their food.
- Poor farmers are forcibly removed from fertile farms.
- Subsistence farmers move to marginal land with lower yields, as in Brazil, or steeper slopes leading to soil erosion, as in the case of Lesotho.
- **Intra-village inequalities** develop. Class structures in many rural societies mean that only the larger and wealthier landowners have access to seeds and capital or credit to pay for irrigation. Poor families, on the edge of subsistence, cannot afford the risk of new methods and techniques. Over time **diffusion of innovations** does occur, but at the same time, inequalities intensify and become entrenched. Overall, the Green Revolution was **widening inequalities** in rural areas.

Governments' willingness to adopt the ideas of the Green Revolution varied. India and the Philippines were facing famine conditions and land scarcity, and so enthusiastically adopted the Green Revolution. By contrast, Thailand was the world's largest rice exporter and had an abundance of land. It feared that the poor taste of HYVs would harm the reputation of Thai rice. Consequently, rates of adoption varied from 13% in Thailand to 85% in the Philippines.

Many geographers argue that the Green Revolution is overtechnical and inappropriate, others say the problems are with insufficient progress in technology and infrastructure and that the spread of this technology was limited. At a global level, the Green Revolution is largely confined to areas where there is sufficient capital and moisture (Figure 4.8). Hence large areas of Africa and Latin America have been excluded from the benefits of the Green Revolution.

Although, globally, yields have increased over the last three decades, this may be due to the increasingly commercial nature of farming, since the products are often for export rather than for subsistence.

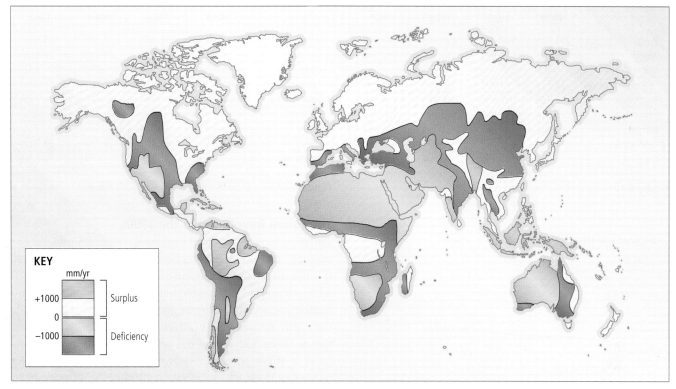

Figure 4.8 *Global shortage and surplus of water*
Source: Dixon, C., 1993, Rural development in the Third World, Routledge

Figure 4.9 *Irrigated area as a proportion of permanently cultivated land*
Source: Barrow, C., 1987

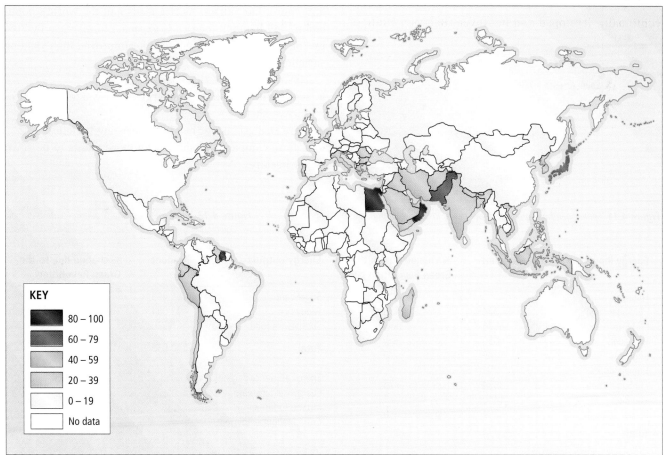

	1978	1983	1988	1993
World	204 281	218 270	230 445	248 125
Africa	9 881	10 533	11 504	12 970
North & Central America	27 233	27 023	26 519	29 391
South America	6 730	7 556	8 375	8 895
Asia	128 684	137 459	145 091	160 017
Europe	13 507	14 684	16 345	16 717
Australasia	1 646	1 869	2 111	2 393
USSR	16 600	19 146	20 500	no data

Figure 4.10 *Global trends in irrigation, 1978-93*

	1970	1980	1991	1992
World	69 245	116 473	134 327	125 931
China	4220	15 335	29 749	29 155
Egypt	373	664	963	882
Japan	2139	1816	1763	1784
South Africa	558	1064	740	785
Thailand	81	296	846	1095
UK	1894	2054	2177	2114
USA	15 535	21 480	18 784	18 983
Zimbabwe	106	173	148	137

Figure 4.12 *Global consumption of fertiliser (000s tonnes)*

The Green Revolution in the 1990s

The need to produce more food is an on-going problem. For example, by 2000 India will need to feed 1 billion people, so it must increase food production by over 40%, from 170 million tonnes to 240 million tonnes. However, of India's 260 million hectares of cultivated land, only irrigated crop lands show any improvement in terms of productivity, and even that is slight. The rest of the land is declining in productivity or is of low potential. Elsewhere, irrigated land is under increasing pressure – salinisation affects 25% of the irrigated land in Central Asia and 20% in Pakistan.

In the mid-1990s, the International Rice Research Institute (IRRI) developed a new variety of rice which yields 25% more than others. As rice feeds half the world's population, and demand for rice is expected to increase by 70% by 2025, there is an urgent need for improved high yielding varieties.

This new breed of rice has:
- seeds on every shoot so energy is not wasted on unproductive shoots
- more rice grains per head than existing varieties
- a more compact shape allowing more plants to be sown per hectare

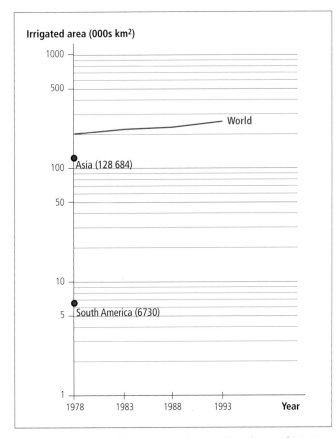

Figure 4.11 *Semi-logarithmic graph to show trends in the use of irrigation*

Figure 4.13 *Some effects of the Green Revolution in India*
Source: Lifford, p.168, in Selmes (Ed.), 1995, World Wide, Hodder .

Energy inputs	Amount	% change due to the Green Revolution	Energy outputs	Amount	% change due to the Green Revolution
Fertiliser			Sugar cane	165 425	+41
(i) Sugar cane	12 324	+138	Paddy rice	43 084	+190
(ii) Rice	3526	new	Subsistence food	1530	-90
Pesticide	650	new			
Irrigation	146	0	**Total**	210 039	+57
Human work					
(i) Sugar cane	3354	+26	Energy efficiency decline		-25%
(ii) Rice	1440	+3	Energy yield increase		+57%
Bullock (draught)	294	0	Income to farmer		+20%
Total	21 734	+111	Casual labour employed		-66%

(Figures in energy units - megajoules)

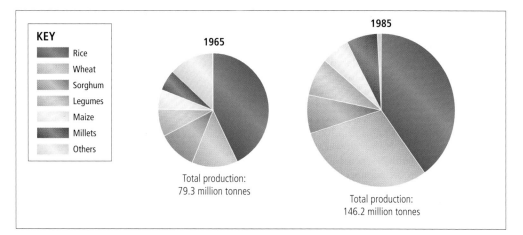

Figure 4.14 *Changes in crop yields in India as a result of the Green Revolution*
Source: FAO, 1967, 1987

KEY
Rice
Wheat
Sorghum
Legumes
Maize
Millets
Others

1965

1985

Total production:
79.3 million tonnes

Total production:
146.2 million tonnes

- yields of up to 13 tonnes/hectare under the best conditions, rather than 10 tonnes/hectare, the current maximum
- equal tolerance to pests, diseases and drought with other varieties.

However, in some of the IRRI's best test plots, rice yields are declining. Centuries of intensive rice cultivation may be depleting the soil of its nutrients. High yielding varieties demand more nutrients, and they may accelerate the process of soil deterioration.

QUESTIONS

1 What is meant by the terms **(i)** the Green Revolution, **(ii)** irrigated crop lands, **(iii)** salinisation, and **(iv)** high yielding varieties?

2 Study Figure 4.10.

a) Plot the figures for changes in irrigation between 1978 and 1993 for the major world regions on semi-logarithmic graph paper. The value for world change has already been plotted on Figure 4.11 and the first points for South America and Asia are indicated.

b) Describe the global trends in irrigation. How does this vary between the major regions?

3 Study Figure 4.12.

a) Describe the changes in fertiliser use between 1970 and 1991.

b) Explain the variations in fertiliser use between 1991 and 1992.

4 'Under the best conditions' the new rice yields up to 25% more than existing breeds of rice. Explain, with examples, what is meant by the 'best conditions'.

5 Study the statistics shown in Figure 4.13. What are the economic, social, political and environmental effects of the Green Revolution? Support your answer with evidence.

6 'The Green Revolution favours the EMDCs rather than the ELDCs.' Evaluate this statement.

7 'History records no increase in food production that was remotely comparable in scale, speed, spread and duration.' How far is this a true representation of the social and economic efforts of the Green Revolution?

APPROPRIATE DEVELOPMENT

We have seen how the Green Revolution has not benefited all places or all people. In some areas conditions have become worse as a result of the Green Revolution. In these places the Green Revolution could be described as an **inappropriate** form of development. **Appropriate development** is any form of development which is:

- **economically affordable**
- **culturally acceptable**
- **technically feasible** (generally with low levels of technology)
- **bottom-up development** – developed by the local community rather than imposed by the government.

These two extracts (Figure 4.15 and Figure 4.16 on page 62) look at the problems in one ELDC, Ethiopia, and outline two appropriate developments.

In the 1984-5 famine in Ethiopia up to 0.5m people starved and over US$2 billion worth of emergency relief was provided. Since then the country has changed dramatically. In 1991 rebel forces gained power and drew up a new constitution allowing local autonomy. However, life expectancy is still only 46 years and a labourer's wage only 30p per day. Nevertheless, Ethiopia's population is set to rise from 53 million in the 1990s to nearly 160 million by 2030.

Famine occurs in Ethiopia due to poverty. If the rains fail, or come at the wrong time, people have to sell their livestock and possessions to buy food.

Increasingly, researchers and aid workers are looking at ways of dealing with Ethiopia's problems. Their attention is focused upon soil, water and fertilisers. The soil is a heavy clay soil, fertile but prone to waterlogging and cracking. Rains are irregular in spring and torrential in summer. Few plants can tolerate this regime apart from the tef grass, Ethiopia's staple food. Each hectare of land cultivated produces just 700 kilogrammes and few farmers have more than 2 hectares. Fertilisers are lacking because people burn animal dung for fuel.

Figure 4.15 *Famine in Ethiopia*
Source: New Scientist, 5 November 1994

High yielding crop varieties, irrigation and fertilisers are not very applicable to many African farmers. Up to 25% of the fertile land in Ethiopia is left fallow owing to waterlogging. Instead, agricultural researchers have looked at ways of overcoming problems of soil, water and fertilisers in a more appropriate manner. By using broad beds, drainage is improved and crops can be grown on the fertile clay. However, making broad beds is exhausting work so researchers have developed a simple plough that can be used with just one ox. Oxen have been replaced by a cross breed of Friesan and local Boran cattle, in order to combine good milk production with an ability to tolerate Ethiopia's climate. By using wheat instead of tef, yields of 2 t/ha rather than 700 kg/ha can be achieved. However, wheat requires chemical fertilisers, hence is relevant for farmers in the commercial sector, not Ethiopia's large subsistence sector.

Figure 4.16 *Broad beds and multi-purpose cows*
Source: New Scientist, 5 November 1994

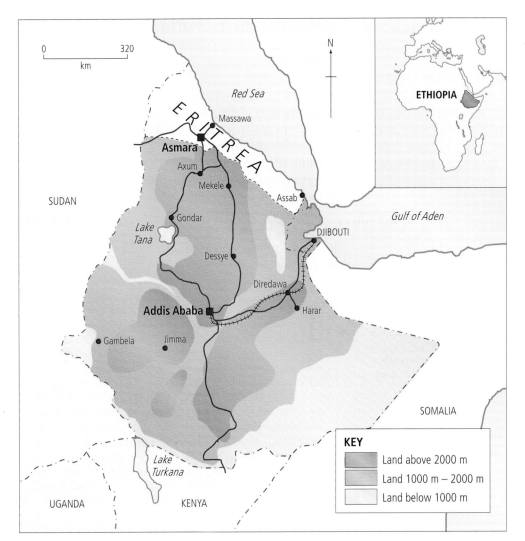

Figure 4.17 *Ethiopia: key geographic information*

KEY

Land above 2000 m

Land 1000 m – 2000 m

Land below 1000 m

QUESTIONS

1 Why are Ethiopia's farmers reluctant to adopt new techniques?

2 Why is it better to expand cultivation into the waterlogged area rather than on to the Ethiopian hillslopes?

3 Evaluate the appropriateness of the Green Revolution to Ethiopia's farmers (Figure 4.17).

4 Using an atlas, explain why most of the people live in the Ethiopian Highlands. What does this imply for development strategies?

Case study:
Agriculture in South Africa

In the last chapter we looked at a case study of health and health care in South Africa. We saw the clear racial differences in the levels of health and type of health care available. South Africa's agriculture also reflects the **dual nature** of the South African economy. The contrasts between the largely white commercial sector and largely black subsistence sector could hardly be greater. **Commercial agriculture** accounts for 90% of agricultural value but the bulk of employment is in **subsistence black farming**. In normal years, South Africa is a food exporting nation and 30% of its non-gold exports come from agricultural products. It produces:

- more than 50% of the agricultural products of southern Africa
- 45% of Africa's maize and wool production
- 27% of wheat in Africa
- 20% of the potatoes in Africa
- 17% of red meat production in Africa.

Agriculture as a contributor to GDP has decreased from 20% in the 1930s to less than 5% in the 1990s. In some years it has been as low as 3%. Agricultural output has generally kept pace with population increase whereas other sectors of the economy have grown at a much faster rate. However, in the former homeland areas agriculture still accounts for about 20% of GDP,

Inset 4.1
Drought

Drought is a major problem in South Africa. In the 1970s, maize yields varied between 4.2 million tonnes and 11 million tonnes. South Africa's annual domestic demand is about 7 million tonnes, so during a drought there is very little surplus and no export. Generally, maize production has been increasing due to the greater use of fertilisers, high yielding varieties of wheat, pest control, and better water conservation in the soil. The record year for production was 1980–81 when 14.2 million tonnes was produced. By contrast, in the drought of 1991–92 less than 2 million tonnes was produced.

although much of it is of a subsistence nature (Figure 4.18).

South Africa's dual agriculture

According to the 1991 census, there were between 1.2 million and 2 million people employed in agriculture. It is estimated that there are about 65 000 **commercial farmers** and 30 000 **part-time farmers**, largely in Kwa Zulu/Natal.

The drought caused serious problems:
- animal production dropped substantially
- nearly 4 million tonnes of maize had to be imported
- up to 100 000 jobs were lost in agriculture.

While drought was a factor causing difficulties in rural areas, underdevelopment and the lack of resources in rural areas were the main causes of vulnerability to drought.

In 1992 the government spent over US$1 billion on drought relief. Critics of the government's relief package claimed that it focused too much on white farmers. Of 10 million people living in rural areas, 93% were black. The government allocated US$160 per rural white in drought aid, but only US$3 per rural black.

Of the 65 000 commercial farmers, less than 5% are black. In 1991, the commercial farmers on average earned more than US$12 000, while part-time and small farmers generally earned between US$1500 and US$5000 from farming. There are also between 1.2 million and 2.0 million **farm labourers** and subsistence farmers in South Africa. These are mostly blacks. Employment on farms is largely in non-homeland areas.

Figure 4.18 Homeland agriculture

QUESTION

1 **How significant was the 1991-92 drought in South Africa? Give reasons for your answer.**

	Non-homeland area	Homeland area	Total
Total area (m ha)	102.3	17.3	119.6
Farmland (ha)	83.1	16.1	99.2
Rural population (m)	5.3	13.1	18.4
Farmland per person (ha)	15.7	0.2	5.4
Average farm size	1300 ha	1 ha	
Share of gross marketed output	96%	4%	
Average productivity per person per year	US$2/ha	US$0.5/ha	
Share of agricultural GDP	90%	10%	

Figure 4.19 *Division of South African farmland, 1990*

The total area of South Africa, including the homelands, is 120 million hectares. In 1993, the homeland areas constituted less than 14% of the total area but were occupied by 44% of the population, nearly 18 million people. 55% of households in the homelands were small-scale landowners with an average of 1 hectare of land and below subsistence production, while only 10% derived a full income from farming. Some 30% of families in the homelands were landless. The 65 000 commercial farms in the rural non-homelands had an average of 1300 hectares each.

The economic division of rural South Africa largely coincides with the racial division, namely white-commercial agriculture in the non-homeland areas and black-subsistence farming in the former-homeland areas (Figure 4.19). Average farm size, productivity and income in the non-homeland areas are relatively large and these areas have benefited disproportionately from government assistance.

Commercial agriculture

Much of the commercial agriculture in South Africa is dominated by **white farmers**, although their numbers are decreasing. For example, in the 1950s there were more than 100 000 commercial farmers but by 1995, only 65 000. The exploitation of black labour has been central to the development of commercial agriculture.

Black and coloured agricultural labour is amongst the most exploited in South Africa. As early as 1894, a tax was introduced to force blacks into paid employment. The **Native Land Act** of 1913 and the **Native Trust and Land Act** of 1936 served only to increase the flow of blacks to white farms.

Working conditions for blacks vary greatly. For most, wages are very low and there is limited security. Wages are frequently only about 10% of manufacturing wages although **payment in kind** sometimes doubles their income. At one extreme there are farms where flogging, child labour, and payment by the 'tot' system (part payment in the form of alcohol) is common. Weekly wages can be as low as US$10 for women and US$15 for men. At the other extreme, some farmers provide their labourers with three bedroomed houses, crèche facilities, a school and a library. Wages can be up to US$45 per week.

Figure 4.20 *Soil erosion caused by overgrazing*

Despite the high levels of unemployment in South Africa, commercial farmers complain about a **labour shortage**. This is because the low wages and poor working conditions offer few attractions to workers. Consequently, farmers in the Northern Province employ between 7000 and 8000 Zimbabwean **migrant workers** during the harvest season and up to 20 000 Mozambicans work on South African farms.

Subsistence agriculture

Black subsistence agriculture in South Africa is very **diverse**. This is partly due to the variety of the physical environment in the former homelands. In 1955 a government commission concluded that, on average, homeland areas had up to 50% more agricultural potential than areas in white South Africa. However, this did not take into account the problems of **accessibility** and **population pressure**. Some of the best farmland in South Africa is in homeland areas, namely Kwa Zulu and Transkei: it also has some of the worst, such as in Ciskei. In a recent survey (1995) it was concluded that the homelands merely performed a welfare function for rural areas.

The **decline of black subsistence agriculture** has traditionally been blamed on the shortage of land relative to the growing population (Figure 4.21) and the increasing poverty of that population. Shortage of land has led to:
- overcrowding
- overgrazing
- use of poor land
- soil erosion (Figure 4.20)
- denudation
- declining yields.

In the period before blacks were forced into reserves and, later, homelands, tribal groups were not confined to small areas. The loss of their traditional lands led to the decline of the black rural economy (Figure 4.22). Increasing

	1970	1980	1990	2000	2020
Cultivated land per person in hectares	0.6	0.5	0.4	0.3*	0.2*
Other	5.5	4.2	3.2	2.4*	1.5*

*estimated

Figure 4.21 *Land per person 1970-2020*

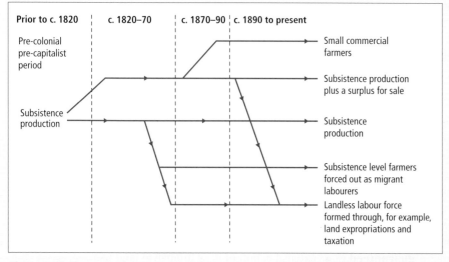

Figure 4.22 *The causes of underdevelopment in rural communities in South Africa*
Source: Webster, D., 1986, The political economy of food production and nutrition in Southern Africa, Journal of Southern African Studies, 2, 4, 447-63

poverty prevented black farmers from affording the inputs necessary to improve yields. As the reserves were unable to feed the needs of the black population, many blacks became migrant labourers and entered the cash economy. Thus, migrant labour was a result and a cause of low productivity in black agriculture. The failure of many migrants to send much of their wages back to homeland areas further weakened the agricultural base.

Hence, the decline in productivity and profitability of black agriculture is a direct outcome of the nature of capitalist and apartheid development in South Africa. Total food production in the homeland areas is sufficient for about one third of the homeland needs. The failure to modernise and to increase output is related to a number of factors:

- the limited size of plots
- yields up to five times less than on white farms
- up to 20% or 30% of the land being left unused.

The low levels of food production in the homelands can be attributed to the state and also to factors operating at a farm level. Factors operating at farm level include:

- availability and use of land
- labour supplies
- availability of capital.

As already mentioned, the 1993 census showed that 44% of the population lived in the homeland areas (which accounted for less than 14% of the land area of South Africa). This **population pressure** came about due to:

- the rapid population increase in the twentieth century
- the **forced removal** of blacks from 'white' South Africa and their **relocation** in the homeland areas
- tightening of influx control, i.e. preventing blacks from moving to white South Africa.

Despite the large numbers of people present in the homelands the quality of labour is very poor. The homelands,

have often been described as a dumping ground for people considered to have no value to the economy and so there is a disproportionate number of women, children, elderly and infirm. The most able labour usually migrates out of the homelands. The census showed that 59% of rural households were headed by women. African **women** in rural areas face oppression on four counts – because they are African, because they are women, because they are poor and because they live in rural areas. Most domestic chores are labour intensive which reduces the female labour availability for agriculture. The position of black women in South African society is extremely low and so female headed households are doubly hit when it comes to agricultural production.

Capital availability is very low in black farms. Wages sent by migrant workers tend to be small, irregular, and therefore unable to provide for farming inputs. One of the paradoxes of farming in the homeland areas is that there appears to be a labour shortage. There is an excess of population, but up to 30% of the land remains uncultivated in any one year. The main reasons for undercultivation include shortage of finance to purchase inputs such as seeds and fertiliser, and lack of access to land in terms of land rights. Low productivity is also due to poor transport, lack of agricultural and managerial skills, and better returns from waged labour.

QUESTIONS

1. Define the following terms: homeland, migrant labour, population pressure.
2. Explain how the migrant labour system could be both a cause and an effect of low productivity in black agriculture.
3. Using any three of the factors mentioned as reasons for low productivity in black agriculture, explain in detail how they led to the underdevelopment of black agriculture.

ENVIRONMENTAL ISSUES AND AGRICULTURE IN THE UK

This section focuses on environmental issues in the UK, such as how soil erosion and nitrate enrichment have been brought about. It also considers the effect of the European Union's Common Agricultural Policy on the growth of intensive farming and the associated soil erosion and eutrophication. Changes in farming policies have led to some environmentally beneficial farming but have also forced many farmers to change their farming activities, diversify or leave farming altogether.

The Common Agricultural Policy

The Common Agricultural Policy (CAP) was set up in 1957:

- to increase agricultural productivity and self-sufficiency
- to ensure a fair standard of living for farmers
- to stabilise markets
- to ensure that food was available to consumers at a fair price.

At the centre of the CAP was the system of **guaranteed prices** for unlimited production. This encouraged farmers to maximise their production as it provided a **guaranteed market**. By 1973 the European Union (EU) was practically self-sufficient in cereals, beef, dairy products, poultry and vegetables.

CAP led to intensification, concentration and specialisation. **Intensification** is the rising level of inputs and outputs from the land as farmers seek to maintain or increase their standards of living (or margins of profitability). The inputs included fertilisers, animal feed, fuel and machinery. The increased levels of outputs were typified by beef and butter 'mountains' and wine 'lakes'. **Concentration** is the process whereby production of particular products has become confined to specific areas, regions or farms. **Specialisation** is related to concentration and refers to the proportion of total output of a farm, region or country accounted for by a particular product. For example, wheat has become more concentrated in France and the UK as farmers have specialised in its production.

Since the early 1980s there has been a reform of the Common Agricultural Policy because price guarantees and intervention storage created surpluses in cereals, beef, wine and milk. By the 1990s the EU was overproducing cereals by 20% while demand had dropped. In some sectors, technological and scientific improvements boosted yields, further increasing surpluses. Consequently, a larger proportion of EU funding was used to store and sell off **surpluses** at subsidised prices on the world market.

The first modifications came in 1979, with other major changes introduced between 1984 and 1988. In 1984 a system of quotas was introduced in order to reduce overproduction by farmers. Quotas were limits on how much a farmer could produce. Farmers who produced too much were penalised.

The CAP after 1992

The most important changes to the CAP were introduced in 1992. Five objectives were identified:

1. to increase Europe's competitive agricultural base
2. to match production with demand
3. to support farm incomes
4. to stop the drift out of agriculture
5. to protect and develop the potential of the natural environment.

To achieve this, a variety of changes were introduced:

- reduction of price support where surpluses existed
- encouragement of alternative rural land uses
- extensification of (less intensive) land use
- reduced quotas on milk, wine, cereals and olive oil
- guaranteed maximum quantities
- concentration on quality rather than quantity
- income support to farmers in less favoured areas
- early-retirement schemes
- training and assistance for young farmers.

The key elements are **price cuts** and the **withdrawal of land from production**. For example, between 1993 and 1996, milk quotas were reduced by 2% and the price for cereals and beef dropped by 29% and 19% respectively. The prices paid to farmers were reduced in order to make cereal cultivations and beef rearing less attractive. With lower returns from these types of farming, many farmers switched to other types of farming and other non-farming activities, such as recreation, educational visits and golf courses (Figures 4.28 and 4.29, see pages 70 and 71).

The **set-aside scheme** was introduced on a voluntary basis in 1988, allowing farmers to take up to 20% of their land out of production and to receive up to £200 for each hectare set aside. The land could be left fallow, converted to woodland or used for non-agricultural production. While many farmers took advantage of set-aside, many intensified production on the other land and made their least favourable land the set-aside!

QUESTIONS

1 Briefly outline the aims and methods of CAP. How have these changed over time?

2 How successful has CAP been in achieving its goals? Justify your answer.

The environmental effects of agriculture

Soil erosion

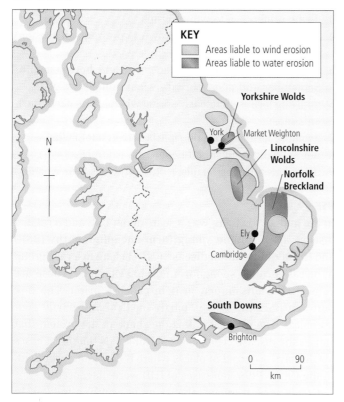

Figure 4.23 *Soil erosion in England and Wales*
Source: Nagle, G. and Spencer, K., 1996, A Geography of the European Union, OUP

Soil erosion is widespread in the UK on **sandy**, **loamy** and **peaty** soils which are vulnerable to erosion by wind and water (Figure 4.23). Since 1945, the potential for overland run-off and soil erosion has increased as pasture has been converted to arable land and more winter crops are sown.

For example, on the South Downs, traditional sheep pastures have been replaced by arable fields on slopes as steep as 20°. There the switch to winter crops in the mid-1970s was accompanied by hedgerow and bank removal and **field enlargement**. The use of heavier, more powerful **machinery** not only compacts the soil but creates 'tramlines' for overland run-off to follow. The use of fire to burn stubble (which was banned in the early 1990s) briefly enriched the soil but removed organic content from it. This organic material bound the soil and helped it to resist erosion. The optimum growth of winter crops requires light, fine soils and the selective use of herbicides. However, fine soils are easily eroded whereas coarser soils with stubble can resist most storms. The consequences are striking: soil losses of up to 250 tonnes per hectare have been recorded on the South Downs and gullies several metres deep have been initiated in storms.

Elsewhere in the UK, soil erosion is a familiar problem: in the Midlands it is associated with potato and sugar beet fields in the summer months after the harvest.

Future levels of soil erosion in the UK largely depend upon whether there is a return to grass or whether the acreage of arable crops continues to expand, which in turn depends to a large extent on the CAP.

The nitrate issue

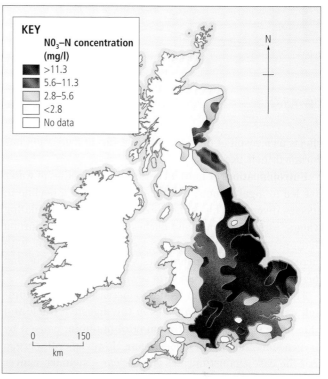

Figure 4.24 *Mean annual nitrate concentration in England, Scotland and Wales*
Source: Nagle, G., 1996, Agricultural issues in the UK GeoActive 160, Stanley Thornes, Publishers

There is a very distinct geographic pattern in the level of nitrates in Britain's water (Figure 4.24). Highest levels, over 11.3 mg/l-1 (milligrams per cubic litre) are mostly found in eastern parts of England, whereas the lowest levels, less than 2.8 mg/l-1, are found in Scotland, north-west England and central Wales. In general, there is an east-west trend with higher values in the east and lower values in the west. There are, however, certain anomalies. Parts of south-east England have very low values, less than 2.8 mg/l-1, while there are quite high rates, 5.6-11.3 mg/l-1, in the south-west and in parts of north-west England.

Nitrogen is a key component for plant growth and so farmers are keen to apply nitrogen fertilisers. Moreover, national and European policies promote agricultural self-sufficiency and the manufacturers of nitrate fertilisers are also keen to see an increase in their use. In the UK their use rose from just 200 000 tonnes in 1945 to a peak of about 1.6 million tonnes in the late 1980s (Figure 4.25 on page 68). However, there are serious ecological, economic and health

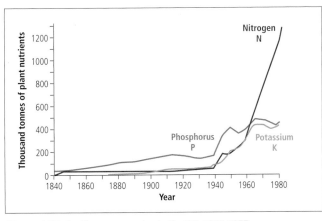

Figure 4.25 *Fertiliser consumption in the UK, 1840-1977*
Source: Ilbery, B., 1992, Agricultural change in Great Britain, OUP

effects as a result of this increase, and recent legislation has curtailed their use.

Eutrophication, or nutrient enrichment, of bodies of water has led to algal blooms, oxygen starvation and a decline in species diversity. This is most evident in poorly circulating waters, especially ponds and ditches. While there is a strong body of evidence to link increased eutrophication with increased use of nitrogen fertilisers, some scientists argue that increased phosphates from farm sewage are the cause.

The concern for health relates to increased rates of **stomach cancer**, caused by nitrates in the digestive tract, and blue baby syndrome, **methaemoglobinaemia**, caused by oxygen starvation in the bloodstream. However, critics argue that the case against nitrates is not clear – stomach cancer could be caused by a variety of factors and the number of cases of blue baby syndrome is statistically small.

Of more general concern is the amount of nitrates in tap water. The pattern of nitrates in rivers and groundwater shows marked regional and temporal characteristics. In the UK, it is concentrated towards the arable areas of the east, and concentrations are increasing. In England and Wales over 35% of the population derive their water from the aquifers of lowland England and over 5 million people live in areas where there is too much nitrate in the water. The problem is that nitrates applied on the surface make their way slowly down to the groundwater zone, and this process may take up to forty years. Thus, increasing levels of nitrate in drinking water will continue to be a problem well into the twenty-first century. The annual cost of cleaning nitrate-rich groundwater is estimated at between £50 million and £300 million.

Since the late 1980s, the problem has been tackled in a number of ways:

1 changing land use – less arable land, either due to set-aside, afforestation or pastoral farming
2 changing inputs – extensification of agriculture
3 giving preference to winter crops
4 sowing cover crops (crops grown to prevent soil erosion) early
5 avoiding the use of nitrogen fertilisers between mid-September and mid-February when rainfall is higher
6 applying fertilisers in early spring when plants need nutrients most
7 avoiding fertiliser use on riparian (riverside) fields
8 not applying fertilisers if heavy rain is forecast
9 using less nitrogen fertiliser if the previous year was dry.

BSE

In the mid-1990s there was a scare about BSE and a related disease, CJD. **Bovine spongiform encephalopathy** (BSE) and **Creutzfeldt-Jakob disease** (CJD) belong to a rare group of diseases called spongiform encephalopathies. These are caused by a misshapen protein called a prion. The link between BSE and CJD is partly medical and partly geographical. The medical link is the shape of the protein that causes the disease. The geographical link is that most cases of CJD have occurred in places where BSE is more prevalent. In the UK in 1996, ten cases of CJD were diagnosed.

CJD is rare: it affects about one person in a million. In Papua New Guinea, CJD is known as *kuru* or *laughing death*. It seems to have been spread by ritual cannibalism.

The first case of BSE in Britain was in 1986. Most of the infection in cattle took place in the late 1980s, peaking in 1992. It takes at least four years for CJD to incubate in humans and therefore at the very earliest it would have peaked in 1996. It is widely believed that BSE was transferred to cattle due to feeding them meal that was infected with scrapie, a disease common in sheep. Cows that were fed on infected sheep tissue developed BSE. As these cows were then slaughtered, crushed and fed back to other cows, some of these became infected.

Why is BSE/CJD a problem in the UK?

A number of reasons can be put forward. First, few places outside the UK suffer from scrapie and also raise large numbers of cattle. Second, cattle carcasses in the UK are burnt to make bonemeal at a relatively low temperature. Third, cattle in the UK derive up to 5% of their ration from meat and bonemeal. These three factors make Britain particularly vulnerable (Figure 4.26).

QUESTIONS

1 Describe Figure 4.25 which shows fertiliser use in the UK. Explain why fertiliser use has been linked with eutrophication of streams and groundwater.

2 How does the distribution of soil erosion (Figure 4.23) in the UK compare with that of nitrate pollution (Figure 4.24). Which farming practices link the two?

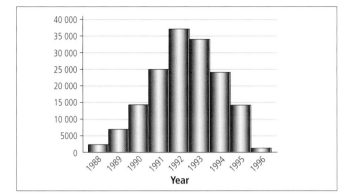

Figure 4.26 a) *BSE: reported cases in the UK*
Source: Ministry of Agriculture, Fisheries and Food

UK	161 663	France	13
Switzerland	206	Germany	4
Ireland	123	Italy	2
Portugal	31	Denmark	1

Figure 4.26 b)
BSE: reported cases in Europe
Source: The Economist, 30 March 1996

Feeding animals ground-down meal is not uncommon. However, cattle are herbivores (plant eaters), whereas the meal they consume is ground-up sheep and cattle. Moreover, in the 1970s a new technique for burning carcasses, which involved lower temperatures and was supposed to make the bonemeal taste better, became widespread. In the UK, temperatures of less than 100°C were used to incinerate cattle. These temperatures would not kill off all bacteria. In France and Italy, by contrast, temperatures of 130-140°C are the standard.

In 1997, the CJD Surveillance Unit suggested that the rising number of UK cases of CJD might reflect better diagnosis rather than any real change in the incidence of the disease. Another report indicated that the disease may have originally been brought into the UK by infected game from Africa.

As soon as other EU countries suspected that animals might be spreading BSE they banned British beef and bone-meal exports. France and Ireland destroyed all animals in any herd that contained even one case of BSE. This was not done in the UK.

The economic and political implications of BSE are severe. To eradicate BSE in the UK could cost up to £15 billion. The problem has not only affected farmers but all those employed in the beef and dairy industry.

Groups such as the National Farmers Union claim that the BSE issue has been exaggerated and blown out of all proportion. Their publications suggest that beef is safe, and that in fact British beef is much safer than beef from elsewhere.

Protecting environments in the UK

Figure 4.27 Environmentally sensitive areas in the UK
Source: Nagle, G. and Spencer, K., 1996, A geography of the European Union, OUP

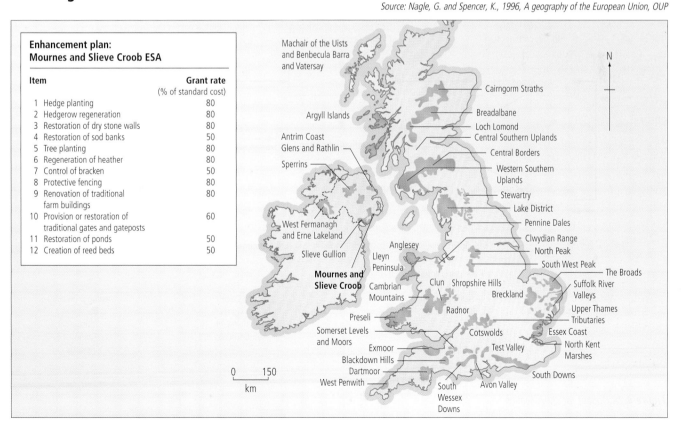

**Enhancement plan:
Mournes and Slieve Croob ESA**

Item	Grant rate (% of standard cost)
1 Hedge planting	80
2 Hedgerow regeneration	80
3 Restoration of dry stone walls	80
4 Restoration of sod banks	50
5 Tree planting	80
6 Regeneration of heather	80
7 Control of bracken	50
8 Protective fencing	80
9 Renovation of traditional farm buildings	80
10 Provision or restoration of traditional gates and gateposts	60
11 Restoration of ponds	50
12 Creation of reed beds	50

The British government has responded to the environmental impact of agriculture with a number of schemes. Along with the expansion of set-aside and environmentally sensitive areas (ESAs) (Figure 4.27 on page 69), a number of measures addressing specific issues have been introduced:

1 **Nitrate sensitive areas scheme** to protect groundwater areas
2 **Habitat schemes** to improve and create wildlife habitats
3 **Organic aid schemes** to encourage farmers to convert to organic production methods
4 **Countryside access scheme** to provide public access to set-aside land and suitable farmland in ESAs.

Payments are available for a variety of activities such as hedge planting, restoration of drystone walls, bracken control and so on (Figure 4.27).

In 1985, the EU agreed to provide farmers with the means to farm ESAs in traditional ways which would preserve important biological and heritage landscapes. Less intensive, organic methods were favoured, with increased amounts of fallow. By 1994, 10 500 farmers in the UK had signed or applied for ESA agreements, and payments during 1994-5 totalled almost £25 million.

Diversification

Diversification refers to the variety of farming and non-farming activities that farmers adopt in order to make a profit (Figure 4.28). Diversification is a recent trend but is increasingly important. It developed as the costs of farm inputs increased more than the price received for farm products, and profits fell. Diversification allowed farmers to increase their earnings from alternative sources.

There are a number of forms of diversification:

● **direct marketing** – pick-your-own (PYO), farm gate sales and farm shops
● **accommodation** – bed and breakfast, camping and caravanning
● **recreation** – golf courses, 'horsiculture', and nature trails
● **commercial** – new crops or livestock.

Diversification requires a number of conditions:

● availability of capital
● effective marketing and advertising
● planning permission to develop on Green Belt land
● no conflict with farming activities at key times of the year.

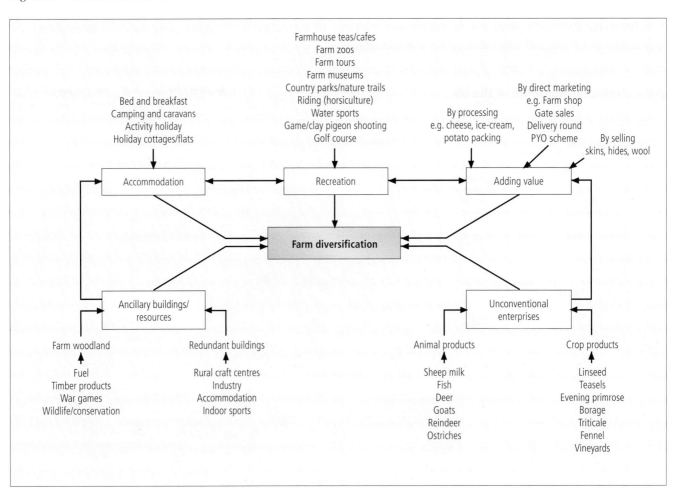

Figure 4.28 *Options for diversification*
Source: Ilbery, B., 1992, Agricultural change in Great Britain, OUP

Figure 4.29 *Diversification in the farming industry – ostrich farming*

SUMMARY

This chapter has focused upon four main aspects of agriculture:

- contrasts between EMDCs and ELDCs
- food supply and the Green Revolution
- agriculture in South Africa
- environmental issues and agricultural change in the UK.

The first section showed that the contrasts in agriculture between EMDCs and ELDCs are related to levels of development, technology, capital availability and environment. Moreover, many of the processes in EMDCs, such as price control, intervention, storage and production of the inputs needed for the Green Revolution, keep ELDC agriculture at an impoverished state.

In the second section, we saw that despite impressive changes in food supply, there are worrying trends. Growth of yields from HYVs is slowing down, lands are becoming degraded and there are widening rural inequalities. Not all areas are able to benefit from the Green Revolution, as the cases of Ethiopia and South Africa showed. In the case study on South Africa we saw in detail the importance of political factors in determining patterns of agriculture. Many ELDCs were former colonies and have similar problems to South Africa, if not as acute. In the UK's farming sector environmental issues dominate.

QUESTIONS

1   Describe the changes in the numbers of tractors as shown in Figure 4.30. Why do you think the numbers of tractors decreased in some countries between 1980 and 1992?
2   Using Figure 4.30, describe the contrasts in the level of technology between EMDCs and ELDCs. How useful is the number of tractors as a means of measuring levels of technology and mechanisation? Justify your answer with examples.
3   Define the following pairs of terms: capital intensive and labour intensive; arable and pastoral; commercial and subsistence; EMDCs and ELDCs.
4   Explanations of rural poverty in ELDCs frequently mention **(i)** physical or ecological characteristics, and **(ii)** economic and political factors as contributing to the low levels of development in ELDCs. Using at least two examples from both categories explain why farming in some ELDCs is said to be undeveloped.
5   'The Green Revolution: curse or blessing, and for whom?' What are the geographic implications of this statement?
6   'Large farms and freehold tenure do not guarantee increased productivity.' Discuss.
7   'Agriculture is very much a live issue.' What are the live issues in agriculture in the UK? Explain at least one of these issues in detail. How do they differ from the issues in South Africa, or any other ELDC that you have studied?

BIBLIOGRAPHY AND RECOMMENDED READING

Cole, J., 1987, *Development and underdevelopment*, Routledge
Dixon, C., 1993, *Rural development in the Third World*, Routledge
Findlay, A. and Findlay, A., 1987, *Population and development in the Third World*, Routledge
Hodder, R., 1992, *The West Pacific Rim*, Belhaven
Lemon, A., 1987, *Apartheid in Transition*, Gower
Lemon, A., 1995, *The Geography of Change in South Africa*, Wiley
Nagle, G., and Spencer, K., 1996, *A Geography of the European Union*, OUP
Nagle, G. and Spencer, K., 1997, *'Sustainable agriculture'* in *Sustainable development*, Hodder and Stoughton
South Africa Institute of Race Relations, Annual, *Race relations survey*, SAIRR

WEB SITES

ANC Home page - http://www.anc.org.za/
Oxfam - http://www.heinemann.co.uk/oxfam
Queen Elizabeth House Library, Oxford - http://www.info.ox.ac.uk/-qehlib

CD-ROMs that are useful for information on agriculture include:
Encarta - latest version (Microsoft Works)
3D Atlas (Electronic Arts)
World Reference Atlas (Dorling Kindersley Multimedia)

	1950	1970	1980	1992
World	6046	15 483	21 742	26 137
China	1.3	135	745	774
Egypt	–	17	36	61
Japan	0.7	278	1471	2003
South Africa	48	155	180	166
Thailand	0.6	8.0	73	164
UK	302	456	512	500
USA	3640	4617	4740	4810
Zimbabwe	4.2	17	20	16

Figure 4.30
Distribution of tractors (000s) 1950-1992

Chapter 5
Industry in the economy

Chapter 1, What is development?, showed how a country can change from being a predominantly agricultural society, first to an industrial, and then to a service or post industrial society. As labour is released from agriculture, as a result of mechanisation, people move into other sectors. But there are major problems for ELDCs as they follow the road to industrialisation. Many of them lack raw materials, skilled labour and markets, and, in addition, they are in competition with countries that are already industrialised.

This chapter looks at the benefits of industrialisation, global patterns of manufacturing, new and traditional models of industrial location, and then examines a number of issues with the use of case studies. Examples of contrasting industries are taken from India, South Korea, South Africa, Mexico and the UK. These suggest that many of our preconceptions about industry and development may need to be reassessed.

THE BENEFITS OF INDUSTRIALISATION

Having a strong and varied industrial base is an advantage for a number of reasons. Manufacturing adds value to products. It takes raw materials and converts them into finished and semi-finished goods. This added value is crucial for countries that wish to earn foreign currency. In the past, ELDCs have supplied raw materials to EMDCs, which EMDCs have manufactured into finished products and then sold back to the ELDC at higher prices. By manufacturing the goods themselves, ELDCs can increase their export earnings and reduce their import costs, allowing them greater self-reliance.

ELDCs are constrained, however, in their attempts to industrialise. First, many of these countries are small and have limited home markets. Being large can be an advantage because there is a large home market, as the case study of India (see page 78) shows. It is not coincidental that the world's largest countries all have large industrial bases; small countries do not have a large enough market for many goods. Although small countries, such as Zimbabwe and Ghana, can support some industries, such as textiles, food processing and cement industries, they cannot support industries which need a much larger market, such as the car industry or the computer industry.

In addition, small countries are not always able to offer sufficient skilled labour.

ABBREVIATIONS

EOI – export orientated industry
ISI – import substitution industry
MNC – multinational corporation
NAFTA – North American Free Trade Agreement

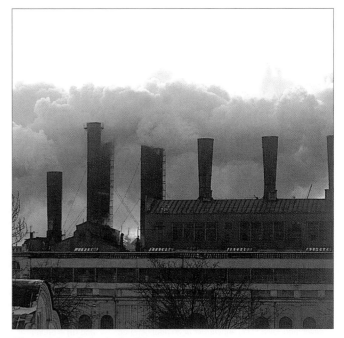

Figure 5.1 *Pollution in the CIS*

GLOBAL MANUFACTURING

The world pattern of manufacturing is very uneven. The main industrial powers are the USA, Western Europe and Japan. In addition to these there are countries with a smaller, but increasingly important industrial base, such as Brazil, Mexico, India, and China. The pattern is complex. Moreover, it is also difficult to measure the importance of manufacturing. For example, which measures should be used – number of factories? size of workforce? value added? amount of exports? investment in new technology?

One of the most widely used indicators is volume of steel production. (Other indicators can be used – employment, number of factories, value of exports, value added, may be used, but volume of steel production is still used, despite its shortcomings.) Steel production is dominated by the CIS, USA, Europe and Japan. There are also a number of emerging producers such as Brazil and South Korea but very few ELDCs. In addition, many EMDCs are experiencing a decline in their steel production. This is due to a variety of reasons such as depletion of resources, falling demand, over-capacity, and a shift to a post industrial society.

Inset 5.1
Data response: analysing tables

Rank	Country	Manufacturing value added (US$ million 1986)	% of world total	Cumulative (%)	Average annual growth rate (%)		
					1960-70	**1970-80**	**1980-87**
1	United States	1 037 243	24.0		5.3	2.9	3.9
2	Japan	591 038	13.7		13.6	6.5	6.7
3	USSR	516 741	12.2	50.0	-	-	3.7*
4	China	456 434	10.5		-	-	12.6
5	West Germany	279 365	6.5		5.4	2.1	1.0
6	France	174 286	4.0		7.8	3.2	-0.5
7	United Kingdom	152 214	3.5	74.6	3.3	-0.5	1.3
8	East Germany	94 813	2.2		-	-	4.0*
9	Italy	93 512	2.2		8.0	3.7	0.9
10	Canada	79 077	1.8		6.8	3.2	3.6
11	Brazil	74 032	1.7		-	8.7	1.2
12	Spain	48 795	1.1		-	6.0	0.4
13	India	38 311	0.9		4.7	5.0	8.3
14	South Korea	36 644	0.9		17.6	15.6	10.6
15	Mexico	33 869	0.8		10.1	7.1	0.0
16	Taiwan	33 812	0.8		-	-	-
17	Switzerland	33 692	0.8		-	-	-
18	Sweden	31 107	0.7		5.9	0.7	2.5
19	Netherlands	30 564	0.7		6.6	2.6	-
20	Romania	26 810	0.6		-	-	4.8*
21	Poland	24 972	0.6	90.4	-	-	1.4*
22	Czechoslovakia	23 983	0.6		-	-	2.8
23	Yugoslavia	23 825	0.6		5.7	7.1	-
24	Belgium	23 654	0.6		6.2	3.0	2.3
25	Argentina	23 533	0.6		5.6	0.7	0.0

* Gross industrial production - No data

Figure 5.2 The world 'league table' of manufacturing production
Source: based on data in UNIDO (1988) Industry and Development: Global Report 1988-1989; World Bank World Development Report, various issues; United Nations Economic Commission for Europe (1990). Economic Survey of Europe in 1989/1990

A Using the data in Figure 5.2, describe the global variations in manufacturing production by value added. (8 marks)

Look for these main points:
- maximum
- minimum
- trends
- exceptions.

In this question, we are only shown the top twenty-five countries so look for:
- geographic areas
- types of country
- economic importance.

And remember, time is short. In an exam there might only be 40 minutes to answer an essay, so allow 12-15 minutes to answer an 8-mark section.

An answer might read:

The largest manufacturing producer in the world in 1986 (over a decade ago) was the USA. This country accounted for over US$1 billion of manufacturing production – almost 25% of the world's total. Japan and the USSR each accounted for over US$500 million in manufacturing production. These three countries together accounted for half of the world's manufacturing production by value added. China in turn added a further ten per cent, and the European countries about another 20%.

Among the top manufacturing producers there were:

- *EMDCs such as the USA and Japan*
- *socialist countries such as the USSR*
- *ELDCs such as China.*

The rest of the countries produced less than US$100 million each. However, there was a wide range from all continents with the exception of Africa.

B How has growth in manufacturing changed since 1960? (8 marks)

There are a number of approaches that can be taken with this question:

1 We could compare the data for 1960-70 with that of 1980-87.
2 We could look at the fortunes of EMDCs against NICs, socialist countries, ELDCs and NICs.
3 Another approach is to divide the countries into those that have declined continuously since 1960-70, those which declined and then grew, and those which grew and then declined.
4 We could look at the data for each column and analyse the trends within each time period.

Before starting it is important to assess the data available. There are certain factors which might be important:

- is all the information available? – some columns here have missing data
- is all the information the same? – here some data refers to industrial production not value added
- are the time scales the same? – here we have three different time scales: 12 years, 11 years and 8 years; in this case it is not important as the data shows average **annual** growth rate but we need to be aware of the pitfalls.

This answer takes the fourth (time based) approach:

In 1960–70 the average annual global growth rate was about 7%. Highest rates of growth were recorded in South Korea (17.6%), Japan (13.6%) and Mexico (10%). There were also above average growth rates in Italy and France. By contrast, the lowest growth rates were found in the UK (3.3%), Spain (4.7%) and the USA (5.3%). However, there are a large number of countries for which data are lacking. These are generally the socialist countries such as the former U.S.S.R, China and former East Germany.

By 1970–81 the average global growth rate had fallen to about 3.5%. The highest growth rate was again found in South Korea (15.6%), followed by Brazil, Mexico and Yugoslavia (between 7% and 8%). These are all NICs. By contrast, the lowest growth rates were found in the UK, which fell by 0.5%, Argentina and Sweden. Other countries with below average growth rates included Germany (2.1%), the Netherlands (2.6%) and USA (2.9%).

In the final phase, 1980–87, growth rates were still high in South Korea (10%). However, China was by then experiencing the fastest growth at 12.6%. Japan's average annual growth had increased slightly to 6.7% but all other countries had growth of less than 5%. Of these there are mixed fortunes:

- *some countries grew compared to the 1970s, for example, USA, UK, Canada and India*
- *others decreased compared to the 1970s, for example, Germany, Italy, Brazil and Spain.*

C Explain the changing distribution of manufacturing production since 1960. (9 marks)

This part of the question wants us to summarise the main geographic trends from the table and to explain them. The main trends are:

- declining importance of some EMDCs, such as the USA, UK and Germany
- the growth in NICs, such as South Korea and Taiwan
- the growing importance of China
- the varying fortunes of ELDCs such as India.

The best answers will be supported by information from case studies. As always, plan your answer. Write down important factors, such as:

- availability of raw materials
- skilled labour
- access to cheap labour – the spatial division of labour
- changes in demand
- competition
- government assistance
- access to markets, especially trade blocs
- development of new markets
- government policies, such as import substitution industries (ISIs) and export orientated industries (EOIs).

An answer might read:

One of the major changes in the distribution of world manufacturing in this period was the decline of many EMDCs and the growth of many NICs. In addition, some large countries such as India, China and the former USSR are major industrial producers largely on account of the size of their population (and hence their potential markets).

There was a decline in the value of manufacturing in many EMDCs for a variety of reasons. In the UK these included the depletion of resources such as coal and iron ore, increased competition from overseas producers, and declining demand for their products. For example, many textile producers went out of production as a result of synthetic fibres such as nylon and rayon.

British steel production declined partly due to a decrease in demand. The need for steel for ships, railway carriages, armaments and construction declined. In addition, large, modern factories in South Korea and Taiwan are more efficient and competitive. Many of the UK's steel manufacturing firms were out-dated, with old methods and small premises. Moreover, the UK has moved towards being a post industrial society. There is more value (profits) to be made in the service industries, especially banking, finance and insurance.

In NICs, industrialisation has been sponsored by their governments. Governments see industrialisation as a good thing because:

- *it adds value to products*
- *it reduces imports*
- *it increases exports.*

Many NICs, such as South Korea, experience a period of time when industry is dominated by ISIs (import substitution industries). These aim to reduce the reliance on expensive imports from EMDCs. Once the country has established an industrial base, it develops EOIs (export orientated industries), exporting their goods to other countries such as EMDCs. So the decline of manufacturing in many EMDCs is closely linked to the growth of industry in many NICs. And because the industries are new, they are usually more competitive.

INDUSTRIAL LOCATION MODELS

Early attempts at explaining the location of manufacturing stressed the historical development of industry.

The early analyses concentrated on the distribution of physical factors such as the availability of energy resources, raw materials, water and cheap flat land. Later analyses stress the role of labour, governments and access to markets. Geographers have tried to explain industrial location by the use of simplified models. A number of models can be identified which include urban-industrial location, least cost location, spatial margins, behavioural approaches, spatial division of labour, and the product life cycle.

Models of urban land use have shown manufacturing industry located in inner city areas (Burgess's concentric model), along major routeways (Hoyt's sector theory), and in industrial suburbs (Harris and Ullman's multiple nuclei model). These models reflect the variety of manufacturing industries and their differing locational requirements: they describe the location, but little explanation is given as to why manufacturing is located there.

A number of models have been developed to explain location of manufacturing.

Weber: least cost location model

In 1909 Alfred Weber predicted that industrialists would locate factories at the least cost location (Figure 5.3) since industrialists' main aim was to increase their profit margins. His model was based mostly on transport costs but also took into account labour costs and agglomeration economics, that is, the savings that could be made through sharing costs, for example in industrial estates (Figure 5.4). He predicted that production which involved significant weight loss during manufacture would locate close to the source of raw materials. The location of the iron and steel industry close to the coalfields is a classic example. Industries, such as brewing, which experienced weight gain during processing, would locate close to their market.

There are many weaknesses with Weber's model. For example:

- industrialists may not only be concerned with maximising their profits
- there can only be one least cost location although many profitable ones
- transport costs are of less importance with higher value industries.

However, some of the model's predictions can be seen to work:

Many multi-national corporations (MNCs) seek supplies of **cheap labour**, not only in ELDCs but in peripheral parts of EMDCs, such as Northern Ireland and Wales.

Second, industries such as iron and steel works on the coast are in the **best locations** for the import and export of goods.

The **concentration** of high tech industries together on sites, such as the Cambridge Science Park where companies share in new developments and technologies, illustrates Weber's principle of **agglomeration**.

Finally, the increasing global importance of MNCs, with their huge financial and human resources, is creating a type of **rational man**, intent on maximising profits and backed by the necessary information and financial resources to implement research findings.

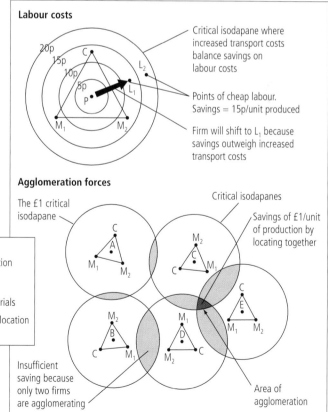

Figure 5.4 *The effect of labour costs and agglomeration – Weber*
Source: Nagle G. and Spencer K., 1997, Advanced geography revision handbook, OUP

Figure 5.3 *Weber's least cost location model*
Source: Nagle G. and Spencer K., 1997, Advanced geography revision handbook, OUP

Smith and Rawstron: spatial margins of profitability

An alternative model is Smith and Rawstron's **spatial margins** (developed in the 1950s and popularised by Smith in 1971), where industries are attracted to areas rather than points, which offers a more realistic method of analysing locational preference. The spatial margin is an area within which a particular industry can be undertaken profitably. Within the margin, revenues exceed costs and a profit can be made. Beyond the margin, cost exceeds revenue and production would incur a loss (Figure 5.5).

The significance of the spatial margin is that it focuses attention on limits to locational choice on the part of the entrepreneurs (or planners) who have imperfect ability and knowledge, and does not concentrate on one single point where profit may be maximised.

Behavioural models

The behavioural school states that people are not rational beings, and that their decisions are influenced by a variety of factors such as personality, wealth, skills and education. It suggests that predicting human activity is unwise. These behavioural models were developed in the 1950s and 1960s as a reaction against the scientific predictive bias in earlier models.

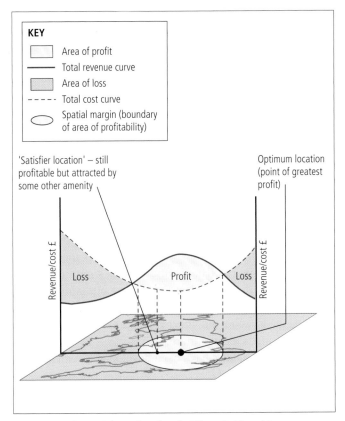

Figure 5.5 *The spatial margins of profitability – Smith and Rawstron*
Source: Nagle G. and Spencer K., 1997, Advanced geography revision handbook, OUP

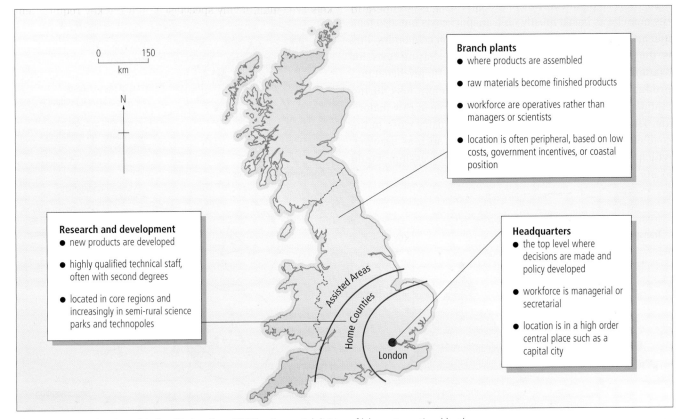

Figure 5.6 *Humphrey's model of multi-plant firms (1988) – the spatial division of labour at a national level*
Source: Nagle G. and Spencer K., 1997, Advanced geography revision handbook, OUP

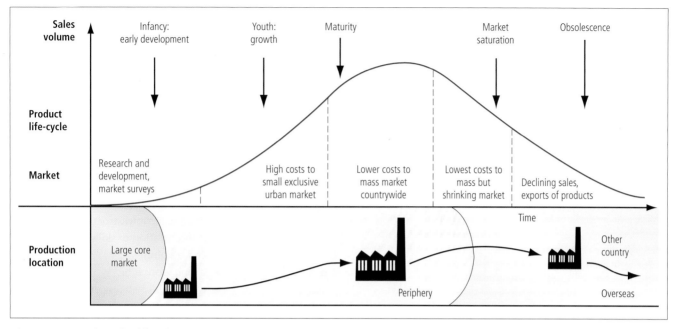

Figure 5.7 *Vernon's product life cycle*
Source: Nagle and Spencer, 1997, Advanced geography revision handbook, OUP

Behavioural approaches include Greenhut's notion of 'psychological income'. Psychological income is an **unquantifiable benefit** or happiness. For example, an industrialist might choose to move from the central least cost location to a small rural location, with less congestion, pollution and crime; profit would not be maximised but there would be a higher quality of life.

A number of new models are particularly relevant to ELDCs. These models include the spatial division of labour and the product life cycle. The **spatial division of labour** is the way highly paid, qualified labour and unskilled, low paid labour is concentrated in different areas. On a global scale, the highly skilled labour is concentrated in EMDCs and, within EMDCs, in large cities; a low paid, unskilled workforce characterises many ELDCs. Within a single country, highly skilled, trained workers are likely to be found in large cities (core locations) whereas unskilled workers will predominate in the periphery (Figure 5.6). One of the major forces that has shaped global industrial location since 1945 has been the way in which large companies have moved their assembly functions to areas of low labour costs. At the same time, decision-making and research and development are concentrated in a core location.

Another interesting model developed by Vernon looks at the product life cycle (Figure 5.7). Unlike the other models, Vernon considers changes in the product that is being sold and changes in the company. When a product is new, markets are small, highly specialised, and the key requirement is market access. Once the product has proved successful, expansion occurs and assembly in areas of cheap labour begins. Once the home market is saturated, it is necessary for the company to locate overseas if it is to continue to sell its product.

All of these models have their weaknesses. But by their very simplicity they help us to concentrate on one factor at a time. The explanation of industrial location is complex. But the explanations for its change are even more complex.

INDUSTRIAL DEVELOPMENT IN INDIA, AN ELDC
So far we have looked at industry at a global level, and examined some of the models of industrial location. In the rest of this chapter we look at a number of examples from ELDCs and EMDCs. These show how complex the pattern of industry can be. We start by considering the growth of high technology industry in India, in particular the state of Maharashtra.

QUESTIONS
1 Describe the location of industry as shown in Figure 5.4. Explain why industry has located where it has. Give real-life examples to support your answer.

2 In what ways do you think industrial location in ELDCs differs from industrial location in EMDCs? Give reasons for your answer.

3 Why is Weber's model increasingly important in explaining industrial location in EMDCs?

4 Which of the models of industrial location best explains the location of industry in ELDCs? Give reasons for your choice.

Case study:
Industry in Maharashtra

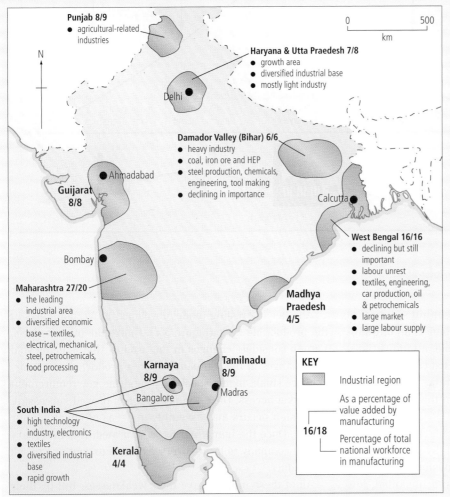

Figure 5.8 *India's industrial regions*
Source: Carr, 1997

efficiency. This is reflected in the level of inward investment into the state – it is the highest in India. A recent survey among investors listed a wide range of attractions, including:

- well-developed physical infrastructure
- reliable power supply
- proximity to ports
- good social infrastructure (concentration of skills, education and training)
- strong work ethic
- well-established law and order
- political stability.

Nevertheless some recent developments suggest that Maharashtra is becoming 'over heated', that is, it is becoming less attractive for investment, less competitive, and a victim of its own success. Labour costs in Bombay (the centre of Maharashtra's industrial base) are among the highest in the country. In addition, it has a severe transport problem and vastly excessive office costs. This has led to some companies, such as Coca-Cola, moving north out of Bombay to Delhi, where accommodation is cheaper and more accessible. Although Maharashtra is India's main centre for the car industry, new developments are taking place outside the state. Mahindra and Mahindra, a company which has always been based in Maharashtra, decided to locate its US$600 million plant in the southern state of Tamil Nadu. Hyundai, the South Korean carmaker, is also setting up a US$1 billion plant there.

Office rents in Bombay are much higher than in New York or London, yet the quality of office accommodation is very poor. Many firms rent luxury hotels rather than offices: the management consultants McKinsey have occupied a floor of the five-star Oberoi hotel since 1992. Some firms have moved out to

Maharashtra is an excellent example of how and why industrial development takes place in an ELDC. Maharashtra is India's third largest state, its undisputed financial centre and industrial powerhouse (Figure 5.8). In addition it has the best irrigation, power supply and communications in the country, a large reservoir of skilled manpower and management personnel, and proximity to ports. It is attractive to investors: between 1991 and 1996 it attracted over US$64 million worth of foreign investment.

The state's 80 million people, less than 10% of India's population, produce 23% of the country's output. The state's chemicals, rubber, metals, and plastics industries each account for more than a third of India's total production. 40% of income tax in India comes from Maharashtra.

Its infrastructure is among the best in India (Figure 5.9). It does not suffer from the power cuts that affect most of the rest of India, it has two large ports, and it has an efficient telecommunications network. The state's government and bureaucracy are famed for their suburban locations where rents are cheaper, more space is available, and it is more convenient for staff. Yet, even there, traffic congestion is a major problem.

Maharashtra's industrial concentration is proving unpopular with firms who believe that greenfield sites offer not only cheaper production costs but also offer greenfield markets, that is, largely untapped areas.

Yet, for all these problems, some new developments are taking place in Maharashtra. Growing congestion, energy problems, and a shortage of trained engineers in Bangalore in the south of the country, have led to an overspill of high technology industries northwards to Pune, Maharashtra's second largest city.

Industrial policy

Maharashtra has to work hard to maintain its position as the industrial giant of India. New industrial policy is attempting to address the problem of overloaded infrastructure by developing nine industrial townships, ranging in size from 2000 to 7000 hectares, throughout the state (Figure 5.9). These will spread industrial activity throughout Maharashtra in a shift of emphasis from cities to large towns.

The state government believes that as a result of the dispersal of industrial infrastructure, local employment will grow, and it is planning to set up technical institutions to train potential employees in these areas. Private sector involvement is also being encouraged, and the state sees its role as a 'facilitator' rather than a controller.

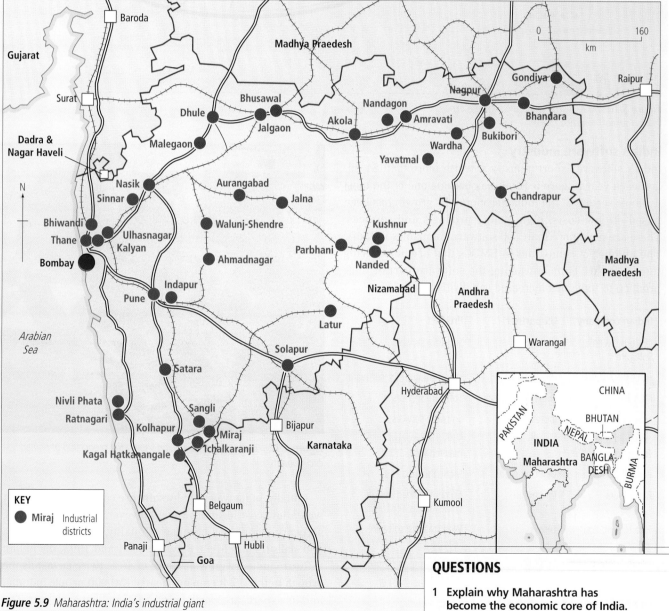

Figure 5.9 *Maharashtra: India's industrial giant*
Source: *Financial Times, 1996*

QUESTIONS

1 **Explain why Maharashtra has become the economic core of India.**

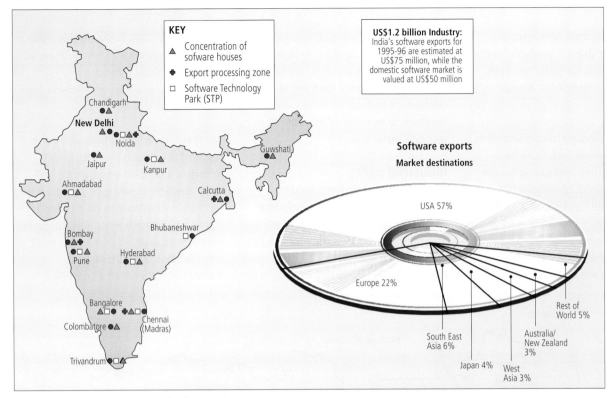

Figure 5.10 *India's silicon cities and software exports*
Source: Financial Times, 1996

India's software industry

India's software export industry is worth more than $1 billion each year (Figure 5.10). It has become one of the most dynamic sectors of the Indian economy. Its growth has been based on low costs, high quality products and services. There are now more than 700 software companies in India. The number of companies in EMDCs that are outsourcing their software (subcontracting the software part of their product) to India has increased rapidly (Figure 5.11).

Indian company	US partner	Product
Citicorp Overseas Software	Citicorp	Software services
HCL-HP	Hewlett Packard	Workstations, PCs, software
ITC	Lotus Development	Software services
Mastak	Ingres	Software services
Onward Computer Technologies	Novell	Software services, maintenance
Pertech Computers	Dell Computers	Motherboards, PCs
Rotta India	Intergraph	Computer-aided design workstations, services
Tata Information Systems	Unisys	Workstations, software services
Wipro Infotech	Sun Microsystems	Workstations, software services

Figure 5.11 *Indian-US partnerships in the electronics industry*
Source: Bunce and Studd (Eds.), 1997, The developing world, Hodder and Stoughton

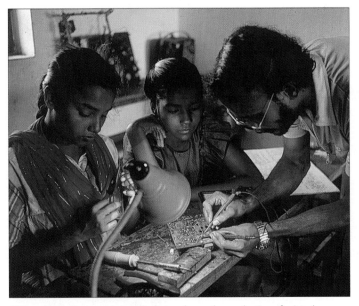

Figure 5.12 *Young girls in India being shown the production of printed circuitboards*

Initially, India was used by software companies because it was a low cost location. Now, however, India is attracting software companies because of quality, speed, innovation and skills (Figure 5.12). Between 1991 and 1995, the Indian software industry grew at a rate of 46%, twice as fast as the growth in the US. It employs nearly 150 000 people in India, and its exports are worth over US$75 million each year. The Indian domestic market is worth a further US$50 million.

India is keen to develop the software industry for several reasons:

- it demands high skills
- it does not damage the environment
- it is a growth industry
- there is a great deal of investment money available.

A number of factors explain why India has been so successful and how it has outshone competition from China, the Philippines and Eastern Europe. These include:

- the availability of a huge pool of relatively low cost, technically qualified software professionals
- high levels of quality
- a time zone advantage with both the US and Europe.

In addition, there have been attempts to improve India's telecommunications.

In the USA and Europe there has been a growing shortage of software engineers. After the USA, India has the largest number of English-speaking scientific workers. The sheer size of the workforce in India, its technical competence and relative low cost have been paramount in explaining the development of the software industry in India.

Inset 5.2
Bangalore

Bangalore has been described as the 'silicon plateau' of India. It is home to a cluster of high technology firms: IBM, Hewlett Packard and Motorola. Bangalore has attracted investors for a number of reasons:

- a skilled workforce
- Bangalore has a number of research institutions and universities
- compared to the west of India, Bangalore offers low labour costs – a first class graduate can be recruited for as little as US$4200 a year
- Bangalore has low rainfall and pleasant temperatures on account of its plateau location
- India is an important base for western firms trying to enter the Asian markets.

One company that has located in Bangalore is Motorola, the US electronics and equipment company. In order to overcome the power cuts that plague most of India, Motorola has its own generator. It chose Bangalore for a number of reasons:

1 it is the high tech centre of India
2 other US multinationals, such as Hewlett Packard and 3M, have located there
3 there is high quality but relatively cheap labour
4 it wanted a foothold in the expanding Indian market.

The Bhopal disaster

Bhopal is the capital of Madhya Pradesh in central India. In the 1970s, the US firm Union Carbide established a factory in the northern part of the city to produce chemicals for pesticides. For Union Carbide the site allowed access to a pool of cheap labour, to the vast Indian market, and it gave them a location where environmental and safety procedures were not strictly enforced. At the time it was a popular decision as:

- it provided much needed employment for local people
- it reduced India's dependence on imported chemicals.

There were, however, a series of leaks, spills and accidents at the plant. The plant management did not consider these serious enough to take any action.

In December 1994, some 36 tonnes of methyl isocynate (MIC) leaked from an underground storage tank. (MIC is a toxic chemical used to manufacture carbamate pesticides.) When water accidentally entered the storage tank, the cooling system failed. This caused the mixture of MIC and water to overheat and explode. Once exposed to the air, some of the MIC was converted into poisonous hydrogen cyanide gas. Huge quantities of the gas leaked out, and the plant's safety procedures were unable to cope, and in fact, not even the warning alarm was properly sounded.

The gas covered an area of 40 square kilometres and affected about 200 000 people (Figure 5.13 on page 82). People woke up coughing and with severe breathing problems. Those who managed to escape the area, on whatever transport they could get, survived. Many of those who remained in Bhopal died. The worst affected area was close to the Union Carbide factory. Over 5000 people were killed. Of these, about half were as a direct result of exposure to MIC and the rest due to the after-effects. Close to the factory, the high density shanty towns made of wood, straw, tin, and plastic allowed the gas to seep into people's homes. In the wealthier areas further away people were able to close windows and doors and protect themselves against the gas.

Thousands were evacuated by railway staff, and the Indian army was called in to help with the evacuations. The day after the accident, over 25 000 people were crowded into Bhopal's hospitals, suffering from respiratory problems and blindness (Figure 5.14). Estimates of the number made seriously ill by the explosion vary from 10 000 (Union Carbide estimate) to 200 000 (Indian officials' estimate). The problem was made worse by the fact that little was known about the hydrogen cyanide gas and the company were not prepared to give out much information.

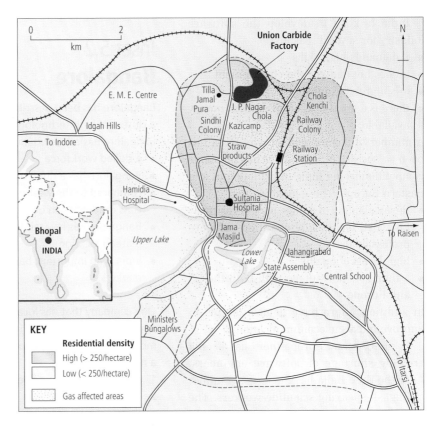

Figure 5.13 *Bhopal - the spread of the MIC gas*
Source: A. Agarwal and S. Narain (eds), 1986, The state of India's environment 1984-85, New Delhi, Centre for Science and Environment

Figure 5.14 *The Bhopal disaster*

A number of factors explain the disaster and the scale of the effects:

- far too much MIC was stored at the factory
- normal safety procedures were inadequate
- there was a failure to sound the warning system once the leak occurred
- few details were released about the nature of the gas
- shanties were allowed to be developed close to a hazardous factory.

Over a decade later, large numbers of people in Bhopal suffer from respiratory problems, blindness, digestive problems and stress related illnesses. Many have never worked since, and will never work again. The company was brought to court, and ordered to pay US$470 million in settlement. In addition the clean up operation cost a further US$570 million. It has been estimated that the tragedy could have been prevented had the company invested US$1 million in safety equipment.

QUESTIONS

1 Describe the reasons why high technology industry has been attracted to Bangalore.

2 Describe and explain the environmental and social impact of industrialisation in India. Give examples to support your answer.

INDUSTRIAL DEVELOPMENT IN SOUTH KOREA - A NIC

Figure 5.15 *Shipbuilding in South Korea*

South Korea is often described as the 'model' newly industrialising country (NIC) whose economic growth has been spectacular. The reasons for this growth were discussed in Chapter 1, page 11. However, there are now signs that the growth rate is declining and undesirable side-effects are becoming apparent. It provides similarities and contrasts with India.

South Korea's future growth industries are likely to be in research and development, and high-value industries, including computers, biotechnology and aerospace. In order to become more flexible and competitive the Government is helping small and medium sized industries which can compete in specialised markets.

South Korea maintains many economic strengths (Figure 5.16). Economic growth is high, at 7% per year (Figure 5.17). The country invests heavily in expanding its industrial base. It has a young, well-educated workforce, and there is full employment.

But despite its economic strength, there are signs that South Korea, like many NICs, is losing its international competitiveness. South Korea likes to claim that it is the Japan of the future. However, it is beginning to resemble the Japan of the present – a sluggish economy beset by serious structural problems.

What are the warning signs?

- a weak yen has benefited Japanese car and shipbuilding at the expense of South Korea
- a slowdown in the global demand for semi-conductors, which account for up to 20% of South Korea's exports
- South Korea is a 'high cost/low efficiency' economy
- production costs have risen rapidly since the mid-1980s
- wages are the highest in Asia after Japan

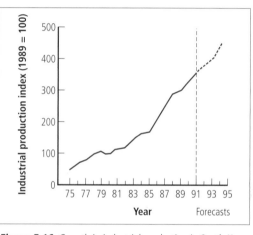

Figure 5.16 *Growth in industrial production in South Korea*
Source: UNIDO Report, 1993-94

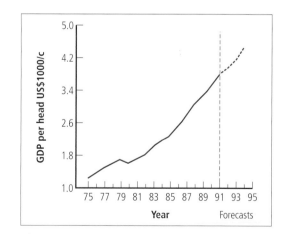

Figure 5.17 *Economic growth – gross domestic product per head*
Source: UNIDO Report, 1993-94

	1963	**1992**
GNP per capita (US$ per head)	82	7220
Infant mortality rate (per 1000)	85	11
Urban population (%)	29	77
Population with access to safe water	63	93
Employment in primary industry (%)	63	19
Employment in secondary industry (%)	9	28
Employment in services (%)	28	53

Figure 5.18 *Changes in South Korea, 1963-92*
Source: Bunce and Studd (Eds.), 1997, The developing world, Hodder and Stoughton

- the transport system is overburdened, and its costs are twice those of US and Japanese producers
- labour productivity has not kept pace with wage increases
- most of South Korea's exports are in a narrow range of highly cyclical industries – electronics, cars, ships, petrochemicals and steel – and are facing increased competition from China and South East Asia
- there has been a lack of spending on research and development
- the South Korean industry has built large factories to achieve economies of scale, that is, to gain benefits from being large, there is little flexibility or innovative industrial development.

South Korea is now faced with having over production (over capacity) in many sectors, and a lack of cutting edge technology. In the past it relied on low wages and a cheap currency to sustain high growth. Both these factors are disappearing. State support for the chaebol (large corporations), is being phased out. The chaebol dominate the economy at the expense of small businesses. They maintained their competitiveness on a diet of state subsidies, and their sheer size allowed them to achieve economies of scale. But they have caused an absence of innovative entrepreneurial activity. In addition, trade barriers are falling and there is increased competition from other producers.

Women in South Korea

The status of women in South Korean employment and society remains extremely low (Figure 5.19). South Korea – more than many countries – is a male dominated society. Women are subjected to sexual discrimination, forced to leave their jobs when they marry and have to retire earlier than their male counterparts. The percentage of South Korean women in the workforce was 44% in 1995, compared with 37% in 1975. However, most women are in low paid jobs in manufacturing and services. Women's wages average 55% of men's, and few women reach the higher ranks of industry, finance and politics.

To help rectify the situation, in 1996 the government introduced a Women's Development Act. One measure includes greater access to childcare facilities. At present less than 20% of South Korean children under the age of six have access to facilities: the state aims to raise this to 60%.

Figure 5.19 *Low status women's work in South Korea*

INDUSTRY IN SOUTH AFRICA: THE TASK AHEAD

'We must not be fooled by the existence of new factories, offices and shopping malls into thinking that the underlying industries are globally competitive. Underneath the attractively painted body panels, the engine is rusty and out-dated.'

Michael Holman, Roger Matthews and Mark Suzman, quoting the Monitor Company Financial Times, May 2 1995

So far we have considered two countries which are successful industrial economies – India on account of its size, and South Korea on account of its planned industrialisation. South Africa, an ELDC, although it is the largest industrial economy in Africa, is inefficient and economically uncompetitive. It is said to have the 'most expensive low labour costs' in the world.

QUESTIONS

1 Explain why South Korea's workforce is so important for its economic development.

2 What do you think the term 'cyclical industries' means? Explain why electronics, cars and steel are considered to be cyclical industries.

3 What are 'economies of scale'. Why are larger factories thought to be more efficient than smaller factories?

For example, it costs more to transport steel from the centre of South Africa to Durban than it does to transport it from Durban to Europe. Many South African industries have survived only because of state protection and subsidies; some companies have served very small markets, and therefore have very high costs. Moreover, South Africa is not as rich as it first seems: GDP per head is lower than Hungary and on a par with Brazil or Botswana, and it loses its labour cost advantage because of its very low productivity.

South Africa needs an economic transformation just as far reaching as that achieved in the political arena. The Government of National Unity has to reach growth rates comparable with the Asian NICs in order to redress the inequalities brought about by apartheid. South Africa needs higher productivity, more flexible labour markets and more efficient management if it is to become internationally competitive. Although it has received overseas investment, many investors are reluctant to invest too much, fearing political instability.

To have a successful economy, South Africa needs a thriving black middle class. Until the early 1990s, most blacks were forbidden from owning company premises in cities, denied skills and training and had virtually no access to capital. Hence the main route into industry for blacks was as workers.

Unemployment in South Africa

There are 4.7 million South Africans, mostly black, without jobs, half of them under 30. This is more than 30% of the potential workforce. Each year 400 000 school leavers join the search for work, but in 1995 only 3% found formal sector employment. Unemployment is 32.6% and is a potential economic time bomb. Both industry and the government are over-staffed and under-productive. However, the government's commitment to reconstructing an economy previously distorted by minority rule, sanctions and isolation, creates new opportunities.

	Labour costs per hour	Labour hours per car	Labour cost per car
South Africa	5.6	64	......
Mexico	6.0	24	......
USA	38.0	19	......

Figure 5.20 Labour costs and the time taken to manufacture a car

MODERNISING MEXICO

Mexico is another example of a country attempting to modernise. Proximity to the USA has proved a blessing (access to a large wealthy market) and a curse (the USA dominates Mexico). In 1994 Mexico signed the North American Free Trade Agreement (NAFTA) with the USA and Canada. This created one of the largest free trade zones in the world. It is the first agreement which joins countries from the developed and developing worlds.

NAFTA is an agreement to phase out restrictions on the movement of goods, services and capital between the three countries by the year 2010. Its aim is to:
- eliminate trade barriers
- promote economic competition
- increase investment opportunities
- improve cooperation and trade between the three countries.

Until 1982, Mexico followed a policy of government-sponsored industrialisation based upon ISIs. However, financial crises as a result of overspending in the 1970s and 1980s forced the Mexican government to seek aid from the USA, the World Bank and the International Monetary Fund. Aid was provided, at a price – Mexico was forced to rearrange its economy along free market lines. The government was keen to agree, partly to receive the aid and partly in fear of being ignored by the USA. Mexico hoped that by joining NAFTA, economic growth would follow, employment would increase and development would take off; Mexico hoped to become a NIC.

However, there has been opposition to NAFTA within the countries themselves. Critics argue that it will not necessarily bring economic growth.

Experience in Canada has shown that:
1 Many small firms have closed due to competition from lower cost US firms
2 Many firms left Canada for lower cost areas in the USA
3 Mergers and takeovers have led to increased unemployment.

With respect to Mexico, it is predicted that:
1 US industries will move to Mexico to take advantage of its very low labour costs, thereby creating unemployment in the USA and reinforcing a low-wage mentality in Mexico.
2 Up to 15 million farmers in Mexico will be affected by the removal of subsidies, decline in communal ownership of the land and the removal of border restrictions on trade. US and Canadian grain producers will dump their surpluses in Mexico, forcing uncompetitive Mexican peasants out of agriculture.

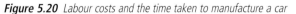

QUESTIONS

1 Give two contrasting reasons why investors **(i)** want to invest in South Africa, and **(ii)** do not want to invest in South Africa.

2 Using Figure 5.20 which shows labour costs and manpower hours involved in constructing a car, work out the cost in labour hours of producing a car in South Africa, Mexico and the USA. How do you account for the difference between the three countries?

According to NAFTA, Mexico's rural areas will become export orientated: industrial and service growth will replace agriculture. However, where there has already been growth, its value has been questioned. Along the USA-Mexican border there are about 2000 US-owned, labour-intensive, export-orientated assembly plants, employing about 500 000 Mexican labourers. Many of the workers are children, wages are low and working conditions often unsafe.

Environmentalists point to Mexico's poor record of enforcing environmental laws. They fear that Mexico may become a dumping ground for hazardous material and show that Mexico's rivers and air are already heavily polluted (Figure 5.21).

Maquiladora development in Mexico

Mexico has attracted many US-owned companies to build low cost assembly plants in places such as Cuidad Juarez, Nuevo Laredo and Tijuana (Figure 5.22). These factories, called *maquiladora* operations, are foreign owned but employ local labour. Since 1989 over 2000 US firms have set up in Mexico's border cities. The main attractions are:

- low labour costs
- relaxed environmental legislation
- good access to US markets.

Figure 5.21 *Environmental pollution in northern Mexico*

Many Mexicans are in favour of the maquiladora as they bring investment, money and jobs to northern Mexico.

However, Mexico is becoming more dependent upon the USA, and the USA would seem to be benefitting more from this development than Mexico.

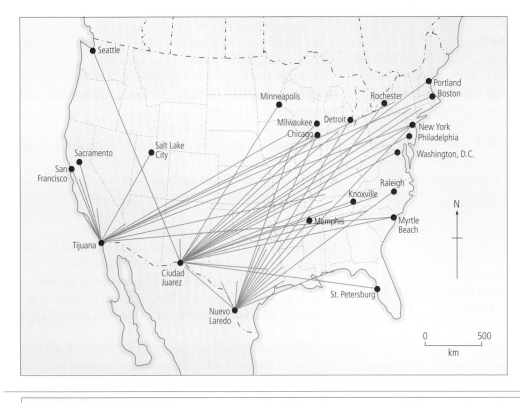

Figure 5.22 *Destination of goods from maquiladora plants in Mexico*
Source: Bunce and Studd (Eds.) , 1997, The developing world, Hodder and Stoughton

---

QUESTIONS

1 In what ways does NAFTA differ from other trading blocs such as the European Union? Why is this important?

2 Who are likely to be the main **(i)** winners and **(ii)** losers as a result of NAFTA? Explain your answer.

3 List **three** advantages and **three** disadvantages of maquiladora developments in Mexico.

4 How far will maquiladora developments provide long-term development for Mexico? Give reasons for your answer.

INDUSTRIAL CHANGE IN THE UK, AN EMDC

Case study:
The north east of England

So far we have looked at industry in ELDCs and NICs. This case study from the north east of England looks at industrial change in an EMDC, and provides a number of contrasts with industrial development in ELDCs and NICs. There are also, however, a number of similarities.

The north east of England is associated with heavy industries, such as coal mining, shipbuilding, iron and steel manufacture and engineering. It has suffered huge job losses as a result of **deindustrialisation**, the decline of heavy industry. There has been some regeneration, largely due to **inward investment** by Japanese and German investors.

The region's heavy industries have all declined, and unemployment in the North East is above the national average. Some heavy industry still remains: British Steel and ICI are major employers on Teeside, and there are still numerous engineering companies such as Vickers and Rolls-Royce.

Here we look at the changes to one company, Swan Hunter, and at some of the new inward investment to the North East.

The decline of Swan Hunter
Since the middle of the nineteenth century, Swan Hunter has played a leading role in British maritime history. For many decades, more than a third of the world's ships were built in its shipyards. Altogether, it built over 2700 ships – including more than 400 warships and fleet auxiliaries.

Figure 5.23 *The height of shipbuilding on the Tyne*

Swan Hunter comprised several Tyneside shipyards. In the 1880s, Swan Hunter expanded rapidly as the North East entered its golden era of shipbuilding (Figure 5.23). Among the company's greatest triumphs was the *Mauretania*, which held the Blue Riband for 22 years, as the world's fastest liner across the Atlantic. Tyneside was a centre of **technical innovation**, its main triumph being the steam turbine.

By 1930, Swan Hunter had an unbroken **river frontage** of some 1.2 km, and works covering nearly 80 hectares. The company dealt with all aspects of shipbuilding, including design and construction, repairs, overhauls and renewals. During the two world wars, it constructed, repaired and converted all types of ships. After the war there was massive replacement of shipping lost during the war. It was clear that the layout and structure of the shipyard had to be changed if the company was to be competitive in the modern shipbuilding industry. The main reason was the change in **production techniques** with

the steel structure of the ship being welded instead of riveted; the ship was constructed from large prefabricated units instead of single plates, and bars were welded on site. The main advantages of carrying out a large percentage of the welding under cover, were continuous employment and freedom from weather conditions. Ship sizes were also increasing, therefore shipyards had to reorganise to accommodate these changes as existing berths were too narrow.

There were problems with reorganising and redesigning the shipyards:
- the awkward shape of the sites, which were long but lacked depth (to give access to railway lines and roads)
- yards needed to be complementary to each other rather than duplicating facilities
- yards needed to be rebuilt without disrupting the building of ships to make larger berths
- the design had to improve handling of goods and raw materials at the yards.

In recent decades, increasingly strong **competition** from Far Eastern shipbuilders has made shipbuilding much less profitable. Following the Geddes Report on shipbuilding (1966), discussions were opened with the owners of other shipbuilders on the Tyne about the possibility of merging all the shipyards on the Tyne into one company. The resulting company, Swan Hunter Shipbuilders Limited, was **nationalised** in 1977. Approximately 11 500 people were employed and the yards built cargo vessels, bulk carriers, tankers and container ships of all sizes. In the five years prior to nationalisation almost £16 million was spent on modernising the yards.

Swan Hunter was **privatised** in 1986. Thereafter, the company decided to concentrate on warships and auxiliaries for the Royal Navy. Shipbuilding was concentrated at Wallsend on the Tyne and employed some 3500 people.

In the face of increasing competition, a decrease in orders from the UK Ministry of Defence (MOD) and a failure to win significant export orders, Swan Hunter was forced to close. The key factor was the decision of the MOD not to use the Swan Hunter shipyard. The company was bought by THC Fabricators, who reopened the yard and have managed to keep it operating at 60% capacity. Recent work has included converting the bulk carrier *Solitaire* into the world's largest pipeline-laying vessel. A much smaller Swan Hunter has managed to survive, unlike many firms in the North East.

Inward investment in the North East

There has been a considerable amount of aid to the North East since the 1960s (Figures 5.24 and 5.25). Communications were improved and industrial estates developed. The big breakthrough came when Nissan decided to invest in the North East. It has ploughed nearly £1 billion into the area and employs some 4500 people. Since then, other investors have followed, the latest and largest being the German electronics group, Siemens.

In 1995, Siemens announced a £1 billion investment in Tyneside (Figure 5.26). It chose the Hadrian Business Park to develop its semi-conductor manufacturing and research centre. The investment will create about 2000 jobs, which balances the 2000 jobs lost at Swan Hunter. There was strong competition from a number of European countries to attract the investment, but Tyneside won it with an attractive package of incentives, labour and site characteristics.

The attractions included:
- research facilities – the Hadrian Business Park is within thirty minutes drive of four universities
- existing skills – the region has a tradition of engineering works
- government incentives – the area receives special assistance from the government and has received as much as £50 million
- labour – the region offers a supply of skilled but relatively cheap labour
- the site – there is plenty of high quality water (required for the cleaning and rinsing processes), good building land, and room for expansion
- behavioural factors – the Chairman of the Northern Development Corporation spoke fluent German.

Inset 5.3
Decline in shipbuilding

Since the Second World War, shipbuilding and ship-repair industries in Europe have declined for a variety of reasons:
- a decrease in orders due to overseas, mainly Far Eastern, competition
- world recession and rationalisation of shipyards
- overcapacity of shipping in relation to demand
- competition from other forms of transport
- more widespread political stability leading to reduced demand for naval warships
- lack of investment in the industry.

The decline is not confined to the UK or Europe: world orders fell from 74 million tonnes in 1973 to 25 million tonnes in 1985 and this downward trend has continued into the 1990s.

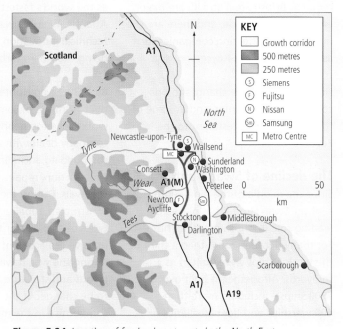

Figure 5.24 *Location of foreign investments in the North East*
Source: Geofile, Jan 1997, The North East region

Company	Date	Location	Activities
Nissan	1984	Washington	Japanese car manufacturer
Fujitsu	1991	Newton Aycliffe	Japanese computer company making micro-chips
Samsung	1995	Teeside	South Korean computer and electrical company
Siemens	1995	Tyneside	German semi-conductor manufacturer

Figure 5.25 *Major companies investing in the North East*
Source: Geofile, Jan 1997, The North East region

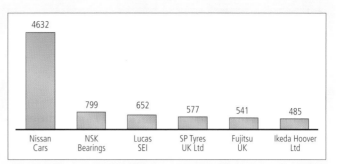

Figure 5.27 *Japanese firms in the North East - numbers employed, 1997*
Source: Geofile, Jan 1997, The North East region

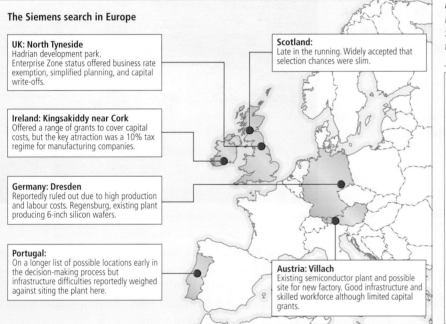

The Siemens search in Europe

UK: North Tyneside
Hadrian development park.
Enterprise Zone status offered business rate exemption, simplified planning, and capital write-offs.

Ireland: Kingsakiddy near Cork
Offered a range of grants to cover capital costs, but the key attraction was a 10% tax regime for manufacturing companies.

Germany: Dresden
Reportedly ruled out due to high production and labour costs. Regensburg, existing plant producing 6-inch silicon wafers.

Portugal:
On a longer list of possible locations early in the decision-making process but infrastructure difficulties reportedly weighed against siting the plant here.

Scotland:
Late in the running. Widely accepted that selection chances were slim.

Austria: Villach
Existing semiconductor plant and possible site for new factory. Good infrastructure and skilled workforce although limited capital grants.

Figure 5.26 *Siemens decision to locate in the North East*
Source: Nagle G. and Spencer K., 1996, The geography of the European Union, OUP

QUESTIONS

1 State two similarities between inward investment in the North East of England and industrial developments in India and Mexico.
2 Describe two contrasts between the type of industrial development that is taking place in the North East with that taking place in Mexico.
3 Briefly explain two contrasting reasons why the Japanese, South Koreans and Germans want to locate in the UK.

SUMMARY

In this chapter we have seen how important manufacturing is to many countries; even EMDCs need new industries to regenerate areas of decline. Manufacturing is seen as a means to achieving economic development and increases in standards of living, with riches available at the end of the journey. And yet in many ELDCs and NICs there is a heavy price to be paid for the benefits of industrialisation:

- pollution, disease and death in India
- economic exploitation in Mexico
- industrial stagnation in South Africa
- exploitation of female and child labour, in many countries.

Industrialisation in EMDCs has also created many problems. (See *Changing settlements* in this series.) Industry needs to be properly managed and carefully controlled; ELDCs should not necessarily copy the experience of those in the West, they should learn from their mistakes, whilst emulating the success stories.

QUESTIONS

1 What is the difference between communism and capitalism? Why do you think that capitalist countries, but not communist countries, have become NICs?
2 For any **two** contrasting countries:
a) Describe how manufacturing industry has changed in the last thirty years.
b) Explain why these changes have taken place.
c) Examine the effects these changes have had on the economy and society of the countries involved.
3 With reference to specific examples, account for the increasing proportion of manufacturing industry located in NICs.
4 Compare the advantages and disadvantages that industry can have an ELDC.

BIBLIOGRAPHY AND RECOMMENDED READING

Baker, S., et al., 1995, *Pathways in senior geography*, Nelson
Blunden, J. and Reddish, A., 1996, *Energy, resources and environment*, Hodder and Stoughton
Carr, M., 1997, *New patterns: progress and change in human geography*, Nelson
Dicken, P., 1992, *Global shift*, Paul Chapman Publishing
Foster, I., 1991, *Environmental pollution*, OUP
Hodder, R., 1992, *The West Pacific rim*, Hodder
Nagle, G., and Spencer, K., 1996, *A Geography of the European Union*, OUP

WEB SITES

ANC home page - http://www.anc.org.za/

Chapter 6
Tourism

Tourism is big business: it is one of the most efficient, organised and marketed commodities in the world. It is as much about money as it is about holidays.

This chapter examines the patterns of global tourism, models of tourist development, factors affecting tourism, and the impact of tourism on culture, society and the environment. Examples from the UK, Thailand, South Africa and the Mediterranean are used to illustrate the range of impacts, both positive and negative, that tourism makes.

GLOBAL TOURISM

Tourism is defined here as all temporary visits (over 24 hours) in another place. This includes visits for:

- leisure
- recreation
- holiday
- sport
- health
- study
- religion
- business
- family and friends.

Since World War II, there has been a huge increase in the number of international tourists, brought about by improvements in transport, communications and affluence. In 1950, there were 25 million international tourists; by the 1990s, over 500 million international tourists. These were mostly from EMDCs to other EMDCs. There is, however, increasing demand for tourism to ELDCs: although tourists may seek remote places, they often demand food, shelter and hygiene of an EMDC standard.

World-wide tourism is growing at about 4% per annum. For example, the number of international tourists to Hawaii grew from 15 000 in 1964 to 3 million in 1974.

There are many different types of tourism. These include:
- elite tourism, such as ecotourism
- offbeat tourism, such as experience of the Arctic
- unusual holidays, such as educational tours
- mass tourism, such as coastal holidays in Mediterranean resorts and Florida
- short breaks, such as cultural and historical breaks in a famous city (Figure 6.1)
- visits to theme parks, such as Disneyland.

Figure 6.1 *Kinkaku-Ji Temple, Kyoto*

The main reason for tourism is holidays. These account for 70% of all journeys undertaken. Visiting relatives is second and business travel is third.

Mass travel dates initially from the nineteenth century. Its growth is closely linked with:
- improvements in transport, notably railways and steamships
- the growth of conducted tours, such as those by Thomas Cook
- an increase in leisure time, disposable income and personal mobility.

Tourism has an important role in development. It accounts for about 70 million jobs worldwide, and global spending on tourism in 1990 exceeded $70 million. Internal tourism (within a country) accounts for as much as four times the amount of international tourism. It is the world's largest industry; the oil industry is second and the car industry is third. Tourism is important in terms of economic development. It generates employment in construction activity. Airports, hotels, roads, and other facilities need to be built and maintained. In addition, it has links with many important service industries. These include accommodation, entertainment, food and catering, tour guides, travel by air, road and rail, banking services, shops, laundry, cleaning, taxi, bus, car hire, insurance, luggage suppliers, medical services, travel agencies and duty free shopping.

These service industries are very diverse. Many are small-scale operators, such as restaurants and taxi firms. There are a small number of very large-scale operations, such as hotel companies and air travel operators.

Although tourism may inject money and help development, there can be negative impacts such as:

- destruction of local culture
- changes in land use
- increased demand for buildings, leading to overdevelopment
- reduced agricultural production
- increased imports, leading to budget deficits
- families are fragmented as workers migrate to tourist locations
- money is spent on tourists to provide water, food, shelter, waste disposal and entertainment.

Global patterns

Between 1965 and 1993 there was a five-fold increase in the number of tourists worldwide from 110 million to over 510 million, with a slight dip in the 1980s due to economic recession.

The location of the most popular tourist destinations varies over time. For example, in the 1920s and 1930s Nice and Monte Carlo were fashionable. Spain was popular in the 1950s, whereas the Caribbean was renowned in the 1960s. Africa was favoured in the 1970s, the Pacific in the 1980s and increasingly, in the 1990s, Asia has attracted larger numbers of tourists.

Changes in the global nature and distribution of tourism are taking place (Figure 6.2a). Europe and North America accounted for 75% of visitors in 1993, compared with 82% in 1980. There has been a slight increase in Africa, East Asia, the Pacific and the Middle East. This is due to a combination of favourable exchange rates, competition between airlines and the growth of specialised tourism such as **ecotourism**. Visits to China and Eastern Europe are increasing as these countries become more 'open' to visitors.

Over 80% of all tourists come from just twenty countries, mostly EMDCs. The destination of tourists varies:

- most tourists to Africa are from Europe
- Australasia is increasingly important for East Asian and Pacific travellers but less important for European and North American tourists
- the Middle East market is largely comprised of European and East Asian travellers, but not Americans
- Europe remains internationally popular, particularly with Europeans, and with North Americans (because of historic ties)

North America, Europe and Japan account for most of the global expenditure, Europe alone accounts for 48% of expenditure. The global contribution of tourism to tax is huge. In 1994, US$655 billion were spent and it is estimated this will rise to US$1578 billion by 2005. In 1991, Asia earned over US$30 billion from tourism.

Rank		Country	Arrivals (000s)		World share of arrivals (%)	
1990	1995		1990	1995	1990	1995
1	1	France	52 497	60 584	11.43	10.68
3	2	Spain	37 441	45 125	8.15	7.96
2	3	USA	39 539	44 730	8.61	7.89
4	4	Italy	26 679	29 184	5.81	5.15
12	5	China	10 484	23 368	2.28	4.12
7	6	UK	18 013	22 700	3.92	4.00
5	7	Hungary	20 510	22 087	4.47	3.90
8	8	Mexico	17 176	19 870	0.74	3.39
27	9	Poland	3400	19 225	0.74	3.39
6	10	Austria	19 011	17 750	4.14	3.13

Figure 6.2 a) Top tourist destinations, 1990-95

Rank		Country	Receipts (US$ m)		World share (%)	
1990	1995		1990	1995	1990	1995
1	1	USA	43 007	58 370	16.25	15.70
2	2	France	20 185	27 322	7.63	7.35
3	3	Italy	20 016	27 072	7.56	7.28
4	4	Spain	18 593	25 065	7.02	6.74
5	5	UK	14 940	17 468	5.64	4.70
6	6	Austria	13 410	12 500	5.07	3.36
7	7	Germany	11 471	11 922	4.33	3.21
8	8	Hong Kong	5032	9075	1.90	2.44
10	9	China	2218	8250	0.84	2.22
9	10	Singapore	4596	7550	1.74	2.03

Figure 6.2 b) Main tourist earners, 1990-95

QUESTIONS

1 Describe the geographic pattern of international tourist destinations, as shown in Figure 6.2a. How do you explain this pattern?

2 Which countries in Figure 6.2 b) earn more money from tourism in relation to the percentage of tourists they attract? How do you explain the differences between the percentage of tourists and the percentage of spending?

Inset 6.1
Recent growth of tourism in Australia

Tourism is one of Australia's biggest industries. It accounts for over US$7.5 million, 11% of total export earnings. The number of international visitors has tripled since mid-1980 - there were about 1 million visitors in 1984-85, 2 million in 1990 and over 3 million in 1993-94. The growth rate is about 14% per annum. The number of tourists is expected to reach 6 million by 2000, and the Olympic Games in Sydney in that year will provide a big boost. Employment at Homebush Bay, site of the Olympics, increased from 405 000 in 1986 to 460 000 in 1993. It is estimated that by the year 2000, 600 000-700 000 people will be employed in tourism in Sydney.

Japan is the largest source of tourists to Australia and there are big growth rates in other Asian markets. The emerging Asian middle class, especially in the NICs such as Taiwan, Hong Kong, South Korea, Malaysia, and Singapore, are especially important. Australia is their nearest country with a 'western' culture. To promote Sydney to the Asian market, the New South Wales government had a US$4.8 million advertising campaign for Sydney, in 1993.

MODELS OF TOURIST DEVELOPMENT

Butler's model of evolution of tourist areas

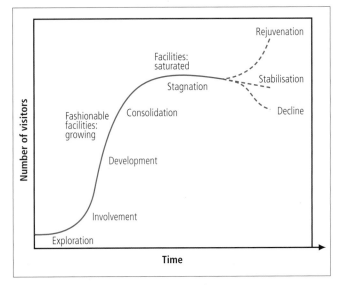

Figure 6.3 *Butler's model of the evolution of tourist areas*
Source: Chrispin, J. and Jegede, F., 1996, Population resources and development, Collins

A model of tourism has been devised by Butler (Figure 6.3). He observes phases of emergence, growth, prosperity and decline. This equates with exploration, involvement, consolidation, and stagnation and decline. Single product towns, that is, towns very much dependent on tourism, such as Killarney in south west Ireland (Figure 6.5), are very similar to mining towns which only prosper while the raw material exists.

There are six main stages in Butler's model:

1 Exploration

A small number of tourists visit a newly-discovered location seeking exotic adventurous travel. There is minimal impact.

2 Involvement

If tourists are accepted and if tourism is acceptable, the destination becomes better known. There are improvements in the tourist infrastructure. Some local involvement in tourism may begin.

3 Development

Inward investment takes place. Tourism becomes a big business. Companies from EMDCs control, manage and organise tourism. This leads to increased package tours, more holidays and less local involvement.

4 Consolidation

Tourism becomes an important industry in an area or region. It is not just the provision of facilities but also includes marketing and advertising. Former agricultural land is used for hotels. Facilities, such as beaches and hotel swimming pools, may become reserved for tourists. Resentment may begin and there is a decelerating growth rate.

5 Stagnation

There may be increased local opposition to tourism and an awareness of the problems it creates. Fewer new tourists arrive.

6 Decline

The area decreases in popularity. International operators move out and local involvement may resume. Local operators may be underfunded, however. Hence there is a decline in tourism. It is possible for the industry to be rejuvenated, such as UK coastal resorts in the 1990s. It is a very simple and generalised model, nevertheless it allows us to see how a resort has developed and it enables comparisons between different tourist areas to be made.

The core periphery enclave model

This model is based on the economic core periphery model (see Chapter 1, What is development?). It examines the social and economic influences on tourism and the effects of tourism (Figure 6.4).

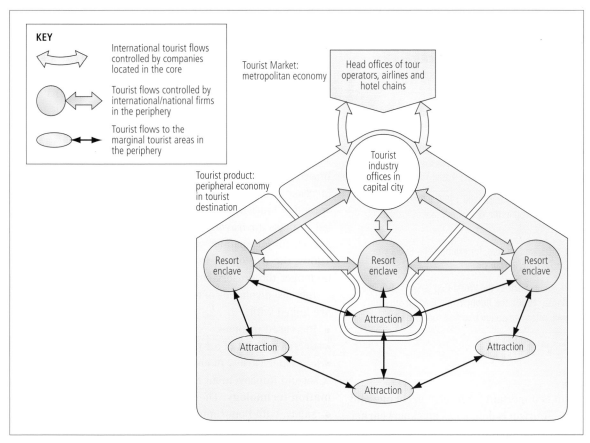

Figure 6.4 *The core periphery model of tourism*
Source: Chrispin, J. and Jegede, F., 1996, Population resources and development, Collins

Figure 6.5 *Tourists admiring the Lakes of Killarney, Eire*

The model shows that the flow between EMDCs and ELDCs perpetuates core (rich) and periphery (poor) relations. Most of the hotels, tour operators and airlines are owned by companies in EMDCs. The ELDCs are often former colonies.

Tourist resorts and enclaves are specifically designed for tourists. These contain specialised facilities such as hotels, restaurants and recreational activities. Hence, there is very little contact between the resident population and the tourist population. Consequently, there is little experience of the reality of economic, social and cultural life. Many tourists see ELDCs as being less developed (as they are) without realising that funds which could be used for development purposes are often directed into tourism, and benefit the tourists rather than the local people.

FACTORS AFFECTING TOURISM

1 **Natural landscape** – mountains (the Alps); natural history (Galapagos); coasts (Great Barrier Reef); forests (Amazon Rain Forest); rivers (Grand Canyon); deserts, polar areas, wildlife

2 **Climate** – hot, sunny, dry areas are very attractive to most tourists; seasonality of climate leads to seasonality of tourism

3 **Cultural** – language, customs, clothing, food, architecture and theme parks. Examples include recreation, Nice; religion, Lourdes; administration, Brussels; and education, Oxford

4 **Social** – increasing affluence, leisure time, longer holidays, paid holidays, better mobility, better transport, more working women

5 **Economic** – exchange rates, foreign exchange, employment, multiplier effects, investment in infrastructure, leakage (the money being transferred out of the country)

6 **Political** – political unrest, for example the 1992 military coup in Thailand led to a 20-30% drop in the occupancy rate in luxury hotels

7 **Disease** – malaria, AIDS, and cholera, for example the Ebola virus in Zaire in 1995 led to a drop in tourism

8 **Sporting events** – events such as the World Cup (USA, 1994), the Olympic Games (Atlanta, 1996), the Rugby World Cup (South Africa, 1995), lead to a small, often temporary boom in tourism.

Figure 6.6 *Factors affecting tourism*

Economic factors

International tourism is important for foreign exchange and balance of payments. Tourism is defined as an export earner because it brings new money into the economy (external import). For example, in Egypt and Jamaica over 60% of export income is often derived from tourism. It is also very important in EMDCs – in Spain, it is the highest export earner.

Tourism creates much unskilled employment, such as porters, maids, and cleaners, as well as highly skilled employment, including accountants, managers, and entertainers. In ELDCs, wages from tourism often exceed the national average. By contrast, in EMDCs wages in tourism are usually below the national average. Tourism is also very seasonal and this can lead to problems of seasonal unemployment and under employment.

Tourism also leads to developments in the infrastructure, notably roads and utilities. These do not, however, always benefit the local people, but tourists. For example, in Kenya up to 17% of tourist expenditure leaks out of Kenya, very

often to EMDCs. Leakage takes place in various ways:

1 foreign workers in the tourist industry send their earnings home
2 travel costs go to airlines and shipping companies
3 goods and services imported for tourism are paid for
4 foreign owners of hotels and other amenities are paid
5 money is used to pay off foreign debt.

Economic factors can also influence the tourist. A strong exchange rate, such as a good rate against the German Deutschmark or the Japanese Yen, influences many tourists to go abroad. These tourists seek relatively cheaper places, where they get better value for their money.

Technological factors

Improvements in travel safety, decreased travel time and increase in communications and information have aided the spread of tourism. Technological changes in **transport** have led to mass air travel. The 707 jet aircraft, the world's first successful jet airliner, was developed in 1954 and by the 1960s, the world was in the jet age. Moreover, air travel is no longer the preserve of the rich and the middle class.

Increased volumes of tourism, and more accessible travel, are linked with:

● increased incomes
● decreased cost of air fares
● a greater variety of cheaper package tours.

A second improvement has been in **computing and information technology**. These have led to increased:

● safety, with better monitoring of aircrafts and ship
● satellite navigation
● booking, reservations, and itineraries.

Thirdly, **medical advances** are important. Before the 1950s, international travel was associated with a risk of infectious disease. Now, however, with better immunisation, vaccination, improved water supply and sanitation, the risk of infectious diseases is greatly decreased.

Political factors

As we have seen in other chapters, political involvement is central in the development process. This is also true of the tourist industry (Figure 6.7).

Changes in political and economic influences

Trade barriers and **agreements** play an increasingly important role in tourism. The **World Trade Organisation (WTO)** (formerly **GATT**) should increase tourism by allowing easier

---

QUESTIONS

1 Locate and classify the following sites in terms of their attractions for tourism: The Great Wall of China; Egyptian pyramids; Red Square, Moscow; The Vatican; Mecca; Disneyworld; Salt Lake City; Oxford; Disneyland, Paris.

2 For a tourist area in an EMDC **and** in an ELDC show how the factors listed in Figure 6.6 have influenced their development as tourist centres. List the main similarities and differences between the two places.

Political factor	Explanation	Example
1 Development strategies	Land use control, building control, pollution control	Restrictions on number of tourists e.g. Namibia
2 Travel documents	Track the flows of tourists and immigrants	Passports, visas, permits. Lack of control into the EU
3 Quarantine regulations	Check spread of plant and animal diseases	Channel Tunnel between France and UK could aid the spread of rabies
4 Infrastructure	State funding for all kinds of infrastructure	Government sponsored developments such as sports events
5 Control of exchange	Limit the amount of money taken into a country	In Egypt and Bulgaria proof of money spent is needed
6 Legalised gambling	Casinos	Las Vegas; former homelands in South Africa
7 Advertising, promotion	To increase the number and /or change the type of tourist	Northern Ireland and the Republic of Ireland's joint campaign from 1995
8 Deregulation	Decrease government control	US airline industry
9 Geo-political conflicts	War and political upheaval	Northern Ireland, former Yugoslavia
10 Sanctions by other countries	Boycotts	South Africa pre-1992
11 Government Dept. of Tourism	Coordination, planning, regulation	Yellowstone National Park
12 Legislation	Creation of national parks, heritage areas, etc.	National parks in the UK
13 Taxes	Direct and indirect	Departure tax in Japan, VAT in the UK

Figure 6.7 *Impact of political factors on tourism*

and fairer flow of goods across international borders. Fewer government restrictions on foreign ownership, multinational controlled hotels and travel agencies will also lead to increases in tourism. The **generalised agreement on trade and services (GATS)** is part of WTO and is working towards freedom of movement across borders, hence any restrictions at borders are against their plans. There is still potential for foreign domination of the hotel industry, however. In addition, foreign aid may be determined by the level of liberalisation of ELDCs. This effectively means more aid for more hotels. Within major trading blocs, tourism may be promoted, limited border controls may exist and passports may not be needed.

Figure 6.8
Japanese schoolchildren visiting the Hiroshima Peace Park

THE IMPACT OF TOURISM ON CULTURE AND SOCIETY

Tourism is increasing in terms of numbers and also in its environmental impact. Tourism can destroy the very attractions that draw people to a place.

Positive impact of tourism

1 **Employment**

Tourism is labour intensive and has a **multiplier effect**. This leads to more money in the local economy, for example, demand for more buildings, more hotels, more entertainment, guides, and therefore provides increased employment opportunities.

2 **Environment**

The revenue from tourism may be re-invested to maintain sustainable long term use and protect the environment.

For example, Mallorca is using much of its tourist revenue to protect what remains of its unspoilt landscape (much of the south of the island has already been damaged by tourism).

3 **Culture**

Tourism may lead to the preservation of local customs and heritage due to increased local awareness of the importance of architectural and heritage sites; craft and art industries may develop to reinforce local cultural identity.

4 **Education**

Local people may benefit from increased training and demand for skills; this may lead to the growth of information centres which lead to increased knowledge on the part of the visitor.

The study tours run by the Japan Foundation are an excellent example.

5 **Infrastructure**

Although infrastructure developments, for example, roads and utilities, such as electricity, gas and water are mostly for tourists, there is a spin-off effect which may benefit local people.

Negative impact of tourism

1 Alienation

The contrasts between the tourists and the local population can be very great. Local resentment, crime and even terrorism may develop against tourists. Examples of terrorism include Egypt in the early 1990s and the abductions in Cambodia in 1994. Inflated prices for second homes and apartments may develop and local food production may decline making life more expensive for local people.

2 Prostitution and paedophilia

In Thailand and the Philippines, prostitution and paedophilia are very common. They are linked very closely with poverty. One consequence has been a rise in the number of cases of AIDS.

3 Westernisation of culture

Multinational food chains, such as Kentucky Fried Chicken, McDonalds and Coca-Cola, are global and destroy the unique quality of a place. Global patterns in music, fashion and cinema also lead to a westernisation of cultures and society (Figure 6.9). This devalues the tourist experience and damages local cultural systems.

4 Commercialisation of culture

In some countries, for example, religious dances may be commercialised and packaged – glamourised for western audiences and performed out of context. There may be trivialising of local crafts, such as woodcarvings, and there is usually much production of cheap souvenirs.

Figure 6.9 *McDonald's in Tokyo*

Impact on the natural environment

Beautiful environments attract tourism. Unfortunately, the number of visitors may exceed the **carrying capacity** and lead to the destruction and degradation of vegetation which may, in turn, cause soil erosion. For example, mangrove removal for coastal resorts is widespread in many developing countries. The construction of facilities, especially highrise flats, poses huge problems for the natural landscape. Wildlife is also affected by fishing, shooting, poaching and over feeding. Miyajima deer, on Miyajima Island, off Honshu, Japan are one example. Tourism also contributes to the pollution of water and air as well as noise and visual pollution.

Coastal areas: the Mediterranean experience

growth in tourism

	1960s	1970s	1980s	1990s
Tourists from UK to Spain	1960 = 0.4 million	1971 = 3.0 million	1984 = 6.2 million 1988 = 7.5 million	1990 = 7.0 million
State of, and changes in, tourism	Very few tourists.	Rapid increase in tourism. Government encouragement.	Carrying capacity reached – tourists outstrip resources, e.g. water supply and sewerage.	Decline – world recession, prices too high – cheaper up-market hotels elsewhere.
Local employment	Mainly in farming and fishing.	Construction work. Jobs in hotels, cafés, shops. Decline in farming and fishing.	Mainly in tourism – up to 70% in some areas.	Unemployment increases as tourism declines (20%). Farmers use irrigation.
Holiday accommodation	Limited accommodation, very few hotels and apartments, some holiday cottages.	Large blocks built (using breeze block and concrete), more apartment blocks and villas.	More large hotels built, also apartments and time share, luxury villas.	Older hotels looking dirty and run down. Fall in house prices. Only high-class hotels allowed to be built.
Infrastructure (amenities and activities)	Limited access and few amenities. Poor roads. Limited streetlighting and electricity.	Some road improvements but congestion in towns. Bars, discos, restaurants and shops added.	E340 opened – 'the Highway of Death'. More congestion in towns. Marinas and golf courses built.	Bars/cafés closing, Malaga bypass and new air terminal opened.
Landscape and environment	Clean, unspoilt beaches. Warm sea with relatively little pollution. Pleasant villages. Quiet. Little visual pollution.	Farmland built on. Wildlife frightened away. Beaches and sea less clean.	Mountains hidden behind hotels. Litter on beaches. Polluted seas (sewage). Crime (drugs, vandalism and mugging). Noise from traffic and tourism.	Attempts to clean up beaches and seas (EC Blue Flag beaches). New public parks and gardens opened. Nature reserves.

(2 at take off)   3 (peak)   4 (decline)

Figure 6.10 *Tourism life cycle for the Costa del Sol, Spain*
Source: Baker, S., et al, 1995, *Pathways in senior geography*, Nelson

Figure 6.11 *The impact of tourism on the Mediterranean*

Coastal areas are one of the most important types of landscape for tourism. Sandy beaches, combined with hot, sunny climates act as a magnet for tourists. However, the concentration of large numbers of tourist in localised areas can have a detrimental impact on the local environment.

The Mediterranean is the world's most important tourist location, accounting for 35% of international tourists worldwide. The problems there are intense due to the sheer **concentration** of tourists, accommodation, infrastructural development, traffic and the generation of waste (Figure 6.10). The number of tourists in the area has risen from 54 million in 1970 to 157 million in 1990. It is set to rise to at least 380 million by 2025, perhaps up to 760 million if the world economy is strong. In addition, population growth in Mediterranean areas is forecast to rise from 350 million in 1985 to 570 million by 2025.

Over half of the tourists are concentrated in coastal regions causing increased pressures on fishing, industry, urban development and energy supplies (Figure 6.11).

The impacts include:
- loss of habitat and biodiversity
- extinction of species
- inadequate sewage effluent treatment and disposal
- unsustainable exploitation of natural resources
- traffic congestion

- changes in traditional lifestyle.

The growth of tourism has been especially noticeable in Greece and Turkey where the numbers have increased sixfold and fourfold respectively, since 1970. The concentration of tourists has reached alarming levels in places. For example, the Tarragon area of Spain contains up to 4250 tourists per square kilometre. Tourist infrastructure in the Mediterranean area accounted for over 4400 square kilometres in 1984, of which over 90% was in Spain, France and Italy. It is estimated that this area will be doubled by the year 2025. Nearly 3 million tonnes of solid waste was generated in 1984 and is forecast to rise to 8.7-12.1 million tonnes by 2025. Similarly, waste water is predicted to rise from 0.3 billion tonnes to 0.9-1.5 billion tonnes during the same period.

The Black Sea area, which attracts 40 million tourists annually, is experiencing a similar decline in environmental quality and a reduction in tourist numbers. Poor planning, unsanitary conditions, lack of water and limited investment have created environmental stress and disease (for example, cholera). Beach closures have resulted in a transfer of tourists to other, clean, beaches.

The impact of tourism in the Mediterranean

1 Overdevelopment

Unplanned growth of hotels and tourism facilities with little regard to visual impact or local architecture has led to visual degradation over vast areas. Land has been used for recreational facilities such as golf courses and theme parks. Major roads and airports encroach on protected areas such as Ria Formosa National Park in the Algarve.

2 Visitor related development pressure

One example is the agricultural development around the Coto Donana National Park in Southern Spain which is aimed at meeting tourists' food needs. Here, the wetlands of the national park are threatened by water abstraction and pesticide run-off.

3 Loss of habitat and loss of biodiversity

Over 75% of the sand dune systems from Gibraltar to Sicily have been lost since 1960. This has led to the loss of breeding grounds of the Loggerhead Turtle. Over five hundred Mediterranean plant species are threatened with extinction. In Mediterranean France (in particular), one hundred and forty five species are on the verge of extinction or have already disappeared.

4 Species impact

In 1986, the pressure of tourist numbers near the nesting sites of the Loggerhead Turtle and Green Turtle at Dalyan in Turkey led to the Turkish government to curtailing the building of a hotel. However, the very act of protecting the turtles has led to an increased influx of tourists, 5000 every summer, creating other environmental pressures such as waste dumps.

5 Lack of sewage and effluent treatment and disposal

Only 30% of municipal waste water from Mediterranean coastal towns receives any treatment before being discharged. As a result, some Mediterranean beaches fail EU bathing water quality tests. For example, 7% of Spanish beaches and 13% of French beaches failed. The total cost of developing the required level of sewage treatment is over £6 billion. Spillages from pleasure boats were also a major source of pollution.

6 Unsustainable exploitation of natural resources

Abstraction of drinking water and exploitation of fisheries resources is unsustainable. Over-abstraction of water for drinking, bathing, golf courses and water theme parks has led to increased forest fires.

7 Traffic congestion

On coastal roads, traffic congestion is becoming an increasing problem.

8 Changes in traditional lifestyle

Where local populations are outnumbered by tourists, such as in the poorer regions of the Balearics, Turkey, Croatia and Cyprus, over-dependence on tourism threatens traditional lifestyles.

QUESTIONS

1 With the use of examples, describe and explain the impact of tourism on coastal areas in the Mediterranean, or a coast that you have studied.

2 How will pressures on coastal areas change in the future? What impact will they have? Give reasons to support your answer.

Ecotourism

Ecotourism is a 'green' or alternative form of sustainable tourism, operating at a simple level in remote areas, with a low density of tourists. Ecotourism includes tourism that is related to ecology and ecosystems. These include game parks, nature reserves, coral reefs and forest parks. It aims to give people a first-hand experience of natural environments and to show them the importance of conservation. Its characteristics include:

1 planning and control – tourist developments must fit in with local conditions
2 greater involvement and control by local or regional communities
3 a balance between conservation and development; environment and economics.

The key objectives for sustainable tourism are:

• preserving the quality of the environment
• maximising the economic benefit for the local or regional community.

In areas where ecotourism occurs, there is often a conflict between allowing the tourists total access and providing

Inset 6.2
The Mediterranean Blue Plan

By 1970, the Mediterranean Sea had become a dumping ground for untreated sewage, industry and chemical waste, agricultural chemicals and oil. This led to the growth of red algae, toxic to humans and marine life. 'Red tides' of algae blooms made the beaches unsafe and threatened tourism. In 1976, the Mediterranean Blue Plan was signed by eighteen countries bordering the Mediterranean. Their aim was threefold:

• to build more sewage treatment works
• to control industrial waste
• to reduce the use of pesticides.

However, the project is extremely expensive, costing over US$1.5 billion in total. The poorer countries in the south and east cannot afford the cost, and some countries contribute nothing or very little. Hence its continued operation is very much in doubt. The contrast in attitude between the richer countries, France, Spain and Italy, who cause most of the pollution, and the poorer countries is very great. The rich want to clear up the beaches, whereas the poor want to create new industries and develop economically.

QUESTIONS

1 Why is the Mediterranean Sea so polluted?
2 To what extent are the attempts to improve the quality of the Mediterranean Sea influenced by (i) economic motives, and (ii) environmental concerns? Give reasons for your answer.

---

them with the facilities they desire, and with conserving the landscape, plants and animals of the area. Another conflict arises when local people wish to use the resource for their own benefit rather than for the benefit of animals or conservation.

Ecotourism has also been described as **egotourism**. Critics argue that ecotourists are trying to get closer to the environment and are perhaps causing much more damage than mass tourism. Backpackers, for example, are thought to be the greatest threat. They put little into the local economy but want to visit all the best places. As backpackers go off the beaten track, they destroy more of the natural environment. By contrast, mass tourism concentrates visitors into fewer, designated locations.

Case study:
Tourism in Thailand

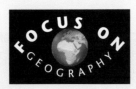

Tourism is Thailand's most important source of foreign exchange. Thailand is an excellent example of an NIC that has developed tourism. This has largely been to attract foreign currency. Almost 7 million visitors entered Thailand in 1995. This was an increase of over 12% on 1994. Nevertheless, this figure represents a slow-down compared with the rate of growth in the 1980s. In 1986-90 the number of tourists almost doubled from 2.8 million to 5.3 million, i.e. 15% per annum over the period. Annual growth since 1994 has been about 5%.

Thailand has emerged as a tourist destination for a number of reasons (Figure 6.12):

- cultural diversity and historic attractions in Bangkok, the capital, and excursions to such places as the famous bridge over the River Kwai
- large, sandy coastal beaches, such as Pattaya and Phuket, set in a tropical climate
- temples and religious attractions, especially in the north around Chiang Mai
- attractive countryside, with irrigated ricefields and orchid cultivation
- hill tribes in the north of the country
- tropical vegetation and wildlife, such as elephants.

In addition, Thailand is only a few hours flight from Tokyo, and is a favoured stop-over on the long haul flights between Europe and Australia. Over half of Thailand's tourists come from south east Asia, but there is a significant number from Europe and North America. There are two main types of tourist:

- package holidaymakers, whose holidays include travel and accommodation
- backpackers with little money to spend.

The majority of tourists are in the package holiday category. They want to visit the attractions of Thailand but to travel in conditions of comfort. Increasing numbers of tourists come from eastern Europe, Russia and China: they typically stay in budget hotels. They spend their money shopping and eating which, paradoxically, increases their total holiday spending to the same as or more than Japanese or western European travellers.

A number of hotels cater for the high spending tourist. One example is the Chiang Mai Regent Hotel which provides a luxurious base for tourists happy to spend a few days in the north of the country.

East European and Asian tourists have transformed Pattaya, a beach paradise in the south, into a holiday resort comparable with a Spanish resort of the 1970s. Places such as Bangkok and Chiang Mai – originally the focus of the 1980s tourist explosion, have become secondary tourist centres.

In 1987 a promotion to increase tourism, *Visit Thailand Year 1987*, increased arrivals by nearly one-quarter. Many countries have since tried to copy Thailand's promotion. One of the most recent has been Myanmar (Burma). There, the military dictatorship optimistically declared a *Visit Myanmar Year* in 1996.

One problem facing Thailand is that tourists are becoming more discerning. The Tourist Association of Thailand (TAT)

believes that Thailand cannot cater for every tourist need and that it must be selective. The TAT's aim is to try to:

- spread tourists around the country more
- encourage more diverse activities
- take more care of the environment.

Thailand's tourist market is going through a structural change. The industry is adjusting itself to cater for niche customers. These include the South Korean honeymoon market, and Chinese and Vietnamese *nouveau riche*. Thailand also expects to benefit from its proximity to Indochina and Burma, the frontier of south east Asia. In addition, it hopes to attract visitors en route to the Olympic Games in Sydney in 2000.

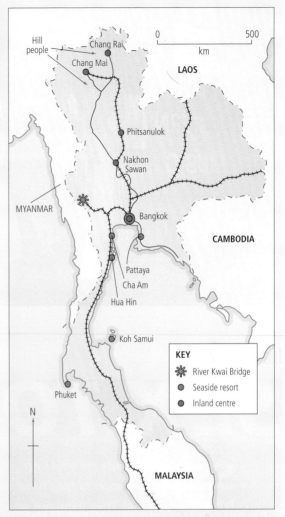

Figure 6.12 *Centres of tourism in Thailand*
Source: Cole, J 1996 A geography of the world's major regions, Routledge

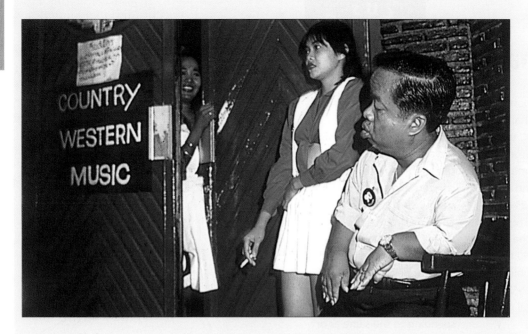

Figure 6.13 *Sex tourism in Thailand, outside a nightclub in Pattaya*

Inset 6.3

SEX TOURISM

Figure 6.14
Prostitution and AIDS in Thailand
Source: Adapted from You magazine, 1 December 1996

Small boys and girls are sold into prostitution as soon as they have left primary school. They hang out on the pavements, among the skinny, diseased dogs lying curled in front of shops that sell very little. Up to 90% of girls from the poorest villages end up in prostitution or some kind of sex work. They are often sold by families who are offered a lump sum of money. They do this to pay off debts that have amassed.

Mae Sai is a village in northern Thailand. It is part of an area of subsistence farming. However, the nature of farming has been disrupted by Thailand's rapid urbanisation. Many families are also dependent upon the heroin trade. Mae Sai lies within the notorious heroin-trading Golden Triangle.

Agents or 'middle men' arrange children for big operators in the large cities. The market for 'sex tourists' has grown dramatically. South East Asia is desperate for foreign currency and is a place where young lives can be bought cheaply. Many children find themselves tied into bonded labour, working in brothels, bars, and massage parlours. They live in appalling conditions. Many children, boys as well as girls, may have to 'service' up to ten clients a night.

QUESTIONS

1 Using an atlas, travel brochures and any other information, describe the attractions that Thailand offers for tourists.
2 Why is Thailand reluctant to stop sex tourism?

Case study:
Environmental impact of leisure and tourism in the UK

Since 1960 there has been a considerable increase in leisure activities of all types in the UK. The tourism industry in the UK had a turnover of over £35 billion in the mid-1990s, double that of the 1980s. In 1994 it accounted for over 5% of GDP and employed over 1.7 million people. In 1994, earnings from recreation and leisure exceeded £10 billion. Consumer spending on sports-related items also accounted for over £10 billion. The sports industry employs over 500 000 people.

Leisure travel has increased by over one-third since the mid-1970s. Leisure now accounts for over 40% of all passenger mileage each year. Over 80% of all leisure journeys are made by car.

The commonest impacts of tourism and leisure include:
- overcrowding
- traffic
- wear and tear
- disturbance and noise
- inappropriate development.

However, it is very difficult to quantify these (Figure 6.15).

	1891	1951	1971	1991
Population (000s)	27 231	41 159	46 412	48 119
Average working week (hours)	56-60	44.8	40.4	40.0
Paid annual holiday (weeks)	rare	1 to 2	2	≥4
Licensed cars (million)	negligible	2.1	10.4	19.7
Foreign holiday-goers (million)	negligible	3	14	30

Figure 6.16 Growth in leisure in Britain, 1891-1991
Source: House of Commons, 1995

Recreational and environmental impact

Rural areas have received much attention in recent years. The Government White Paper in October 1995 considered the options for managing rural areas while recognising that they have altered considerably in recent decades. No longer are they merely areas of food production, but are increasingly used for industrial, residential, commercial and recreational developments. None of these is a particularly new phenomenon but what is new is the intensity with which rural areas are being used.

The increase in tourism and demand for leisure facilities has increased dramatically over the last century.

Improvements in transport, changes in work practices and the growth in disposable income have made places more accessible to a larger number of people, both in a geographic sense as well as in an economic sense. Figure 6.16 shows changes in the working week, the number of weeks paid holiday per year and the increase in the number of cars since 1891.

Recreational pressures can put tremendous strain on resources in rural areas and this varies with the type of recreational use.

Walking

One of the most popular and widespread recreational activities is walking. It is estimated that over 100 000 people are members of the Ramblers' Association and that over 5000 belong to the Long Distance Walkers' Association. The potential impact of so many people on sensitive areas is great. For example, damage to sensitive species on popular walks may lead to soil erosion and create gullies (Figure 6.17, see page 102), as along the route to Red Tarn in the Lake District. Heathlands, chalk and limestone grasslands, and wetlands are particularly fragile, and breeding birds who come to these areas are also affected. In coastal areas destruction of sand dune vegetation and the initiation of blow

Figure 6.15 Tourists in Bath - a honeypot site

Figure 6.17 *The effect of trampling*

out dunes are a widespread problem, as at Studland in Dorset and Ainsdale in Lancashire. Salt marshes are also vulnerable and trampling may lead to localised destruction of vegetation and subsequent erosion of the salt marsh.

In agricultural areas there is conflict between leisure users and farmers over access. For example, people with dogs can cause three main problems: disturbance to sheep, scaring people, especially children, and fouling of footpaths.

Angling

Angling is the most popular sport in the United Kingdom and it is estimated that over 2.5 million people are regular fishermen. Over 350 000 anglers belong to the three main angling organisations, the National Federation of Anglers, the Salmon and Trout Association and the National Federation of Sea Anglers. In addition there are over 2 million fishermen who do not belong to any organisation, but fish on a regular basis.

Angling can have a serious effect on the environment, including visual impact, noise, damage to vegetation, trampling, riverbank erosion and the dumping of rubbish. Other effects include the modification of ecosystems through the introduction of exotic species, such as the rainbow trout introduced from North America at the end of the nineteenth century, modifications to vegetations and habitats, and disturbance to wildfowl and nesting birds.

Not all of the modifications on river habitats are necessarily done by anglers, nor are all bad. Some rivers are regularly stocked and managed in order to attract and maintain fishermen: in the River Cole near Swindon, the National Rivers Authority is undertaking a comprehensive restoration programme, recreating natural pool and riffle sequences and water meadows as well as restocking fish levels.

Golf

The popularity of golf increased dramatically during the late 1980s, although the growth in the number of new golf courses has slowed considerably in the 1990s. Controversy regarding golf courses is intense. Originally, golf courses were located on sandy, heathland areas, such as at Frilford Heath, south Oxfordshire, which had limited agricultural potential. However, as the popularity of the sport has increased, the location of golf courses has altered and increasingly they have been developed in areas with good agricultural potential and close to centres of population. The North Oxford golf course is one example.

New golf courses, it is argued, ruin the environment by water abstraction, modification of natural habitats, the creation of new buildings such as clubhouses, access roads, car parks and the development of new sewage facilities (Figure 6.18). The use of fertilisers and the regular cutting of grass inhibits natural vegetation and creates a man-made landscape. In the case of Penn, Buckinghamshire, a proposed new golf course has created fears not only about its effect on the natural environment but also about its likely impact on the social character of the village.

However, in some areas, golf courses have created diverse semi-natural managed habitats replacing intensive arable agriculture. One example is the Waterstock Golf Course and Driving Range near Thame, Oxfordshire.

Off-road activities

Off-road cycling, like walking, can damage vegetation and lead to soil erosion in particularly popular locations. Chalk downlands, bridleways, peat in wet condition and the New Forest have been identified as especially vulnerable, due to a mixture of environmental sensitivity and population pressure. Some bikers are considered to be over-enthusiastic and this leads to conflicts with other users, especially elderly walkers or those with young children.

The impact of off-road driving in 4x4 vehicles and on motorcycles is more intense. Soil and vegetation losses are increased; there has been extreme damage in parts of the North York Moors, the Peak District and the Yorkshire Dales. Noise disturbance is also a problem.

Figure 6.18 *Cactus damage on a golf course*

TOURISM IN SOUTH AFRICA

South Africa has been promoted as 'a world in one country' and for good reasons. It offers a bewildering array of recreational options in such places as game reserves, mountain resorts, unspoilt beaches and cosmopolitan cities. The scenery is breathtaking, the climate very agreeable, there is great cultural diversity and heritage, and the country's hospitality is well known.

Developing tourism

Since the election in 1994 of Nelson Mandela as president of South Africa, there has been renewed interest in the country. It hosted the 1995 Rugby Union World Cup, and tourism is an increasingly important part of the South African economy. In 1995, investment in tourism was at least US$1.5 billion, and at least US$5 billion will be spent in the late-1990s as hotels are built and upgraded, car rental and airline fleets expanded and airports improved. South Africa is one of the world's fastest growing holiday destinations. Over one million foreign visitors entered the country in 1995 compared with 700 000 in 1994 and 300 000 in 1990. Foreign earnings from tourism were US$3.5 billion in 1995. Tourist numbers are expected to increase by an average of 15% per year until the year 2000, and the tourist industry's contribution to the economy is expected to grow from 3.2% to equal the world average of 7%.

South Africa has a large number of attractions for tourists (Figures 6.21 and 6.22, see page 105):

- its rich and varied wildlife and world famous game reserves, such as Kruger National Park (Figure 6.19, see page 104)
- a tropical climate, which is attractive for European visitors especially in December and January
- glorious beaches in the state of Kwa Zulu Natal
- a rich cultural heritage and the traditions of the Zulu, Xhosa and Sotho peoples
- it is relatively cheap compared to developed countries
- English is widely spoken and there are many links with the UK
- it is perceived as a safe destination since the collapse of apartheid and the election of the new ANC government.

South Africa's successful and peaceful transition to a democracy, the popularity of President Mandela, and marketing by the South Africa Tourist Board, led to a tourism boom in the mid-1990s (Figure 6.20, see page 105).

Tourism has brought a number of benefits to South Africa:

1 **Foreign currency:** the number of foreign tourists has increased by 15% per annum during the 1990s and they contribute 3.2% of South Africa's gross domestic product (GDP)

2 **Employment:** thousands are employed in formal (registered) and informal (unregistered) occupations ranging from hotels and tour operators to cleaners, gardeners and souvenir hawkers

3 **Land use:** it is more **profitable** to use semi-arid grassland for tourism; estimates of the annual returns per hectare of land range from US$12-16 for pastoralism to US$50 for dry-land farming and US$200 for game parks and tourism

4 **Investment:** over US$2.5 billion was invested in South Africa's tourist infrastructure in 1995, upgrading hotels, airlines, car rental fleets, roads.

However, a number of problems have arisen:

- a weak Rand attracts tourists but makes imports (for tourists) costly and marketing abroad expensive
- there is pressure on natural ecosystems, leading to soil erosion, litter pollution, decline of animal numbers
- much tourist-related employment is unskilled, seasonal, part-time, poorly paid and does not provide rights for the workers
- resources are spent on providing facilities such as air conditioning, piped water, electricity, sewage facilities for tourists while local people may have to go without
- a large proportion of profits goes to overseas companies, tour operators, hotel chains
- many of the tourist facilities are owned by whites, and there are serious imbalances in the race-profile of people involved in tourism
- crime is increasingly directed at tourists; much is petty crime but there have been very some serious incidents
- tourism is by nature very unpredictable, varying both with the strength of the economy and a number of factors outside the country's control, for example the lure of alternative holiday destinations.

The tourist infrastructure in South Africa is already showing the signs of strain: check-in queues lengthen, flights are over-booked, car hire companies are turning business away, hotels are packed and game reserves are booked up months in advance. In 1995, the number of foreign tourists increased to over one million, but tourism needs investment if it is to grow. International and local groups of companies have became increasingly active. For example, Inter Continental hotels linked with the Southern Sun to run three 5 Star hotels in Cape Town, Durban and Johannesburg.

The role of tourism in **local economic development** is to boost jobs in rural areas. This includes private game farms and making local handicrafts. In addition, small hotels and bed and breakfasts are a big growth area. These link tourism with the local community.

Ecotourism in South Africa

In 1996 South Africa was promoted under the banner 'Go wild in 1996' and the South African Tourism Board focused its attention on eco- and adventure tourism.

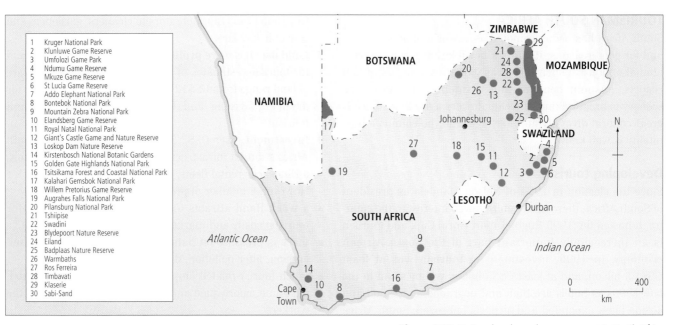

Figure 6.19 *National parks and game reserves in South Africa*
Source: Nagle G. and Spencer K., 1997, Advanced Geography Revision Handbook, OUP

South Africa has many attractions for tourists interested in ecology. It has one of the greatest diversities of bird species in the world, with more than 870 species, about 10% of all species known to man. These include flamingos, pelicans, vultures and eagles.

Similarly, the floral wealth represents some 10% of the world's species. In particular, the Cape Floral region is one of the most spectacular in the world. Fynbos vegetation, a type of macchia or Mediterranean plant, is unique to the area. In Namaqualand in the north western Cape, the desert is transformed into a blaze of flowers following the spring rains, and is an important tourist attraction.

However, it is for its game reserves that South Africa is most famous. These range from desert habitats to subtropical ecosystems and are home to over 290 species of mammal. The National Parks Board runs seventeen National Parks and one National Lake. The most famous and most popular is the Kruger National Park. It contains nine rivers and has an unparalleled diversity of wildlife (Figure 6.23). It has more species than any other park on the African continent owing to its variety of habitats. All of the 'magnificent seven' species, elephant, lion, leopard, buffalo, cheetah, wild dog and rhino, are present in the park.

Kruger National Park stretches for 320 kilometres along the border of Mozambique to the Limpopo River in the north-eastern corner of the Transvaal (Figure 6.24). Its width from west to east averages only 64 kilometres, giving it an area of about 19 000 square kilometres. Vegetation is mostly bushveld, varying from park-like areas, dominated by grass, to thick bush. The landscape is fairly flat with occasional outcrops of rocks (koppies) and low ranges of hills. The rivers which cross the park are surrounded by reeds, palms and subtropical vegetation.

The Kruger National Park was established in 1926. A buffer zone between the Kruger National Park and the farmland nearby is provided by:

- the Timbavati group of unfenced game reserves in the eastern Transvaal
- the Sabi-Sand reserves to the south
- Klaserie to the north.

This is an important part of land-use management as it eases the pressures on the borders of the park, especially from poachers and the gradual growth and encroachment of farmland.

The climate in the Kruger National Park is sub-tropical with the rains concentrated in the summer, between October and March. In the winter, the days are generally sunny and warm, there is little chance of rain and vegetation is less dense; surface water is restricted to rivers and water holes, so animals must use these to find water. As a result, there is a concentration of animals and tourists around water sources during the dry season.

There are a number of potential problems from pressures from tourists. There is an obvious conflict of interest between increasing the number of tourists to increase tourist revenue, and conserving the attractions themselves – the larger the number of tourists the greater the pressures on the land. These pressures include, fire, soil erosion, vegetation removal, feeding and/or frightening the animals, air pollution and litter.

In Kruger, the main way of limiting the damage done by tourists is by limiting the number of tourists that stay there. This is achieved through the booking system for overnight accommodation, whether in chalets, huts or campsites. Facilities are comfortable, but not excessively so: for example, there is only one swimming pool in the park and there are no plans to build any more.

One of the major threats to the area is that of fire. Fire occurs naturally in the dry season and is important for maintaining the ecology of the area, allowing the growth of new grass and the removal of weeds. However, it poses a threat to tourists and tourist facilities. Hence, park authorities light and manage the fires in order to create the natural conditions of a fire but in a controlled situation.

Vegetation removal and soil erosion go hand in hand. They occur as a result of increased pressures by people and vehicles on vegetation that is unable to cope. Normally, this degradation of the land occurs at specific pressure points around water holes and accessible river sites. Limiting numbers and shutting off roads is really the only option in this case.

Ecotourism is a very finely balanced system that links the tourist industry with the conservation of natural ecosystems and it needs very careful management.

- There has been an 11.4% increase in the number of tourists to South Africa in 1995.
- In 1995, approximately 1 million foreign tourists went to South Africa.
- The largest increase (120%) was in French tourists, following an advertising campaign on public transport in France.
- The number of African tourists to South Africa is growing slowly (0.5% per annum).
- The majority (more than 75%) of tourists to South Africa are holiday makers, while business visitors, students and transit visitors (using South Africa to get somewhere else) made up the rest.
- The proportion of tourists visiting South Africa for a holiday is increasing.

Figure 6.20 *Recent trends in tourism in South Africa*

Figure 6.21 *South Africa's game attractions*

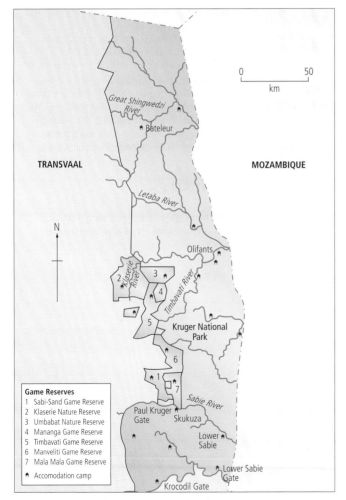

Figure 6.24 *Map of the Kruger National Park*
Source: Nagle, G. 1996, Ecotourism in South Africa, Axis, 2, 3, 22-5.

Game Reserves
1 Sabi-Sand Game Reserve
2 Klaserie Nature Reserve
3 Umbabat Nature Reserve
4 Mananga Game Reserve
5 Timbavati Game Reserve
6 Manveliti Game Reserve
7 Mala Mala Game Reserve
↑ Accomodation camp

Figure 6.22 *South Africa's stunning scenery*

- 300 types of trees
- 49 species of fish
- 33 types of amphibians
- 114 species of reptiles
- 507 species of birds
- 147 species of mammals

Figure 6.23 *Species diversity in the Kruger National Park*

QUESTIONS

1 What kind of visitors do you think are attracted to South Africa? Explain your answer.

2 In what ways could South Africa encourage **(i)** niche markets, such as cultural tourism and adventure tourism, **(ii)** small operators, and **(iii)** marketing areas currently not on tourist trails?

3 Many developing countries are trying to expand their tourist industry.

a) Make a list of all the advantages and disadvantages for a country to expand its tourist industry.

b) Do you think that South Africa should expand its tourist industry? Explain your answer.

4 Ecotourism is one of the most rapidly developing forms of tourism. What conflicts might arise, in an area such as Kruger National Park, between tourists and **(i)** conservationists, and **(ii)** farmers in the nearby areas who wish to expand their farming activities?

SUMMARY

In this chapter we have seen that tourism is one of the world's most important industries. It is also, potentially, one of the most damaging, especially at a local level. This damage may be environmental, social, cultural and personal.

The growth in affluence, leisure time, disposable income and the rise of the Asian NICs will undoubtedly lead to increases in tourism. Cheap airfares, accommodation and package deals will lead to an increase in mass tourism. There is likely to be a growth in theme parks and in the convention and fantasy resort markets. There will be a broadening out from mass tourism into the niche market such as ecotourism, adventure tourism, cultural tourism and environmental tourism.

The prosperity of tourism will be affected by such things as war, unrest, terrorism, disasters, diseases and other hazards. Westernisation appears to be affecting more and more cultures and careful planning is needed to preserve cultural integrity and identity.

QUESTIONS

1 Tourist environments are very dynamic. Explain how and why coastal resorts and nature reserves have changed in popularity since World War II. How useful is the resort life-cycle model (Figure 6.10) as a means of explaining these changes?

2 'Tourism is the fourth revolution in economic activity.' Explain this statement. How accurate do you think it is? Give reasons for your answer.

3 'Recreation is largely the privilege of the rich and the urban.' Discuss.

BIBLIOGRAPHY AND RECOMMENDED READING

Department of Environment, 1996, *Indicators of sustainable development for the United Kingdom*, HMSO

Department of Transport, 1995, *National travel survey 1992/4*, HMSO

House of Commons, 1995, *The environmental impact of recreation*, HMSO

International Passenger Service, 1995, *Transport statistics Great Britain 1995*, HMSO

Jenner, P., & Smith, C., 1992, The tourism industry and environment, *The Economist Special Report 2453*

Mathieson, A. & Wall, G., 1982, *Tourism: economic, physical and social impacts*, Longman

Pearce, D., 1981, *Tourist development*, Longman

Simmons, I. G., 1989, *Changing the face of the earth*, Blackwell

South African Tourism Board, 5-6 Alt Grove, Wimbledon, London SW 19 4DZ, Tel. 0181 944 8080 Fax: 0181 944 6705

Spencer, K. & Nagle, G., 1996, Environmental issues in Europe, *Geofile*, 284

UNICEF (Thailand) 55 Lincoln's Inn Fields, London WC2A 3NB telephone 0171 405 5592 for information on work that UNICEF is supporting in Thailand

World Trade Organisation (WTO) *1993 Year Book of Tourism Statistics 45th Edition*, WTO.

World Trade Organisation/UNEP *1992 Guidelines: Development of National Parks and Protected Areas for Tourism* WTO/UNEP joint publication.

WEB SITES

ANC home page - http://www.anc.org.za/
The virtual tourist - http://www.vtourist.com/vt/

Chapter 7
Sustainable development

Sustainable development has been defined as development which 'meets the needs of the present without compromising the ability of future generations to meet their own needs' (Brundtland, 1987). It is a form of development whereby living standards are improved, whilst at the same time the environment is used, managed, and conserved on a long-term basis. Sustainable development implies social justice as well as environmental sustainability.

This chapter examines the crises or problems facing the world, assesses the human impact on resources, and looks at ways of managing the earth's resources. The role of local sustainable development is stressed. We then focus upon two resources, energy and water, and use contrasting examples from ELDCs and EMDCs to analyse the issues surrounding these precious resources.

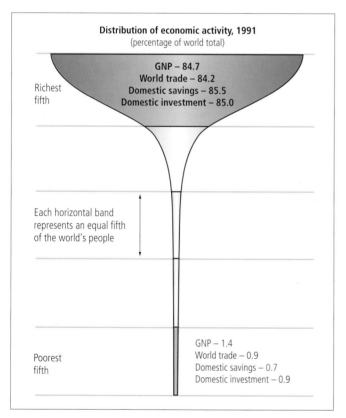

Figure 7.2 *Global economic disparities*
Source: *Nagle, G. and Spencer, K., 1997, Sustainable development, Hodder and Stoughton*

WORLD CRISES

The world is facing a number of interlinked crises which are reducing the chances of achieving sustainable development. The crises encompass social, economic, environmental and political aspects.

The world's 'underclass'

About one-fifth of the world's 5.8 billion population live in desperately poor conditions (Figure 7.2). These are the global 'underclass'. Their lives are at the edge of existence and are continuously close to famine, disease, hunger and death. Since the 1960s, political and economic changes in the world have made some ELDCs even poorer compared with the EMDCs (Figure 7.1). Urban regions have grown at the expense of rural areas. The underclass are constrained by a lack of power and control over their own destiny. Within the underclass certain groups are more vulnerable than others. In particular, women, children and indigenous people and minority ethnic groups are at risk of exploitation. In an average year, fourteen million children in ELDCs under the age of five die. This is the equivalent of 25% of the UK's population or **all** the children born in the UK over a twenty year period. During wars, famines, plagues, economic recession and other disasters, this number increases.

1960	30:1
1970	32:1
1980	45:1
1989	59:1
1991	61:1

Figure 7.1 *Ratio of income of richest 20% of the population to the poorest 20% of the population*
Source: *Reid, D., 1995, Sustainable development: an introductory guide, Earthscan*

The environmental crisis

The environmental crisis is a result of the rate at which the limited resources of the earth are being used or destroyed (Figure 7.3). Moreover, the 20% of the world's population that live in EMDCs consume 80% of the world's resources, whereas the 80% of the population that live in ELDCs use only 20% of the resources. Since many of the resources that are consumed in EMDCs come from ELDCs, much of the costs of producing the raw material or foodstuffs is paid for by ELDCs.

Figure 7.3 *The Tokyo fish market*

Political crises

Political conflict in the form of war, ethnic cleansing, refugee crises, trading blocs, trade wars and economic sanctions has increased. In the 1990s there have been conflicts and renewed violence in Ethiopia, Rwanda, Kuwait, Nigeria, Bosnia, Chechnya, Israel, Sri Lanka and Northern Ireland, among others.

These crises make the task of sustainable development much more difficult. For example, there is little hope for sustainable development in Rwanda if violence and bloodshed

continue. On the other hand, political change in South Africa has allowed freedom of movement for all races. This has reduced population pressure in some drylands (dry areas without the benefit of irrigation). In turn, this has improved the prospects for sustainable dryland agriculture and it has also boosted the hopes for sustainable ecotourism.

THE HUMAN IMPACT ON RESOURCES

Simple models have long been used by geographers to show the relationship between carrying capacity (how many people or how much use the environment can sustain) and population growth or resource exploitation (Figure 7.4).

In 1966, Kenneth Boulding popularised the concept of 'spaceship earth' and provided two scenarios for economic development:

1 The 'robber-' or 'cowboy-economy' had unlimited growth and no checks on conservation. Success was measured in terms of industrial output and there was little thought for the long-term future of the world. Global catastrophe resulted.

2 The 'spaceship-economy' views the world as a closed system with limited resources. In this economy, mankind has to work with the system, conserve resources and plan for future survival. Long-term stability could be achieved this way.

Concern about rapid population growth and resource depletion led to Garret Hardin's *The tragedy of the commons* (1968). His idea is simple but important. He considers the actions of people who have right of access to and use of a com-

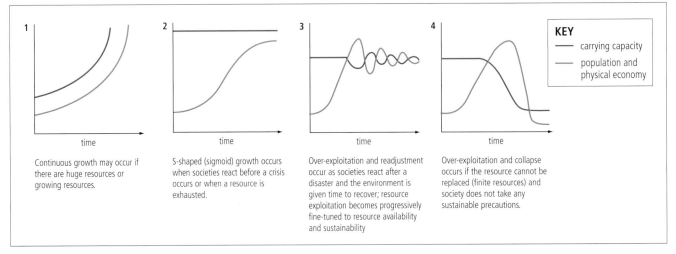

Figure 7.4 *Modelling population and resources*
Source: Meadows, D., et al., 1972, The limits to growth, Pan

QUESTIONS

1 What other types of development are there other than sustainable development? How is sustainable development different from them?

2 Economic growth in ELDCs and NICs will have a serious impact upon the environment.

a) Explain at least two reasons why economic growth in ELDCs and NICs in the 1990s and 2000s will

differ from that in Britain and Germany in the late nineteenth and early twentieth centuries.

b) What implications does this have for the environment and sustainable development?

mon resource, such as a meadow, forest or mineral resource:

1 If an individual continues to increase their yield to improve their standard of living relative to others, then

2 the resource will eventually become depleted, and

3 all those who depend upon it, including that individual, will suffer.

The analogy with global economic growth is clear. The individual in this case could represent a country, a multinational corporation or a peasant farmer. The common resource could be the global or local stock of natural resources.

The limits to growth

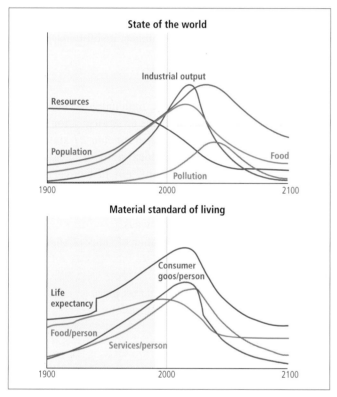

Figure 7.5 *Limits to growth*
Source: Meadows, D., et al., 1972, The limits to growth, Pan

The limits to growth (1972) was a pessimistic view of the state of the world's resources and the likelihood of resource depletion. It concluded that the limits to global growth would occur by 2020. It forecast a severe fall in industrial output and food supplies around 2010 and a rapid decline in population around 2050 (Figure 7.5). Pollution was seen as likely to be one of the main causes of the collapse of the system. The increasing use of resources was also seen as a problem. The report was criticised on a number of counts,

most notably the lack of a regional dimension and the absence of any measures to manage or solve the impending disaster. Nevertheless, the basic message was, and is, correct: the earth cannot sustain economic growth which depends upon an increasing amount of resource consumption.

In a more sophisticated model, the authors built in a number of new scenarios. These include a variety of factors and situations (on a global scale) such as:

● deliberate constraints on population growth

● trade-off between population size and levels of material well-being

● the development of technologies to conserve resources

● increased farming efficiency

● reductions in the levels of pollution

● the rates of pollution do not exceed the tolerance of the environment

● the rates of use of renewable resources do not exceed their rates of regeneration

● the rates of use of non-renewable resources do not exceed the rate at which sustainable renewable substitutes are developed.

With these changes it is possible to see a very different pattern from the one drawn in 1972.

Beyond *The limits to growth*

In the early 1970s, the *Ecologist Magazine* published *Blueprint for survival*. The report predicted that without a change in the way society used resources there would be a breakdown in society and irreversible environmental degradation by the end of the twentieth century.

Blueprint outlined some of the requirements for a stable, sustainable society:

● minimum disruption to ecological processes

● increased conservation of resources

● zero population growth

● a just social system.

However, economic growth is necessary and desirable for a number of reasons:

● industrial growth leads to population growth and this in turn creates demand for more growth (cumulative causation)

● economic growth reduces the risk of unemployment

● growth is needed for profits which are needed for investment

● the success of governments is often measured in growth-related indicators

● recession leads to social and political instability.

QUESTION

1 Study the list of ways of achieving sustainable growth, given in *The limits to growth*.

a) What are the issues connected with the deliberate constraint on population growth?

b) How simple is it to introduce any of these measures into (i) the UK, (ii) an ELDC, and (iii) globally? What hope do you think there is for sustainable development? Explain your answer.

MANAGING THE EARTH'S RESOURCES

Global proposals

The World Commission on Environment and Development (1987) raised the profile of sustainable development. It stated that sustainable development has two key aspects:

- the achievement of basic needs for all people, especially the global underclass
- the limits to development are technical, cultural and social.

This is in complete contrast to the *Limits to growth* idea that the limits to growth were environmental concerns and resource availability.

The Commission suggested seven major proposals for a strategy for sustainable development:

- increase economic growth
- concentrate on the quality of growth
- meet basic needs of food, water, employment, energy and sanitation
- stabilise population growth
- conserve and enhance resources
- use technology to manage risk
- place environment into economics.

Five years later, the United Nations Conference on Environment and Development (UNCED) was held at Rio de Janeiro. The outcomes of the 1992 Rio Earth Summit were five-fold:

- Convention on biodiversity
- Framework Convention on climatic change
- Principles of forest management statement
- a Rio Declaration on Environment and Development
- Agenda 21.

The *Convention on biodiversity* seeks to conserve biodiversity, species and ecosystems. This is important because there may be up to 30 million species in the world, of which only 1.5 million have been described. Up to 25% of the total may face extinction, and up to 100 species a day may become extinct.

The *Framework Convention on climatic change* was signed by 153 countries. EMDCs agreed to stabilise their emissions of greenhouse gases to 1990 levels. ELDCs, however, argued that they should not be prevented from developing and therefore had to fuel rapid economic growth and some refused to sign.

The *Principles of forest management* and the *Rio Declaration on Environment and Development* are unachievable statements, due to their sheer scale and content.

By contrast, *Agenda 21* was a detailed document which spelt out a programme for sustainable development. Four main areas were considered:

1 Social and economic development – international cooperation, poverty, population, health, settlements
2 Resource management – atmosphere, land resource planning, deforestation, mountains, fragile ecosystems, biodiversity, biotechnology, waste disposal
3 Strengthening the participation of major groups – vulnerable peoples, NGOs, local, national and international governments
4 Means of implementation – finance, institutions, technology transfer, education.

Role of local Agenda 21

As a result of the Earth Summit, national governments are obliged to formulate national plans or strategies for sustainable development. These are called *Agenda 21* statements. Sustainable development is a local activity because it is **people** who create development, not just governments. Moreover, according to Chambers (1983), all people, however poor, have some ability, however constrained, of changing what they do, in small ways.

Local authorities have a number of roles in sustainable development:

- as a consumer of resources
- as a force for change in the market place
- as a role model for other organisations
- as providers of information
- as providers of services
- as planners
- as local governments and decision makers.

QUESTIONS

1 What has your local authority provided in terms of an *Agenda 21* statement?

2 Briefly explain how we can use energy, water and paper in a more sustainable way. What factors prevent sustainable development?

ENERGY RESOURCES

This section looks at one of the most important global resources – energy resources. Here we consider some of the main issues, and use two contrasting examples, the UK and India, to highlight the main points. The key sustainable development needs are:

- to ensure supplies of energy at competitive prices
- to reduce the adverse impacts of energy use to acceptable levels
- to encourage consumers to meet their needs with less energy input through improved energy efficiency.

Energy in the UK

Energy consumption

The UK has four main sources of energy: coal, oil, natural gas and nuclear power. It has abundant supplies of fossil fuels and the potential to extend nuclear and renewable sources. UK oil and natural gas production has increased over the past two decades, while production of coal has declined. Production of energy is just over 230 million tonnes of oil equivalent. Oil accounts for over 50% of the total, natural gas 25% and coal 12%.

Consumption of the UK's own resources of oil is currently at a rate of 8% of reserves a year, and for natural gas, 4%. In the long-term, as existing energy resources become scarce, prices will rise, energy efficiency will increase and there will be greater demand for renewable energy sources. Nuclear power accounts for about 27% of the UK's electricity and renewable sources, 2%. However, over 30% of the primary energy is lost in the conversion to electricity.

Consumption of primary energy resources has fallen in the UK for two main reasons:

- the economy has become more fuel efficient
- manufacturing has declined.

Energy consumption has risen, however, in the road transport, commercial and household sectors. Fuel use for road transport now accounts for 25% of total energy consumption.

Oil has been a major source of energy in the UK since the North Sea oil fields were opened in the 1970s. Annual production rose to 130 million tonnes in the mid-1980s, but declined after 1988.

Natural gas is cheap and clean. Production has risen steadily from 1970. Outside the transport sector it is the dominant fuel. It accounts for 65% of domestic fuel, 42% in the commercial and public sector, and 33% in industry. Coal, by contrast, has declined.

Nuclear and renewable energy resources account for about 10% of the UK's energy. The use of nuclear and renewable sources has considerable benefits (Figure 7.6) such as:

- reducing demand for fossil fuels
- producing lower, environmental impacts.

However, there are disadvantages such as radioactive waste, noise and visual pollution, high costs of development and long-term environmental impacts.

Renewable energy in the UK

Renewable energy has been called the 'Cinderella' of the energy sector. It had been left behind and neglected compared with the 'ugly sisters', fossil fuel and nuclear power. By the mid 1990s, that situation had changed. There is now

Technology	Local	Regional	Global
Onshore wind	Noise, visual intrusion, electromagnetic interference	None	None
Offshore wind	Impeded navigation and fishing rights	None	None
Hydro power	Visual intrusion, ecological impact	Ecological impact	None
Tidal power	Visual intrusion, ecological impact	Ecological impact	None
Wave energy	Impeded navigation and fishing rights	None	None
Geothermal	Visual intrusion, noise, water needs, radon release	None	None
Solar	Visual intrusion	None	None
Municipal and general industrial wastes	Particulate and toxic emissions, visual intrusions, fuel transportation	Particulate and toxic emissions, waste disposal	None None
Landfill gas	Particulate and toxic emissions, visual intrusions	Particulate and toxic emissions	None
Agricultural and forestry wastes	Particulate and toxic emissions, visual intrusions, fuel transportation	Particulate emissions	None
Energy crops	Particulate and toxic emissions, visual intrusions, fuel transportation	Particulate emissions	None

Figure 7.6 *The environmental impact of renewable energy*
Source: *The environmental effects of renewable resources- simplified from Walker, 1997*

a clearly identifiable renewable energy sector in the UK (Figure 7.7). Although the output is still small, there has been an important political and symbolic significance in its growth and development. It is closely associated with the move towards sustainable development.

There are a number of forms of renewable energy sources. These include tidal, hydro, wind, waves, biomass and geothermal. These vary in terms of:

- energy generation characteristics
- geographical characteristics
- environmental characteristics.

Renewable energy operates at many scales, from a single wind pump to a large-scale hydroelectric power (HEP) system. Renewable forms of energy differ from fossil fuels in many ways:

- they are often small-scale
- the output of energy is variable and may be unpredictable
- most renewable forms of energy provide electricity
- they are more expensive to produce
- they have a high initial cost of development but relatively low running costs
- the sources of energy are at fixed locations.

However, the costs of renewable energy are falling. They are also increasingly attractive because they do not pollute the environment as much as non-renewable sources. On a global scale, none of the renewable technologies makes a significant impact. At a local scale, however, there may be visual and noise pollution, and ecological disruption. Many sites, such as estuaries and high ground, that are usable for renewable energy, are ecologically sensitive.

Developing renewable resources is complex and costly. It requires a large number of schemes to provide as much energy as a conventional coal-fired power station.

Moreover, renewable sources are only economically viable if they have government support.

Apart from nuclear power, the UK government did not really consider renewable energy until the 1990s. Despite having some of the best resources for renewable energy in Europe, renewable energy was underdeveloped. In the late 1980s, the annual budget for nuclear energy (about £175 million) was twenty-five times greater than the amount spent on renewable sources.

In the late 1980s, the threat of global warming resulted in a need to stabilise CO_2 emissions. Oil prices were falling, too. The UK's fossil fuel industry was becoming less profitable, so the government took steps to increase the supply of renewable energy. It introduced the Non Fossil Fuel Obligation (NFFO) which obliges regional electricity companies to buy a specified amount of renewable energy. Initially this meant nuclear power, but this has since been changed to exclude nuclear energy.

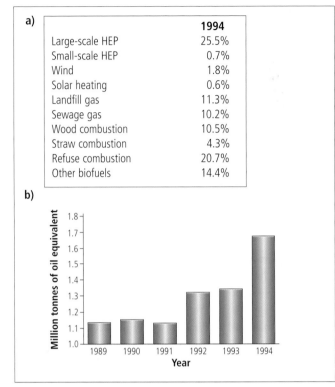

Figure 7.7 *Contributions to the UK's renewable energy sector*
Source: adapted from Walker, 1997

The amount of generating capacity from renewable resources has increased considerably. Waste incineration forms the largest share, followed by wind and landfill gas (Figure 7.7). The companies involved in developing the UK's renewable energy sources are very diverse. Six main groups exist:

- major power generators – National Power owns two-thirds of National Wind Power; PowerGen has also concentrated on wind power and has some small-scale hydro-electric power (HEP) stations
- regional electricity companies – Manweb and South Western Power have wind farms; Norweb is involved with HEP and landfill gas projects
- non-energy utilities – some water companies have formed biogas projects at sewage plants
- renewable energy companies – such as BP Energy Services, comprising wind and biomass projects (biomass is energy produced from living matter or waste materials – such as faeces)
- single project companies – such as South East London Combined Heat and Power.

The NFFO legislation has increased the number and range of companies involved in renewable energy. There is also more competition between the energy companies. Nevertheless, there is still considerable opposition to renewable energy. This is normally organised at a local level and

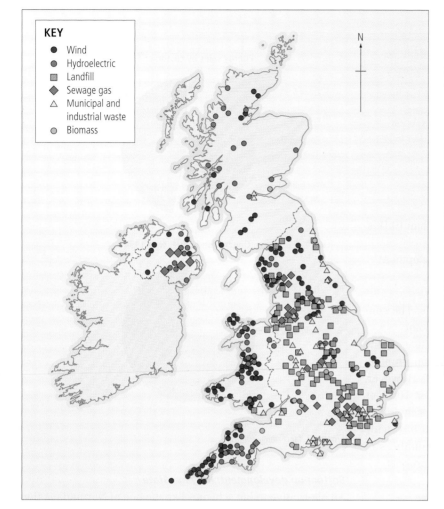

Figure 7.9 *Wind power*

Figure 7.8 *Renewable energy in the UK*
Source: The energy resource: renewable energy in the UK, Geography, 1997

is focussed on environmental issues.

The map of UK renewable energy sources shows their diversity (Figure 7.8). This pattern reflects the supplies of energy as well as the demand. On the supply side there are concentrations of renewable energy in south west England, Wales, Lancashire and Cumbria. Urban areas provide a large amount of energy through landfill and sewage gas.

There has been a noticeable rise in the amount of renewable energy used in the UK since 1990. Biofuels are the main source of renewable energy in the UK; wind power and HEP make only a small contribution. As the price of renewable energy continues to fall, it is likely that there will be an increase in the amount produced (Figure 7.9). With only 1% of the UK's energy provided by renewable forms of energy, there is scope for increase. Moreover, it is a useful form of local employment – wind power employs 1300 people, and a further 900 in associated industries.

New developments in the UK's wind energy

The UK is to build its first, and the world's largest, off-shore wind farm four miles off the Essex coast. The government approved a £35 million project consisting of forty giant turbines. It has guaranteed that electricity prices will remain stable for the first fifteen years of production, which means that the project is economically viable.

Supporters of wind energy favour an off-shore location. This is because:

- winds are stronger
- there is less turbulence
- there will be less noise disruption
- there are fewer environmental objections.

Although off-shore sites produce more energy, they are expensive to develop. Each of the turbines in this scheme is about 70 metres high and together they will generate sufficient energy for a town of about 70 000 people.

The UK has the largest wind resource in Europe. However, Germany, the Netherlands and Denmark produce more wind energy than the UK. In the UK there are only thirty-four wind farms, which together produce enough energy to supply a city the size of Cardiff. It is becoming increasingly difficult to get planning permission for wind farms on land; wind stations at sea do not need planning permission.

The cost of wind energy is declining and is now competing with coal- and gas- fired power stations. This competitiveness has been helped by the NFFO which means that consumers pay a small subsidy to keep the cost of renewable energy competitive.

QUESTIONS

1 Choose an appropriate method to illustrate the data in Figure 7.7 on page 112. Why have you used this method?

2 Study Figure 7.8 which shows the distribution of renewable sources in the UK. Describe and explain the distribution of **(i)** wind and hydro resources, and **(ii)** landfill and biogas resources.

3 Why has Britain made such limited use of its renewable energy resources? How is this likely to change in the future? Give reasons for your answer.

The Indian situation

Renewable energy is more common in EMDCs than ELDCs. This could be due to a number of reasons:

- higher levels of technology, research and development
- a reduction in fossil fuels in EMDCs
- an active environmental movement.

In addition, the type of renewable energy varies. The contrast between the UK and India illustrates this point.

India's population is expected to reach one billion by the year 2000. At present, average annual power consumption is low at about 300 kilowatt hours per head. However, demand is increasing rapidly at a rate of almost 10% per annum (Figure 7.10). The power industry is closely linked to the country's capacity for development. India has made great efforts to industrialise, but increasing numbers of Indian people are questioning the development process.

Top-down development: the Narmada Valley Scheme

The Narmada Valley Scheme is a **multipurpose** scheme which is set to become one of the world's largest hydroelectric power and irrigation schemes. It involves 30 major dams, 135 medium-sized dams and 3000 small dams. It has a number of aims:

- to irrigate 20 000 square kilometres in the drought-prone states of Gujarat and Madhya Pradesh
- to provide drinking water for the whole region
- to generate 500 megawatts of electricity.

The scheme will cost US$40 billion, most of which will be borrowed from the World Bank.

However, the scheme has received a great deal of criticism:

- 144 000 hectares of land and 570 villages will be flooded, and over one million people will be forced out of the region
- the dam will submerge 1500 square kilometres of forest which is home to many rare species of plants and animals
- construction will lead to widespread environmental destruction
- the scheme will only benefit wealthy farmers who can afford expensive inputs
- the area is tectonically active.

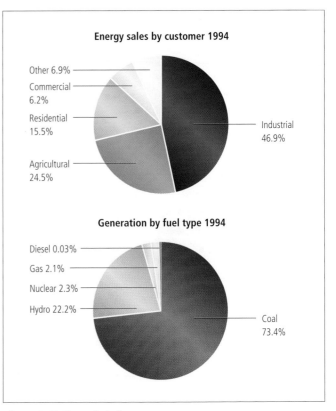

Figure 7.10 *Energy in India*
Source: Flemings Research

Bottom-up development: Haryana State

An alternative to big schemes like the one at Narmada is the sustainable energy project in Haryana State to the north-west of New Delhi. The project has centred on one village, Dhanawas, which has about 300 residents. Participation by the villagers is a cornerstone of the initiative. The production of energy comes from three sustainable sources:

- the development of a number of biogas chambers which use a mixture of cow dung and water – a maximum of 2 cubic metres of cow dung and water each day – enough for five hours cooking or ten hours of lighting; the aim is to make the village self-sufficient in renewable sources of fuel, reducing the consumption of wood
- the building of a gasifer which uses a mixture of shredded mustard stalks, cow dung and water in the form of small pellets and converts them into gas; the equipment is capable of generating the equivalent of 5 kilowatts of electricity, enough to power lighting for the whole village
- the use of solar powered water heaters.

QUESTIONS

1 Describe the pattern of energy consumption in India.

2 What are the main forms of energy in India?

3 What advantages do sustainable energy sources have over conventional sources?

4 What advantages do conventional energy sources have over sustainable sources?

WATER RESOURCES

The water problem

- 25% of the world's population struggle to obtain enough water
- by 2025, up to two-thirds of the world's population will lack sufficient water
- total consumption is increasing at 2.5% per annum
- water demand has increased six-fold since 1900
- by 2025, 27 countries, all but three in North Africa, Asia and the Middle East, will face high water stress – an inability to meet demand
- water shortages will hinder economic growth in many countries
- over 300 major river basins cross national boundaries, leading to competition for water resources
- aquifer water is being used up faster than it can be replaced

Figure 7.11 *The water problem*

In this section we look at one of the most important resources in the world, water. For decades we have taken it for granted. Now we are beginning to recognise its scarcity. The threat of climatic change has led to fears of drought, even in the UK. Overall, the UK has a plentiful supply of water. However, there is an imbalance between supply and demand. There is excess supply in the north and west of the country; the more industrialised, densely populated south and east has a shortage of water. The shortage has become more pronounced due to the hot, dry summers and the dry winters of the mid-1990s.

In many ELDCs and in many semi-arid countries, the problem is much worse. In this section we examine the water problem at a number of scales ranging from urban to international. We also look at some of the political, economic, social and environmental implications of water resource development.

The water problem is enormous (Figure 7.11) and getting more serious:

- two billion people lack access to safe water and three billion lack effective sanitation
- in Africa, the availability of water will be reduced from 9000 to 1600 cubic metres per person per year by 2100
- 40% of the world's population face chronic water shortages
- dirty water in ELDCs causes 80% of illnesses, killing 10 million people annually
- by 2030, there will be nearly 3 billion more people in the world.

Water is an essential part of our daily lives. A clean, fresh water supply is a basic necessity for all societies – for the good health of populations, for agriculture and for industry. As the world's population increases, so does the demand for water. As standards of living increase, the demand for water increases even more. At present, however, many nations, especially EMDCs, use water in an irresponsible and wasteful way.

Of all the water in the world, only 2.5% is fresh, and only 1% of that is available to people. Nevertheless, there is theoretically enough water to support a much larger world population than at present. The problems which are related to water include storage, distribution and pollution, particularly in ELDCs.

There are six main issues related to the world's water resources:

1 **Health**

A WHO report suggests that 80% of the world's diseases are caused by contaminated water. These diseases include cholera, typhoid, malaria, bilharzia and leprosy. About 500 million people suffer from water-borne diseases. Simple preventative measures can achieve massive reductions in the occurrence of diseases. Communal wells and sewage disposal represent the greatest dangers.

2 **Agriculture**

80% of all the water used by people is used in agriculture. In ELDCs, as populations have increased and new high yielding crops have been introduced, there has been a rapidly increasing demand for water. More and more large-scale irrigation schemes are needed.

3 **Environment**

Decisions taken over water supplies can have far reaching effects on the environment. In semi-arid lands, where drought is a recurring problem, the provision of new water holes often encourages overgrazing. This can lead to **desertification**. In addition, **deforestation** increases the rate of run-off, making flooding downstream more likely. This makes water conservation more difficult. Desertification already affects 30% of the land's surface area. It costs US$42 billion in lost food production, and over 135 million people are in danger of having to leave their land.

4 **Technology**

In the past, there has been a concentration on expensive, large-scale schemes with massive dams, complex irrigation networks, and HEP generation. Usually, these have to be funded by EMDCs in return for profitable construction contracts or other agreements. There is now a strong feeling that development should be at village level and that intermediate or appropriate technology is preferable to high technology.

5 **Politics**

As water resources become increasingly important, countries find themselves competing for their use. This can happen where countries share a river as a frontier or where a river flows from one country to another.

6 Money

In 1976, a UN Habitat Conference suggested all settlements should have clean water by 1990. To reach this target, £2 per person would have to be spent in ELDCs. (The world arms budget represents £70 per person in ELDCs.) The 1976 target is not going to be met by the start of the twenty-first century because of lack of funds. In the foreseeable future, water shortages rather than land scarcity will be the biggest constraint on agriculture. The World Bank has lent over US$36 billion for water development projects since 1950. By 2005, ELDCs will need to spend a further US$600 billion on water projects.

Agriculture has been driving the demand for water. About 80% of water is used for irrigation. This is used to produce 40% of the world's food, from just 17% of the cultivable land. Between 1960 and 1980, nearly 60% of all new food output was from irrigated land: Asian agriculture, with its emphasis on rice, faces particular problems. However, urban growth is now causing severe problems in areas such as the Middle East and North Africa.

Traditional water management is unable to cope with the increased demands for water. Between 1960 and 1980, world supplies of water per head fell by 80% from 3430 cubic metres per year to 667. Water supplies of 667 cubic metres per year represent just 15% of the world average water availability per person.

The key sustainable development objectives for water are:
- to ensure adequate water supplies for agriculture, industry and households
- to improve water efficiency
- to maintain the aquatic environment.

Water and health

In 1992, waterborne infections caused 1500 million cases of diarrhoea and four million infant deaths. There are two major types of disease related to water:
- Water-washed diseases, such as skin- and eye-infections. These are transmitted when there is not enough water for personal and domestic hygiene.
- Waterborne diseases. These are transmitted when people use water which has been contaminated by human waste. Cholera and dysentery are prime examples.

In ELDCs, water-washed diseases cause more illness and death than waterborne diseases. Hence, water quantity is more important than water quality. It is better to wash in dirty water than not at all and increasing the amount of water available should decrease these illnesses.

Ironically, some attempts to improve water resources have led to increasing amounts of disease:
- untreated surface waters and poorly built wells
- shallow wells in acidic waters may give harmful concentrations of minerals

- wells built into deep unweathered granite may have high concentrations of fluoride.

Access to water

In ELDCs and NICs, one of the greatest environmental threats is lack of water. Today, the world's supply of water is only one-third of that in 1970. Water scarcity is increasingly becoming a factor in ethnic strife and political tension. In 1990 about 1.3 billion people in the ELDCs and NICs lacked access to clean water (Figure 7.12). And much water pollution is the result of poor sanitation: nearly two billion people lack access to safe sanitation.

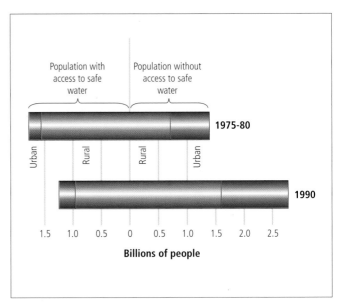

Figure 7.12 Access to water
Source: Human Development Report, 1994, OUP

QUESTIONS

Percentage of population	1975-80 Rural	1975-80 Urban	1990 Rural	1990 Urban
with access to safe water	.....	.....	.....	.....
without access to safe water	....	.....	.....	.....

1 Study Figure 7.12 and complete the table above.

2 With the use of examples, explain why the world's supply of water in 1994 is only one-third of that in 1970.

3 Why is water scarcity increasingly a problem in ethnic and political tensions? Give examples to illustrate your answer.

4 Why are more people in ELDCs subjected to poor sanitation conditions than to poor water conditions?

5 Explain why (i) it is easier to upgrade facilities in urban areas rather than rural areas, and (ii) increasingly higher proportions of the urban population have inadequate water and sanitation facilities.

China: the water shortfall

Millions of Chinese do not have access to clean water (Figure 7.13). In particular, China's northern regions are suffering a severe water shortage. Remedial action is required and will costs millions of pounds. The scale of the problem is immense: more than half of China's large and medium sized cities faced shortages in 1996 and over 100 cities were severely deprived of water. Water pollution adds to the problem.

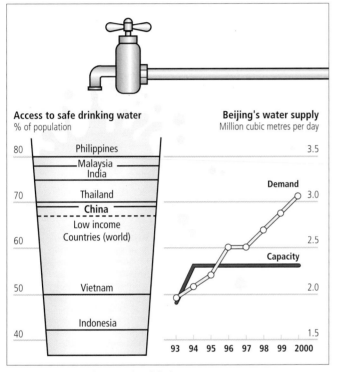

Figure 7.13 *China's water shortfall: the pressure grows*
Sources: World Bank, ADB

Worst affected cities include Taiyuan, capital of Shaanxi province south-west of Beijing, and Datong, also in Shaanxi. Water is available there only at certain times of the day. In the rural areas 70 million farmers and 60 million livestock lack sufficient water. Since 1990, 26 million hectares of China's 110 million hectares of arable land have been affected by drought. In addition, grain outputs have decreased as a result.

China has a total water resource of 2.8 billion cubic metres per annum. This gives an average per capita availability of 2300 cubic metres per annum. However, in the nine northern provinces it is just 500 cubic metres per annum. In Beijing it is less than 400 cubic metres per annum. This is less than 14% of China's average per capita availability, and just 3% of the world average. Local reservoirs cannot meet Beijing's demand. Consequently, Beijing is tapping nearly 3 billion cubic metres of ground water each year. This has caused the water table to drop by 50 metres and subsidence is now an increasing problem. In Tianjin, a city of over 10 million people, and one of China's busiest ports, water availability is the lowest in China.

The water problem in China is so severe largely as a result of its population size. The situation is now made worse by a series of problems:

- 25% of China's urban water supply is lost through leakages
- an even greater share is used in manufacturing
- leaking pipes cost China over £230 million worth of water annually
- in rural areas, porous canals lose 50% of their water
- efficient forms of irrigation, such as drip irrigation and sprinklers, are rarely used, because of their cost.

Indeed, a saving of 1% of the water lost would save 400 million cubic metres, enough water for 6.5 million people for a year. China is looking at schemes to divert supplies from the south to the north, but these are costly, complex projects.

Water in the Middle East

Access to water is one of the most sensitive and intractable problems in the Middle East. It has caused great friction between Arabs and Jews; the example of Israeli-Palestinian tensions illustrates this clearly.

For decades, Israel has obtained up to 80% of the 670 million cubic metres of water provided by mountain aquifers mostly located beneath the West Bank (Figure 7.14). The Israelis have occupied the West Bank since 1967 and have prevented the West Bank Arabs from obtaining better access to the resource.

The mountain aquifers provide Israel with:

- 33% of its water consumption
- 4% of its drinking water
- 50% of its agricultural water.

The 120 000 Jewish settlers in the West Bank use about 60 million cubic metres annually compared with the 134 million cubic metres used by 1.5 million West Bank Arabs. In addition, the West Bank Jewish settlers irrigate 70% of their cultivated land, compared with just 6% of Palestinian land.

QUESTIONS

1 With the help of an atlas, explain which areas of China are most likely to have a water shortage.

2 Explain the human factors which intensify China's water problem.

3 What are the links between water shortages and ground subsidence? Why has the problem of subsidence increased in the UK since the 1980s?

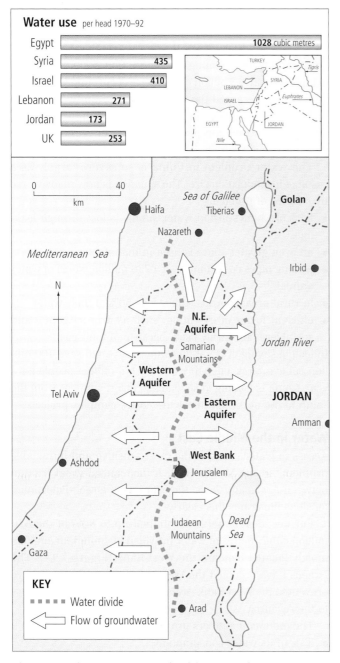

Figure 7.14 *The water issue in Israel and the West Bank*
Source: World Bank Atlas; Professor Hillel Shuval, Hebrew University

In the Peace Talks between Israelis and Palestinians, the Palestinians are asking for more water and a recognition of their rights to water. For the Israelis, it is an emotive issue. They believe that the water is their right to life and their means of survival. Israel has conceded little to the Palestinians; Israel has:

- increased the Palestinian's water quota by 35 million cubic metres
- offered to make available 50 million cubic metres to Palestinians.

The problem of access to water is region-wide. Jordan, Israel and Palestine suffer the most acute water shortages in the region. As part of the Israeli-Jordan peace process in 1995, Israel agreed to provide Jordan with 150 million cubic meters of water per annum.

This will be supplied by:

- diverting water
- building new dams
- desalinisation.

Other possibilities include using the Litani and Awali rivers in Lebanon, cutting back on agricultural usage, and creating a regional water market whereby people pay for the water they use.

Figure 7.15 *Small scale stone dam*

Israel is also quarrelling with Syria, which is demanding the return of the Golan Heights. These provide 30% of Israel's water and its 172 springs are the major source of the River Jordan.

Other potential conflicts exist between Syria, Iraq and Turkey regarding access to the River Euphrates (Figure 7.16, see page 119). In addition, Turkey is developing more dams, reservoirs and irrigation schemes in southern Turkey, thereby reducing the flow of the Euphrates and the Tigris. Syria and Turkey are, in fact, old enemies. They have quarrelled over the Euphrates since the 1960s. Syria and Iraq have protested about Turkey's water development projects. Syria claims that Turkey interrupts water flow, causing power cuts and threatening agriculture. The potential for the conflict to escalate is enormous.

The situation in Egypt is just as intense and bitter.

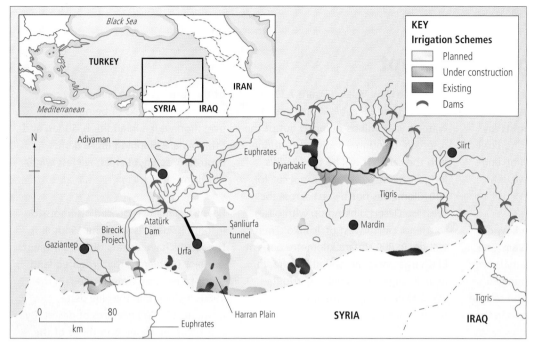

Figure 7.16 *Irrigation schemes in Turkey – existing and planned*
Source: Financial Times, February 1996

Water developments in Egypt

The population of the upper Nile is 10 million. This figure is expected to double by 2010. The expansion of cultivable land and the expansion of settlements in the desert is essential to relieve population pressure in the Nile Valley.

Egypt is the classic example of a country which is in real danger of drying up. It is a poor country, with a low human development index (HDI) (0.551), and a low GNP (US$610 per head). The population size is growing very rapidly (2.1% per annum), and is almost entirely dependent upon the Nile for water. 94% of the population have access to water but only 73% have access to proper sanitation.

Egypt imports most basic foodstuffs. Its main cash crop is cotton, a heavy user of water. The government subsidises the cost of water to farmers, consequently much water is wasted and lost.

In 1997, Egypt's president Hosni Mubarak inaugurated a US$810 million infrastructure in the Upper Nile valley to create a new river delta by 2017. This will irrigate 500 000 acres of desert and also create industrial and tourist complexes. The Sheikh Zayed canal takes the Nile water into the western desert, irrigating land south of the town of Kharga. Long-term government expenditure will finance agricultural, industrial, transport, health and education infrastructures.

Many of the countries in the Upper Nile are unhappy about the way in which the Nile's water is used. Under a 1959 treaty between Egypt and Sudan, all of the Nile water is shared between Egypt (55 billion cubic metres) and Sudan (18.5 billion cubic metres). The rest evaporates. Following decades of civil war, Ethiopia wants to rebuild its economy. It plans a series of mini-dams and HEP dams on the Blue Nile and the Atbara. This will use water that previously went to Egypt. Egypt has formally complained against these plans. The scene is set for a long, bitter battle. The consequences have serious implications for each country.

Figure 7.17 *Water developments in Egypt*
Source: Financial Times, January 1997

Inset 7.1
Expanding irrigation in Egypt

Egypt plans to divert up to a tenth of the flow of the Nile to irrigate its Western Desert. But hydrologists say that this mammoth engineering project, which will cost some £1.2 billion and take twenty years to complete, is a waste of water and money.

Currently, Egypt controls the flow of the Nile at the Aswan High Dam. The dam can hold back the rains that come with the summer flood – around 85 cubic kilometres of water – and release it gradually. This allows farmers in the Nile Valley and its delta to grow crops all year round. Some 90% of its 62 million people live on 4% of its territory irrigated by the Nile. The population is projected to reach 85 million by 2015. But with the narrow Nile valley filled almost to bursting by Egypt's soaring population, the country has designated Toshka as the centre of a plan to make the desert bloom.

The plan is to pump Nile water from Lake Nasser, the reservoir created by the Aswan High Dam, into a canal extending north-west across a vast waste land, creating a lush region,

called the New Valley (Figure 7.17). Between 2 and 9 cubic kilometres of water a year will be pumped out of the reservoir, through a 5 kilometre tunnel, into the canal. It will be the world's longest canal, a concrete canal cut for 240 kilometres north-west across the Western Desert, linking up with oases to the far north-west of Toshka. There will be an 800 square kilometre oasis at El Kharga and then one at Farafra. In its first stages the canal will irrigate 200 000 hectares to create vast new tracts of farmland.

The total cost for the project is estimated at around US$1.90 billion. An official estimate for the first four years has put the construction costs at US$760 million, most of it for the pumping station, the world's largest, which will have to lift up water 55 metres from Lake Nasser to the starting point of the canal. The pumping station will lift 18 litres of water a second from Lake Nasser and deposit it in the new canal.

However, in 1996 Lake Nasser was full for only the first time since 1980. Droughts in 1987 meant that a quarter

of the farmers in the Nile valley came within a few weeks of being denied irrigation water. In addition, Sudan and Ethiopia are planning more dams upstream, so Egypt will have less water in future.

Egypt has made repeated attempts to irrigate its deserts since the 1960s. But the results have been a disappointment. A major problem is that irrigated land tends to become waterlogged. In the 1960s a scheme in the Nile delta irrigated 350 000 hectares of desert. By the 1970s, however, two-thirds of the scheme was not producing crops.

The new scheme is likely to face similar problems, because most of the oases are in depressions with poor drainage. Fields will become waterlogged and provide ideal conditions for mosquitoes to breed. Another problem will be the high evaporation rates the canal will suffer. Moreover, the area is an area of moving dunes which will make maintenance very costly.

Only one-fifth of the volume of the water from the Nile now reaches the Mediterranean compared with five years ago. Other options available for the Egyptians include the use of available ground water and to expand sewage recycling programs.

Source: based in part on New Scientist, 25 January 1997

Figure 7.16 *The Nile at the Aswan Dam, Egypt*

QUESTIONS

1 Why is so much subsidised water in Egypt wasted and lost?

2 What are the implications for Egypt and Ethiopia of Ethiopia's plans to harness the waters of the Blue Nile and the Atbara?

3 What are the physical factors which cause a water shortage in the Middle East? Explain **two or more** human factors that have increased the water problem in the Middle East.

Mexico City – the urban scale

At an urban scale water shortages are acute. Mexico City is renowned for its smog. However, there is now a new problem. Residents claim that if they don't die from air pollution they will either die from thirst or from drowning in their own sewage.

The main source of water for Mexico City's 20 million people is an aquifer below the city which is running dry. As a result, Mexico City is sinking at a rate of 50 centimetres a decade. Dangerous cracks in the clay sediments threaten to allow contamination of the aquifer, which lies just 100 metres below the surface.

Mexico City uses 62 cubic metres of water a second. Two-thirds comes from the aquifer. The rest, 19 cubic metres per second, is pumped from dams 120 kilometres away. The electricity needed to pump the water would support a medium sized town for a day.

Mexico City's demand for water has brought it into conflict with neighbouring states. As the city uses more water, there is less available for irrigation. In addition, up to 30% of Mexico City's water is lost through leakages and theft by individuals and organised gangs, who sell it to those without water.

Two solutions have been offered:
- metering the use of water
- charging residents for what they use.

This is likely to be very unpopular and so far the government has resisted moves to introduce meters.

QUESTIONS

1 Explain **two** contrasting reasons why there is a water shortage in Mexico City.

2 Which parts of Mexico City are likely to experience the lowest levels of water and sanitation? Explain your answer.

3 Briefly describe **two** ways in which water could be used more efficiently in Mexico City.

SUMMARY

The problem of managing resources is getting harder. We have seen how difficult it is for countries with competing needs to work together. Population growth and economic growth is increasing the demand for water and water is being used up at a faster rate than it is being renewed. There are, however, means of improving the situation. These include:
- making the water industry more accountable; less government support
- less water wastage
- more efficient pipes
- better irrigation methods
- desalination of sea water
- more competition; greater efficiency.

But each solution has its own set of problems. For example, desalination is only an alternative for very rich countries, and withdrawal of subsidies is likely to be politically unpopular. For proper long-term sustainable use of resources, short-term political and economic advantages have to be sacrificed. Few are willing to accept the challenge.

QUESTIONS

1 'In the twenty-first century wars will be fought over water.' Discuss.

2 Where, and for what reasons, would you expect to find inadequacies in water and sanitation facilities in EMDCs? Give examples to support your answer.

3 How, and why, is water related to the spread of diseases such as diarrhoea and vomiting?

4 What ways are there of improving access to water and sanitation?

5 With the use of examples, explain the options for sustainable energy development. How do these differ between ELDCs and EMDCs?

6 Explain what is meant by the term sustainable development. Illustrate the potential for the sustainable development.

7 Explain the following terms: limits to growth; spaceship earth; tragedy of the Commons.

BIBLIOGRAPHY AND RECOMMENDED READING

Brundtland, 1987, See WCED

Chambers, R., 1983, *Rural development - putting the last first*, Longman

Elliot, J., 1994, *An introduction to sustainable development*, Routledge

HMSO, 1995, *First steps - Local Agenda 21 in practice*, HMSO

HMSO, 1996, *Indicators of sustainable development for the United Kingdom*, HMSO

Kirby, J., et al. (eds.), 1995, *The Earthscan reader in sustainable development*, Earthscan

Meadows, D., et al., 1972, *The limits to growth*, Pan

Meadows, D., et al., 1992, *Beyond the limits*, Earthscan

Nagle, G., and Spencer, K., 1997, *Sustainable development*, Hodder and Stoughton

Reid, D., 1995, *Sustainable development: an introductory guide*, Earthscan

UNDP, 1995, *Human development report 1994*, OUP

Walker, G., 1997, *Renewable energy in the UK: The Cinderella sector*, Geography, 82, 1, 59-74.

WCED, 1987, *Our common future*, OUP

WEB SITES

Environment Agency home page -
http://www.environment-agency.gov.uk/

Friends of the Earth home page -
http://www.foe.co.uk/

Greenpeace International home page -
http://www.greenpeace.org/greenpeace.html

The Rainforest Action Network home page -
http://www.ran.org/ran/

Abbreviations

CAP	Common Agricultural Policy
CPE	Centrally planned economy
ELDC	economically less developed country
EMDC	economically more developed country
EOI	export orientated industry
EU	European Union
FAO	Food and Agriculture Organisation
GATT	Global Agreement on Tariff and Trade
GDP	gross domestic product
GNP	gross national product
HDI	human development index
HYV	high yielding varieties of genetically altered crops
IMR	infant mortality rate
ISI	import substitution industry
MNC	multinational company
NAFTA	North American Free Trade Agreement
NIC	newly industrialising country
PPP	purchasing power parity
R & D	research and development
WHO	World Health Organisation
WTO	World Trade Organisation
UN	United Nations

Glossary

AIDS (acquired immuno deficiency disease) A disease which destroys the human immune system.

Agglomeration A clustering of people or activities, such as manufacturing and services, which benefit from being in close proximity, e.g. they can share amenities, communication links and labour supply.

Backwash effect Exploitation of the poorer, more peripheral areas in order to sustain economic growth in the rich core. This often involves a flow of resources and labour from the periphery to the core. The long–term effect of the flow from the periphery is polarisation, as poor areas become poorer and rich core areas gain more wealth.

Behavioural model Model which shows that decision–making is not concerned solely with profit, but is a result of a combination of factors, e.g. psychological, emotional, cultural, educational, access to capital, chance. *See also* Rational model.

Branch plant A production unit (factory) of a multinational enterprise. Local decision making is limited, and research and development facilities are often minimal. Output is generally mass produced and does not require a highly skilled labour force.

Branch plant economy A region that depends upon branch plants (of *MNCs*) for much of its employment. It is relatively unstable as (i) it lacks control over the decision making and (ii) many of the jobs are unskilled assembly positions.

Centrality The advantage of a central location, enhanced by good transport links and access to surrounding areas.

Common Agricultural Policy (CAP) Established in 1952 to develop European agriculture in terms of self–sufficiency, reliability and profitability.

Comparative advantage Cost advantages of a country or region for the production of manufactured goods. Such advantages include abundant resources or human skills. The factors that make one region more attractive for certain industries.

Core The centre, or focus, of an area. It usually contains the largest population cluster (frequently the capital city) and the most developed economic base of a region or country.

Core–periphery model The essential differences between the well–developed *core* and less developed *periphery* are the result of initial comparative advantages. The flow of resources between core and periphery generally adds to the differences in their levels of prosperity.

Cumulative causation *See* Multiplier effect.

Degenerative disease A disease leading to a long term decline in health, such as stroke, cancer and heart disease.

Deindustrialisation The decline of manufacturing industry caused by increased mechanisation, foreign competition or exhaustion of resources, e.g. use of robots in car manufacturing plants greatly reduced the need for labour. In the UK, it has been most drastic in regions of traditional heavy industries.

Density (population) The number of people per square kilometre.

Dependency ratio The proportion of the population supported by people in paid employment.

Dependency theory A set of inter–related propositions that identify the process of unequal exchange in economic and social relations between ELDCs and EMDCs; the economic performance and social structures of the less developed countries are dominated by those of the richer countries.

Development Frequently considered to mean the growth and modernisation of an economy, and an increase in per capita income and *gross national product* (GNP). While these are important aspects of development, increasing recognition must be given to improving the quality of life of a population, e.g. education, health care, cultural values and housing.

Distribution (population) The pattern of population location.

Economic man *see* Rational model.

Endemic A disease native to an area.

Epidemic An outbreak of a disease not usually found in a region.

Epidemiology The study of diseases.

Export orientated industries Industries which earn foreign capital by targeting global markets. *See also* Import substitution industries.

Formal/informal sector of employment The formal sector consists of large–scale capitalist or government enterprises with fixed conditions of employment and job security; the informal sector consists of small–scale labour–intensive activities with job insecurity, multiple occupations and low monetary returns.

Gross domestic product (GDP)/gross national product (GNP) GDP is the total value of all finished goods and services produced by an economy in a specific time period, usually one year; GNP is GDP plus income accruing to residents of a country from abroad, less incomes accruing to foreign residents investing in the country.

Growth pole A town or region in which there is a concentrated investment of resources in order to stimulate self–sustaining growth and to encourage *multiplier effects*.

Import substitution industries Local industries and production developed to replace imported goods, reduce dependency on imports, conserve foreign exchange and improve the balance of payments of a country.

Industrial inertia   The process whereby an industry remains in an area long after the initial attracting factors have disappeared, e.g. steel in Sheffield.

Infectious disease   A disease that can be passed through contact, e.g. measles, cholera.

Inward investment   Capital investment by a foreign company into a country, e.g. Nissan in the North East of England.

Migration   A long term, sometimes permanent, change in residence.

Multinational company (MNC)   An organisation having operations in a large number of countries. Generally, research and development is concentrated in growth areas of developed countries whereas assembly and production is located in developing countries or depressed regions. MNCs wield considerable economic and political power.

Multiplier effect   A process which leads to the formation of *core* and *periphery* areas. New economic development in the core often stimulates the local economy and attracts migrants searching for work. The cumulative effect of movements of people and resources increases wealth in the core.

Natural increase   The growth in population as a result of birth rates exceeding death rates, rather than in–migration.

Neo–colonialism   The reassertion of economic control by EMDCs over former colonies, replacing colonial authority with economic authority.

Newly industrialising countries   Countries characterised by rapid economic growth rates due to successful industrialisation in recent decades, e.g. Singapore and Malaysia.

Non–governmental organisation (NGO)   A voluntary, non–political, non–commercial organisation which seeks to help disadvantaged members of society.

Optimum population   The number of people who can be provided with the best standards of living when using currently available resources and technology.

Pandemic   A global epidemic.

Periphery   Areas near the margins of a country or region. They generally have poor links to core areas and are under–developed problem regions, e.g. west of Ireland, Mezzogiorno.

Post industrial society   Societies in which deindustrialisation has occurred and the majority of employment is in service industries.

Primacy   In many ELDCs the urban hierarchy is 'top heavy', with the largest city substantially larger in population than the other major cities. *See also* Primate city.

Primary industries   Extractive industries such as farming, fishing and forestry and mining.

Primate city   A city with a population several times as great as the second largest city. It is most expressive of the national culture, and is usually the capital city as well.

Product life cycle   Vernon's theory that manufactured products pass through a series of stages: development, maturity and standardisation. Each stage varies in terms of locational requirements.

Quaternary industries   Industries associated with research and development, generally located close to the company head office.

Rank–size rule   A rule whereby the population of any town can be estimated by dividing the population of the largest city in a country by the rank of the settlement under consideration.

Rational model   Decision–making where the primary aim is to maximise profits. It assumes access to all necessary information, and the ability to use that information. Increasingly, decision making by MNCs could be said to be 'rational'.

Secondary industries   Manufacturing industries involving the transformation of raw materials into finished and semi–finished products.

Services   *See* Tertiary industries.

Spatial division of labour   The concentration of highly paid, skilled workers in developed countries, compared with low paid, unskilled workers in the periphery or developing world.

Spatial margins of profitability   A locational theory stating that industries can operate profitably in a variety of places but some locations are more desirable than others; the desirability of locations may also change over time.

Sustainable development   'Development that meets the needs of the present without compromising the ability of future generations to meet their own needs' (Brundtland Commission, 1987). This classic definition emphasises inter–generational equity and also assumes the possibility of development that can be accompanied by environmental stability or even environmental improvement.

Tertiarisation   The rapid growth of the service sector in developed economies.

Tertiary industries   A wide variety of service industries, including financial, legal, commercial, public, administrative, educational and health services.

Transnational corporations (TNCs)   *See* Multinational company.

Index